ART
Another Language for Learning

Third Edition

Elaine Pear Cohen
Sculptor and Art Consultant

Ruth Straus Gainer
Visual Arts Specialist,
Montgomery County (Maryland)
Public Schools

ART
Another Language for Learning

Third edition

Heinemann
Portsmouth, NH

Dedicated to the memory of
Kate Pear Arvins and Bernard Straus

Heinemann
A division of Reed Elsevier Inc.
361 Hanover Street
Portsmouth, NH 03801-3912
Offices and agents throughout the world

Every effort has been made to contact the copyright holders for permission to reprint borrowed material where necessary. We regret any oversights that may have occurred and would be happy to rectify them in future printings of this work.

The authors and publisher wish to thank those who granted permission to reprint borrowed material:

"Dolphins in Blue Water," Fireworks," and "Sea Shell" from *The Complete Poetical Works of Amy Lowell.* Copyright © 1955 by Houghton Mifflin Company. Reprinted by permission.

"People" from *City Poems* by Lois Lenski. Copyright © 1971 by Lois Lenski. Reprinted by permission of Henry Z. Walck, Inc.

Photo credits:
Jan Dorfman, p. iii
Iccy, p. 85
Judy Sugar, pp. 38, 59, 75, 79, 189, 236, 239, 240

Library of Congress Cataloging-in-Publication Data
CIP is on file with the Library of Congress.
ISBN 0-435-08847-5

Editor: William E. Varner
Production: Melissa L. Inglis
Cover design: Barbara Whitehead
Cover photo: Bill Mills

Printed in the United States of America on acid-free paper
99 98 97 96 95 EB 1 2 3 4 5 6 7 8 9

"All this has been said before—but since nobody listened, it must be said again."

André Gide

Contents

Foreword

The authors of this book are right to insist that drawing and painting (when observed, studied, or engaged in) are emphatically educational experiences. They have documented their claim well, providing us with a comprehensive view of what has been done in many classrooms, and as well, a number of suggestions of what might be done in many more were this book's message widely understood. I know from my own work as a child psychiatrist interested in how children of various backgrounds grow up that crayons and paints are indeed "another language." Sometimes, actually, they are the *only* language; an apprehensive, skeptical or badly frightened child has no desire to talk to someone he or she considers strange, inscrutable, or potentially hurtful. Children, anyway, even with those they know or trust (or yes, love) are often exceedingly reticent, or all too nervously but evasively talkative—unwilling to speak about, commonly, what is not so much "on" their minds as "in" their minds, waiting (it turns out) for a proper expressive occasion.

Again and again I have had a "conversation," so to speak, with children through the drawings or paintings they have done. Not that the boys or girls have set out, self-consciously, to tell me a story, or (God forbid!) analyze themselves. Rather, in a quiet and unassuming way they have responded to the possibilities of a particular medium: with a few crayons or a paintbrush they can indicate what they see, what they consider important, what silently crosses their minds. And there are, as the authors show, many thousands of other such children—willing and able to draw and sketch their sense of themselves, their hopes and fears; and just as important, willing and able afterwards to use their own artistic productions (or those of others, be they fellow students or distinguished artists) as a means of having a discussion, using words which otherwise would not have been forthcoming.

The point, of course, is not to claim for "art" yet another messianic "solution" for the various educational difficulties (or worse) that face the world's children. Rather, one wants to emphasize that children—for all the noise they often make—are commonly discreet, wary, tactful creatures, not as inclined as many grown-ups to talk about themselves, or even, to volunteer readily what they (as opposed to their parents or their teachers) have been thinking about and trying to make sense of. Yes, boys and girls shout and scream and make their various claims on us (not to mention themselves). But often they keep for themselves much that is lively, canny, speculative. The ferment of their minds may be conveyed in their artistic efforts—especially if those efforts are encouraged by respectful parents or teachers. And if those children end up sharing more of themselves and learning more about themselves, we who are older usually get to learn a few things ourselves from these younger (and occasionally) quite gifted artists and teachers.

DR. ROBERT COLES
Harvard University

Preface

A harried classroom teacher traced an illustration from the book she had just read to her class, dittoed it, and asked the children to "color it in."

"Fill in the spaces with different colors and stay within the lines," she directed. And that was "art" for the week because, although she would like to do better, she finds art a bit of a mystery. She simply doesn't know how to go about teaching it.

*   *   *

A principal glared across his desk at the art teacher. "More money for paint?" he asked. "My budget is overextended; the children in this school can't even read and you want more money for paint!" It never occurred to him that art, properly integrated with language arts, can actually help children's reading (nor has it occurred to many an art teacher).

*   *   *

At home the newborn infant was howling, the two-year-old was spilling her lunch all over the floor, and the oldest child, all of five years old, demanded, "Momma, help me draw a picture." The distraught mother shoved a coloring book in front of the boy, "Here—color!" For her art represented "busy work," something to keep a child quiet.

It was early December, and the Christmas holidays were just two weeks off. A tired teacher pulled out stencils of wreaths, which she had used for the last five years, and suggested that the children make "decorations" for their room. And this too was "art" for the week. This teacher too would like to make art available and meaningful to her children. "But," she explains, "I cannot even draw a straight line. How can I teach them art?"

*   *   *

It is the writers' concern for all these adults, as well as for children, that prompted the writing of this book. As art teachers who have worked in many different situations, we write here for educators who have not had any specialized training in art and are fearful or skeptical about introducing art into the curriculum. We write for administrators who think of art as an extra and, therefore, easily dropped. As parents ourselves, we sympathize with other parents who wish to understand more about the importance of art in the lives of their children. This book is written for them too.

This is not a standard how-to-do-it book; we do not dictate procedures "recipe" style. Instead, by describing actual elementary school classroom experiences, we suggest a quality of discussion—a style—an approach—a reaching for the one-to-one exchange of ideas that constitutes real conversation, indispensable for good teaching. An anecdote about each art activity is juxtaposed with a simple explanation of its philosophical and psychological rationale. These anecdotes are not unique; we could easily substitute many others, all equally interesting. The ones we have selected are typical of children's reactions to art experiences, as observed in many different classrooms, under many different conditions. Individual stories are told not because the children were exceptional, but to make their reactions significant and immediate to readers. We know that teachers who use the approaches described here will have similar experiences. The anecdotes are used to define our philosophy in which art in the classroom is considered an expression of the uniqueness of each individual and a means of understanding the social and physical environment.

Most teachers are overworked and tired. Most parents are bewildered by the diversity of advice offered them. Administrators frequently have more problems then they can handle. We are not suggesting additional projects to worry any of them; rather we are suggesting more effective ways of realizing the aims for which they struggle at present, objectives such as improving reading, classroom behavior, and the quality of learning by making them pleasurable rather than dreary.

At present many adults regard art as a dispensable frill in the curriculum or a subject requiring exceptional talent to teach or learn. They may agree that it is a pleasing activity for some students and that art products are occasionally worthy of respect, but the predominant judgment in American schools about the subject of art can be stated simply—pleasant, but not really very important. There are, of course, exceptions, but basically our society puts a low value on aesthetic experiences. Most schools and homes reflect these societal attitudes.

We believe both children and adults are being cheated as a result of this misconception. Symbolic representations of the the environment though pictures and sculpture are as natural to human beings as the development of speech. In fact, children's understanding and use of visual symbols frequently precedes speech and always precedes written language. As will be revealed in this book, children relish art, not only for its symbolic value but also for the aesthetic pleasure that they derive from the use of materials.

*   *   *

Billy was a five-year-old kindergartner, sturdy, healthy looking, and a bit tall for his age; his eyes told me that he was alert. "But," his teacher reported, "he simply will not talk in school."

Billy was enrolled in a Head Start-Follow Through school where I was the traveling art teacher. One day I brought poster paint to the kindergarten class. I approached this boy who would not speak and gently led him to the painting table. I put a large brush in his hand, showed him the primary colors, the water jar and sponges, patted him on the shoulder, and said, "Have fun!" Then I left to attend to the others.

Anyone who has visited kindergarten rooms knows that the noise level is frequently fairly high. However, at one point there seemed to be a lull, and through the sudden quiet a happy voice rang out, "YELLOW." We turned in surprise to find that our quiet little friend had covered much of his paper with thick, rich yellow paint. He was so delighted with the color that he forgot to be silent.

The startled teacher reacted constructively. She approached him immediately, and they talked about "yellow"—what a beautiful, happy color it is, how his favorite sweater was yellow, and how many yellows they could find right there in the room. It was a real breakthrough. Children often chatter as they work, and in this case Billy's reaction to color was so strong that it led him back to speech.

*   *   *

Although this episode demonstrates art as a valuable tool for stimulating language and perceptual skills, we also want to emphasize the intrinsic value of the arts for their own sake. In a time of growing concern about the quality of life, the preservation of natural resources and the appreciation of beauty, aesthetic education merits increased attention.

It might be well at this point to state what this book is *not*. It is not an attempt to evaluate the relative merits of open classrooms, traditional classrooms, team teaching, ungraded schools, free schools, alternative schools, or other educational experiments. We do not minimize the importance of the controversies about these questions for we recognize that they will determine the very important setting in which art education will take place. But here we address ourselves to the manner in which aesthetic experiences are made available to young children at an individual level, regardless of what their schools' philosophy happens to be. We are concerned about what happens between two people who talk to each other about art—and especially when the two are student and teacher, or child and parent.

Teachers are more than distributors of materials. When children evidence restlessness or boredom, they may be sending signals that they are ready for a higher level of stimulation. They need ideas and suggestions. Teachers must be alert and ready for this important moment. We are opposed to the practice of never giving information or ideas until children ask for them. If they do not know what alternatives exist in life, or in art, how can they know what to ask for? Intervention or suggestions, strategically used, can often be of enormous help.

For example, in chapter 6 on learning to look, mixing colors is discussed. No doubt if children were given points and

Art experiences often give students and teachers opportunities to talk over problems involving space, color, or design. Such one-to-one conversations help build trust and self-confidence for both adults and children.

encouraged to "play around," they would probably discover many of the combinations described and derive great pleasure form their discoveries. However, by preliminary experimentation together in a group (not meant by any means to take the place of later individual experimentation), children can be introduced to a disciplined method of working (washing the brush between colors, utilizing the sponge for excess water, and the like), which will permit them much greater scope and pleasure in experiencing colors. The "discipline" described does not have to be interpreted in a rigid way. For some children, there is value in messing up their paints, but not indefinitely. When youngsters become bored with this, teachers should be ready to provide an alterative, and this is what our introduction to a color session suggests.

Activities are aimed at single objectives, but, as clearly shown in chapter 5 on learning to think, several outcomes invariably occur. Several activities and several objectives may be realized at the same time with one classroom; it is for clarity only that we have defined each subject area separately.

Although the approaches suggested here are placed in the context of work with an entire class, they are valid for a team teacher working with a small group, or a teaching aid working with one child, or a parent working with a child.

And finally, the provocative question raised in *The Rubaiyat of Omar Khayyam* should further help identify the point of view presented throughout this book—"Who is being shaped, the potter or the pot?" If the response is "Both," the questions that follow immediately are perplexing: In what way is the potter shaped along with the pot? What changes are taking place within the artist?

Potters produce pots; painters paint pictures; sculptors create sculpture; the work of each possesses an individual style. Young potters, painters, and sculptors produce new sensations, thoughts, and attitudes along with their pots, paintings, and sculpture. The unique styles reflected in their finished works have developed *simultaneously* with styles of thinking, learning, and working. The shape of the art products is easy to see. This book looks at the *shaping* of the youthful producer of art. It examines art both as a language and a process.

Art functions as a language because it is a communication system in which visual statements clarify ideas and stimulate further ones. Necessary to this communication is a process involving selection and organization of ideas and application of those ideas to art media. This process can help children to learn about themselves, learn to think, learn to see, and learn about feelings. The total educational process will profit from such understandings.

Acknowledgments

The point of view expressed in this book would never have been developed without the help of the many outstanding individuals, who, collectively, are our families. We wish to express our deepest appreciation to all of them. Their own creativity and unwavering support have been constant sources of inspiration and encouragement. This is especially true of our husbands whose questions, growing out of a different context (that of science), and cooperation, growing out of a mutuality of concerns, have enriched our professional lives immeasurably.

Early encouragement, when it was most important, was offered by Barbara S. Waters, Jean Dresden Grambs, Louise Ballinger, Charles Leidenfrost, Patricia Ogburn, Neal Gross, Richard Giboney, and Virginia Plunkett. Fred R. Schwartz didn't know it, but it was he who suggested a book in the first place.

We thank the many people who read chapters and made helpful suggestions. They are not to be held responsible for the end product for which we take full responsibility. We mention with appreciation Herman A. Witkin, Beth Taylor Lerman, Elaine Troll, Michael A. Cohen, Maja Apelman, Elsie

Levitan, Thelma Nason, Herman Epstein, Ellen Dorfman, Claire Rodney, Ann Hornbein, and Mary Robinson.

Of invaluable assistance were our colleagues among class-room teachers and administrators who were willing to give our ideas a try. They include Hans Fickenscher, Charlotte DeCosta, Martha Wolkin, Connie Gregory, Margaret Efraemson, Roseanne Skinner, Carolyn Starek, Mae Streety, Irene Glaser, Joyce Poling, Dr. Howard Graves, Roy Gilham, and Rita Will.

Special thanks is due our exceptional editor, May Allison. Her sympathetic and intelligent help is apparent throughout the book. We also note with pleasure the fine assistance of Miriam Brammer, Lucy Bitzer, Karen Gurwitz, and William E. Varner.

We appreciate the help of Sara Elizabeth Cohen in preparing the index. We are grateful for the constant assistance of Ruth and Dave Shephard of the Job Shop in Woods Hole.

Photography credits are numerous, but we must single out for special mention photographer Judy Sugar, who gave an enormous amount of time and skill to enhancing our effort. Others include Ben Gainer, Jack Simon, art education students at the Philadelphia College of Art, classes of '68 and '69, Jan Dorfman, Sally Brucker Cohen, and Donal Moore.

And to those most influential of teachers, the students described in these pages, our deepest gratitude. Their energy, curiosity, enthusiasm, and aesthetic insights continually served to ignite and renew our own.

ELAINE PEAR COHEN
RUTH STRAUS GAINER

Woods Hole, Mass., 1995

ART AND CHILDREN

1. The Significance of Children's Art

Children's art is a universal, naturally occurring phenomenon. It can be a powerful expressive force and avenue of communication when it is recognized as such. It should be consulted for information about children's thinking and development.

Art in general is more than a set of facts, rules and methods; it is more than a standard branch of knowledge. Art is a reflection of life through the sensibilities and experiences of individual artists. Children's art is particularly expressive because facility in other means of creating and communicating is not yet developed. For example, a child's drawing of a favorite animal is likely to include considerably more detail (indicating thoughtful observation) than the child's written or spoken language.

Recent trends in art education have shifted away from a child-centered focus to a "discipline-based" emphasis. Therefore, it is necessary to state at the outset that the approach presented in this book is unabashedly child-centered. Instead of shifting our focus, we choose to sharpen it.

Aesthetic choices—responses to colors, textures and other sensory phenomena—are made by all people from birth.

Through these choices we learn about the world and our roles and relationships within it. Perhaps this is one reason that children are so engrossed in their own explorations of art media, even before instruction is given.

However, inadequate attention is accorded the significance of the content and even deeper meanings of the process of making art in child development. Children are sending messages about thoughts and feelings in their artwork but often communication is stymied because there is no one to receive or interpret the messages. The stories told here will prepare teachers and parents to understand what they see when they look at children's art, and how to respond so that they may extend communication and advance learning.

THE CONDITION OF CHILDREN

The quality of many children's lives has worsened since this book was first written. Greater numbers live in poverty; greater numbers suffer the effects of violence, anxiety, depression, lack of direction, lack of health care and inability to concentrate. The optimistic outlook that should brighten every child's birthright is often replaced by despair, cynicism and withdrawal—even among the very young. All schools are familiar with these issues. Children cannot learn when the problems around them seem overwhelming.

THE ROLE OF ART EDUCATION

Art education does not provide a simple solution and we cannot offer one. We can show, however, that art is a powerful way to create and strengthen lines of communication. It is also a way of convincing children that their actions, thoughts and feelings really matter. Other people react immediately to art; we and our surroundings are different because of it. These realizations impart a sense of power. That sense is a critical factor for learning and achievement because it underlies feelings of responsibility. Art is also a way to develop imagination and vision about the future. Wherever art is valued, it performs these functions.

EFFECTS OF TECHNOLOGY

The valuing of art in today's schools is endangered by preoccupation with technology. Providing students with computers will not solve their problems or assure that they are well-educated. Yet acquiring more and more computers is a top priority in most schools. Advances in media technology are impressive and will have lasting impact. But the ends to which they are means have not been thoughtfully analyzed. The technology alone is overemphasized as an end in itself. There are cavernous gaps in comprehension between what is happening technologically and young children's characteristic ways of learning.

We don't teach children to talk by handing them a telephone. A lot of playful babbling with a touchable, loving human being is necessary first. Learning in the early stages of every subject requires direct, personal interaction with caring people. All children need to learn the possibilities of the human hand and eye before receiving sophisticated apparatus. Premature emphasis on the latter is intimidating, distracting and demeaning.

These words are not intended to sabotage technological advances in the manner in which French workers attempted to deter machinery by pummeling it with their sabots (wooden shoes). We do urge more serious consideration of the results of a "screen culture" upon our young people. Many children are alone with a TV (or, more likely, TVs) much of the day. Computers in many schools are supposed to be on at all times whether in use or not, lest administrators stop by. While the colored lights flash, zip, and zoom in constantly changing patterns, many aspects of life continue around them. We eat, chat, answer phones and play games simultaneously. Combining many activities at once becomes an habitual pattern. Is it really any wonder that when teachers ask for concentrated attention, they don't get it?

The rapidly changing images of the screen are confusing to many who don't know which images deserve remembering or how they are connected. Still, the fast-paced, fragmented and jarring qualities of TV now pervade many aspects of daily life. Even relaxation has become a frantic pursuit. Schools are usually driven by rapidly changing schedules rather than the quality of their programs. At the end of each day, many activities can be checked off on multiple documents but few have been probed in penetrating ways.

Outgrowths of these conditions are passivity and boredom. Expressions of individuality are often thwarted or ignored.

Children who are offered choices yet refuse them, unable or unwilling to decide what to do, are lately described as having "an attitude." That attitude may be a response to the feeling that "this activity is just filler; you don't take my ideas or me seriously, why should I bother?" All this isn't stated verbally but through the body language of shrugs and smirks or glares and blank stares. Some students repeatedly crumple papers even when barely a line has been placed on them. They are saying, "I am dissatisfied, I can't get involved, I don't trust myself or you to help me."

THE VALUE OF INSTRUCTION

Art can excite even these children—but not if it's a slide show in the dark—or another approach that is simply checking off progress through skills topics. A small amount of instruction, such as how to sketch with a natural stroke instead of a hard line, can enable hesitant ten-year-old students to become engaged with an idea—one of their own. Varied examples by artists will make this process more intriguing. The instruction is the explicit yet gentle guidance that cuts a channel through a rough passage so as to invite an idea to make its way. Along with the work of art, a sense of accomplishment in having tackled and solved a problem is produced. The smiles that result are more than joy in the product alone. They say, "I startled myself, I saw this through; this is my work and I am thrilled by what I can do when I persist." Seeing this process occur as children work in art is an illuminating lesson for everyone.

THE INTERDISCIPLINARY APPROACH

Instruction in an interdisciplinary setting is much more meaningful than discrete presentations in separate subject areas. Relating subject matter can also remedy the disjointed quality of daily schedules. "Interdisciplinary" simply means teaching concepts that are naturally and logically connected at congruent times. For instance, the study of symmetry can take place in art, math, and science for mutual benefit. The study of physical and chemical changes should be coordinated with ceramics. Any study of ancient civilizations must include the art history of the area. Defining poetic imagery requires visual as well as verbal translations.

The numerous examples of the interdisciplinary approach contained in these pages will demonstrate that art is not sacrificed in favor of other subject areas as some fear. To the contrary, each subject is comprehended more fully as the relationships between them are perceived. Indeed, we would agree that this type of perception is the very essence of education. Consider the role of contrast as it is used in all the arts. The relation through juxtaposition of different elements intensifies the perception of each.

When art techniques are taught, teachers and parents need to make clear that these are subsidiary to the expression of ideas and individual meanings. A technique should not be the sole objective of an art lesson. Technical mastery should be in the service of personal expression. Only then does it become art. Many teachers tell us that they often return to *Art, Another Language* for this reassurance in the face of demands for "instructional objectives" and "basic skills." As David Hawkins has said, "The aim is not to cover a subject but to *uncover* it." This style of teaching invites children to take responsibility for pursuing a subject. The self-direction and determination that result from this approach characterize the most meaningful experiences not only in art but also in general education.

NEW IMMIGRANTS

Schools in many communities are affected by the large number of children arriving in the United States from distant places. Many of these children have not yet learned English. Others may feel uncomfortable because of jolting changes in their lives or the strangeness of new customs. In this situation work in the arts can help children to feel welcome without use of verbal language. Studying the art of other cultures, not only those represented in each classroom, helps create an atmosphere where diversity is prized, thus helping everyone to adjust to the new group composition. However, a tendency to spotlight individuals as representatives of their original cultural groups should be avoided unless the students claim this identification themselves. Care must be taken first to recognize each child's individuality and particular qualities of personal experience. The child's artwork is a fine basis for this process. Building on this foundation, artistic achievements from various countries and periods in history can provide rich, directly observable and highly specific means for demonstrating respect for diversity. In this way, individuality and diversity are jointly valued through art.

DEVELOPMENTAL INSIGHTS

Those of us who have had experience with the art process, the "making of art," know that it requires a great deal of critical thinking. In this volume we describe in detail some of the questions that must be asked and answered to help the "artist," child or adult, decide what is to be put on the blank piece of paper, or shaped with the handful of wet clay. In describing the stages of development of young children we indicate what may seem to be standardized descriptions and sequences that most children pass through in the course of their development. Although the house with the lop-sided roof seems to appear and reappear again and again, the discovery process for each child may be new and exciting. The round sun with its spiked edges may represent a totally new idea for a five year old.

We know that human beings all walk, but do they all walk in the same way? Some people walk mincingly, some glide gracefully, some stride with large firm steps, others walk hesitantly, as if anticipating a fall. All may arrive at the end of the same road, but for each the journey may be very different. And so it is with the art process for young children. As they define their own styles of stepping forward, of drawing, of painting or modeling clay, they are able to gain confidence in themselves. They learn that although they may proceed differently from others, they are able to arrive at a desired destination just as well. Inherent talent is not our concern here; engagement in the art process is. Investigation of art as a universal method of communication is key to using the approach presented.

CHILDREN AND PARENTS WITH SPECIAL NEEDS

Similarly, new policies of including all children in a single classroom regardless of handicapping conditions can be supported by recognizing the power of art to transcend those conditions and focus on individual involvement and expressiveness. To be sure, this role for art must be accompanied by adequate supports for teachers as well as students, particularly in the form of more classroom assistance—extra hands!

We have observed that parents too have special needs. Often fascinated by the almost magical way in which the young child, without prompting, will begin to draw, they find the process interesting to watch. A small fist will grasp a crayon, pencil, or paintbrush, and the big moment of discovery will occur. If one moves one's arm in *this* way, the child will learn, holding *this* object, this or that mark will appear on the paper. This is exhilarating both for parent and child. The process will occur over and over again, still exciting for the child but soon boring or worrisome for the parent. In time, questions develop.

Why do they scribble so much?

Why do they repeat the same patterns or symbols again and again? What do they mean?

Why do the drawings continue to be so messy? Why do they mix the colors together until they look like mud?

Why does the four-year-old draw a head and arms but no body? Is something wrong?

What should I say when my child proudly shows me something which is utterly incomprehensible?

These are among the questions we discuss.

A special need of everyone is to feel needed and useful. Valuing children's art is a way of saying to children that "We value *you*." Our society desperately needs to make this statement.

2. The Art Process in the Classroom

Most teachers feel overwhelmed by the tasks before them. In fact, most people feel overwhelmed by the rush of changes, innovations, and discoveries taking place today. How is it possible to keep informed about the latest developments in politics, economics, science and technology? How is it possible to absorb new findings and use them to function wisely and efficiently? More demanding still, how can we teach children to comprehend and contribute to present knowledge?

In the frantic search for answers, the arts are frequently bypassed. Many people would like to know more about art, "if only there were more time." Many beleaguered teachers would like to devote more time to art, but "there aren't enough hours in the day." Some feel excluded from the world of art because they can't create any themselves, and others confess to knowing nothing about art except what they like. Perhaps, they hope, future leisure will permit indulgence in art's diversions.

Art, however, is not a diversion from the business of learning. Studies of children's development indicate that art activities provide direction, clarification, and reinforcement of new concepts. They are sought out with relish and diligence by curious youngsters.

Paradoxically, the very fact of children's enthusiasm for art has contributed to the denial of it as a legitimate study. "If it is so much fun, it can't possibly be educational" is an implicit attitude in many schools and homes. Explicit comments may acknowledge that art is creative play but then go on to complain that it is messy, expensive, and time consuming.

Even an enlightened acceptance of the arts as cultural enrichment usually fails to recognize the essential role the arts play in all cultures. Without art there is no culture. It is impossible to name a society that hasn't expressed itself and *explained* itself through art. The beliefs, myths, fears, hopes, dreams, values, successes, and failures of every people are revealed in their art. The only record of most of humanity's history is "written" in surviving artifacts. Opera singer Beverly Sills put it very well when, at an arts symposium in Texas, she declared, ". . . art is the signature of a civilization."

Since all people make art, and the arts are part and parcel of the very substance of a culture, the transmission of a culture to its members is a basic aim of education. If expression of our culture is to be continued and renewed, then the arts must become an integral part of every curriculum.

Elevating the role of art in elementary schools need not increase the work of teachers. The pleasures of the arts can alleviate the pressures of daily routines even as they advance educational objectives. While the practice of art is not a panacea for every educational problem, it does provide a channel for learning that can be easily navigated.

ONE TEACHER'S DISCOVERY

The role of art in children's lives became clear to me when I was a beginning teacher trying to learn about a big city school system. Mine was a baptism of fire because I entered the profession as a day-to-day substitute teacher. Many theories try to explain children's behavior when their teacher is absent: they are angry, they are anxious, and they are upset about changes in routine. Often I felt that they wanted a day off, too. Whatever the explanation, such children present an exhausting challenge for substitutes.

Chaos reigned until I came up with a formula that was foolproof: (1) When in trouble, suggest art activities; and (2) to avoid trouble, come prepared with art supplies. Nothing else had as reliable an effect. Children of every age and grade immediately became attentive, purposeful, and absorbed in their own work. It was even possible for children to work together, not only with energy but also with equanimity.

As a substitute teacher, I didn't know where or to what grade level I would be assigned each day. Planning ahead for lessons in most subjects was therefore impossible. This was not true for art. Art activities are not only open-ended, they are also open-beginnings. Children can start at individual levels and progress according to their specific skills and imaginations. The more varied these are, the more varied and interesting will be the results. Although variety among student groups causes problems in devising lessons in other subjects, in art it is most welcome.

My first reaction to these discoveries was relief at the smoothly running classrooms I could now anticipate. Secondly, I enjoyed seeing the industriousness and delight of children creating art. Admittedly, my early reliance on art was in my own self-interest, but I soon decided that I must learn to transfer the children's concentration on art to the other subjects I was supposed to teach. As I puzzled about how to do this, I observed the behavior of children engrossed in art activities.

"This is my football team," one little boy explained as he carefully drew each player in the proper position. "Teacher, how do you spell coach?" Numbers were very carefully lettered onto the uniform of each player.

"I'm drawing my house and my street," exclaimed another child and then, eagerly, "How do you spell grocery and Amsterdam Avenue?"

Motivated by their own interests and needs, the children wanted to label all objects and events correctly. They demanded correctly spelled words because these were needed for what they themselves had chosen to do. How different from their lack of interest in standard spelling lists!

Some youngsters rendered space capsules with precision and with a full complement of complex dials and controls. I saw lofty towers of wood scraps, gleefully begun anew after trial-and-error experiments proved something startling about balance. Some children retold favorite stories in cartoon form, carefully establishing the sequence of events and colorfully emphasizing the dramatic climax. "What animals would really live in an African jungle?" one boy wondered as he painted and then asked to look in the encyclopedia to find out. Clearly, the children were not occupied with busy work but were, in fact, gainfully em-

A typical five-year-old's drawing of people. Note that although there is a groundline, some figures float above it and some are anchored down. The smiling sun is typical too of artwork done by all children of kindergarten age.

ployed. It was apparent that much more than techniques of using crayons and paints was being learned.

Although the schools I visited were located in very different neighborhoods, the paintings and drawings I accumulated had fascinating similarities. Children of the same age seem to share preferences for subject matter and techniques no matter what their backgrounds. People float haphazardly in space in most five-year-olds' drawings. At seven years, most children systematically arrange geometric houses, stylized people, and rigid trees on horizontal groundlines, because part of being seven is painting what you know, not what you see. All of these objects are benevolently smiled upon by radiant suns. Nine-year-olds allow the sky and the ground wider expanses than the marginal inches allotted to them in earlier pictures. They also become more concerned with differentiating sex and clothing details.

According to the standardized test results published periodically in my city, children in different neighborhoods had widely different achievement levels, outlooks, and expectations. Why, then, were there so many common elements in their drawings? I began to wonder whether the standard tests were overlooking certain aspects of children's development and whether the striking similarities in drawing development might provide clues to performance in other areas.

It was clear that most children in the early grades were not drawing to perfect any artistic skills—they drew for the pleasure of expressing their ideas and imaginations. If their thoughts had so many similarities in content, style, and progressive development, why were their achievements in academic areas so unequal? How could the obvious intelligence, acute perceptions, and depths of feeling manifested in their art be applied to the subject matter so many of the children were having difficulty with?

These were some of the questions that prompted me to return to graduate school for additional study in art education and eventually to collaboration on this book. My collaborator, who was teaching under entirely different circumstances, had pondered the same questions. Some of the incidents reported here occurred when she was working as an art teacher in an elementary school covering grades one through six. Some occurred when she supervised practice teaching in schools and in an experimental art education laboratory in an art college. Still others occurred during her graduate work, when she was in and out of many classrooms, teaching, consulting, and asking questions.

Our questions arose from contact with many interesting children. There was a third-grade boy, a "behavior problem," who modeled a life-size head in clay that shocked his classroom teacher into an understanding of his basic intelligence. There was a little girl who drew her view of her father as a spot of baldhead seen over the back of an open newspaper. There was the very quiet boy who revealed the depth of his emotions about the death of Martin Luther King by drawing a powerful portrait. And there were the many others, some of whom are described in the pages of this book.

It was exciting to discover that not only gifted children responded with enthusiasm to art activities. Each class session discussed here has been tried and found successful with children of different backgrounds, abilities, and interests. Colors, forms, and textures delight them all. Very few of the children discussed had special aptitude in art; for the most part, our anecdotes are about average children in average schools.

Teachers who learn to integrate art activities with other subjects will enjoy new insights and understandings of their students. In problem situations when youngsters are shy, angry, bewildered, or unhappy, art may provide insights that can help teachers find solutions. In normal situations, art activities can reveal unexpected facets of children's personalities which can be of help in the learning process.

Although the observations, studies, and experiences of the authors took place independently, the conclusions drawn were strikingly similar. We have come to believe that an understanding of the function of children's art will establish the arts as a focal point in elementary school curricula from which many other skills will develop.

EVERY TEACHER CAN BE A MODEL

Sixty elementary school teachers and administrators recently visited an experimental arts workshop in a neighboring school district. "You are welcome to come," the invitation read, "not to observe, but to participate. Please come dressed accordingly."

Despite this request, the attire of the visitors immediately revealed that most of them had decided to be observers rather han participants. A certain reserved panic characterized their reactions when they were urged to join the "fun."

"Oh, I can't draw."

"I have no talent at all."

"I can't carry a tune in an egg basket."

"Excuse me, but I have back trouble."

Such embarrassed apologies were mumbled repeatedly.

As activities in rhythm, movement, electronic music, improvisational dramatics, costume-making, weaving, and sculpting hummed, echoed, and reverberated around them, more and more visitors were seen tentatively touching lumps of wet clay, assuming slightly irregular stances, or emitting resonant notes of unusual pitch. Initial attempts were made gingerly, even surreptitiously, but within two hours the sixty formerly fearful adults had joined two hundred children in chanting syncopated sentences, parading barefoot to improvised Elizabethan music, pummeling and prodding moist clay, pantomiming slow-motion tennis and fencing tournaments, decorating fanciful masks, and balancing towers of small wooden crescents and triangles. How did this transformation come about?

"I learned from the children," commented one teacher. "Their concentration and enthusiasm were contagious."

Another thoughtful participant described feeling "petrified" at the beginning. "For the first time I understood the way my students feel when I place them in a totally new situation. I was so afraid, that I wanted to resist any demands made upon me."

"I had that reaction too," volunteered another, "but then I felt a sense of relief in taking my cues from the children around me. They were so absorbed in their own efforts and, at the same time, so relaxed. After a while I stopped worrying about being noticed or making mistakes. I just wanted to try my hand."

One animated visitor summarized the feelings of many: "I had a great time sharing this experience with the kids. I found that I could respond the way they did—with pleasure!"

Much to their surprise and delight, the workshop visitors discovered their own responsiveness. The reluctance and hesitancy they first felt were overcome when they accepted the children's joy in participation as a model for their own behavior. They learned that involvement in the process of making art not only provided pleasure but also an impetus for thinking. They became more concerned with their own thoughts and actions and less threatened by outside evaluation. They experienced Susanne Langer's assertion that, "The entire qualification for understanding art is responsiveness."[1]

Many teachers feel that they must always provide a model of excellence and shy away from areas where they fear inadequacy. An impossible standard of excellence in all areas is self-defeating in teaching and is a prime reason why the arts are so outrageously neglected. Were everyone to defer to Picasso or Rembrandt, no one would enjoy or even attempt to produce art objects.

One teacher at the workshop recalled her practice of watching Charity Bailey's music program on television at home and then teaching the same songs to her first-graders the next week. This practice proceeded splendidly until one ebullient youngster burst into school one morning exclaiming, "Teacher, teacher, there is a lady on TV who sings the same songs you sing—only better!"

We're sure that Charity Bailey's emulator did not sing so badly. Although hardly a rival for Ms. Bailey, she provided a model of someone who was alert and responsive to the stimuli around her and who was willing to try new experiences. Being this kind of model, not an infallibly excellent expert, is what is needed to encourage children to have confidence in their own efforts. While teachers' musical abilities may not equal professional musicians, their talents as teachers may be measured by the gusto with which their children sing and by the understanding and zest for music they instill.

One of our objectives is to relieve teachers of the paralysis caused by fear of imperfect technique or lack of "talent." Teachers so often urge children to "go ahead and try" and yet neglect their own good advice. We are all troubled by passivity in students who spend too much time in front of television sets. We want them to become the active agents of their own learning, even if their efforts aren't as polished and entertaining as those seen on television. Children must understand that the process of acquiring skills is a sequential one that takes time and experience. The aim of teachers should be to provide models of this process rather than to exhibit an already attained goal. The goal itself will vary according to the individual, but everyone

---

[1] *Feeling and Form* (New York: Charles Scribner, 1953), p. 396.

must be courageous enough to attempt the process. Teachers who are actively pursuing a goal without embarrassment are conveying something far more important than technique or expertise in any one art form. Their attitude will establish the arts as everyone's province and will open new lines of communication between students and teachers.

Must a teacher be able to draw? The answer is unequivocally "no." It is the willingness to try and the excitement of discovery that lead to learning in the arts—as in all areas—for children and for their teachers. As the teacher mentioned before told her young critic, "Some of you may grow up to be musicians like Charity Bailey. Others of you will have different professions. You may become teachers like me. But all of us can enjoy and learn to understand music and all the arts if we make sure they are always a part of our lives."

WHAT WE MEAN BY THE TERM "ART"

Birds sing melodiously, bees erect structures of symmetry and beauty, spiders weave delicate patterns, and stickleback fish dance rhythmically while mating. Can it be said that these creatures produce art? Certainly their creations have aesthetic merit, but they are the predictable results of involuntary behavior. Instinct rather than intention dictates their forms.

The word art derives from the Latin root ars, which means a skill or special competence that is learned rather than instinctive. In early China the word for art, yi-shu, similarly meant any learned skill.[2] During the Middle Ages in Europe all scholarly pursuits, including mathematics, rhetoric, and the attainment of literacy, were included among the arts.

Today art refers to the conscious efforts of human beings to arrange colors, shapes, lines, sounds, movements, and other sensory phenomena to express their ideas and feelings about themselves and their world. In our highly specialized society, the word "art" has taken on a special meaning. Too frequently, it is considered a form of entertainment for moments of leisure rather than an aspect of everyday life. Yet people are making aesthetic decisions when they select homes, furniture, clothing, and all the objects with which they surround themselves.

[2] Gerald Berreman et al., Anthropology Today (California: Communications Research Machines, Inc., 1971).

The restricted concept of art characteristic of modern industrialized societies is very different from views prevalent in other cultures. There, aesthetic qualities are not separate entities but are integrally bound up with meaning and content and are assumed to be natural elements of the culture.

When anthropologists study a society, they consider the arts as a kind of map. Like the Rosetta Stone, art frequently provides a key to the beliefs, myths, customs, and history of a people. Particularly in societies where literacy is not sophisticated, the arts are relied upon to express the culture, record it, and assure its continuity.

Children are part of the larger society in which they live, but they also have their own styles of thinking, learning, playing, and making art. They have a special "culture." Since literacy is not highly developed in their culture, they utilize other expressive modes. Art is frequently one of these, if opportunities for seeing it and making it are available. Parents and teachers can look at children's art in the same way anthropologists study the Rosetta Stone's hieroglyphics. Art provides a key for understanding children's ideas and concepts. Perhaps more significantly, it enables children themselves to make tangible contacts with their own ideas and so better understand themselves, as the following incident illustrates.

*   *   *

A sixth-grade class became interested in how faces change with the mood of a person. They looked in mirrors as they scowled, cried, giggled, and meditated. They looked at each other, and as they looked, they noticed the changes that took place in the lines and in the forms of the face as expressions changed.

The children agreed that they could draw these moods, but that it would be more fun to try to paint a face, using colors that would also suggest a mood. The children got busy, and soon I saw many different types of faces appearing. When everyone had finished, we enjoyed looking at the paintings and guessing the moods.

George had made a large angry face with a rich dark purple background. "That's interesting, George," I commented. "So you think of purple as an angry color, right?"

George stood there, quiet for a moment, and then he replied, "Well, I guess that is what I think, but I didn't know it until I put it down." He shook his head appreciatively, like a little old man. He had just learned something new about George.

To think clearly and act intelligently, people must examine and compare the bewildering possibilities around them. They must separate the important from the unimportant. The art process is one means of doing this. Subjecting the disorder of life to an orderly arrangement satisfies basic human needs and also provides the pleasure of sensory experiences derived from arrangements of color, line, shape, space, and texture. Art is essentially a quest for order.

Before taking action of any sort, people must make decisions. In art, the first ones involve selection. For instance, if I decide to make a picture, what will I depict? What do I want to express? What medium shall I use to express it? Or shall I choose a medium first and allow it to suggest the subject?

Selection of subject matter and media must be followed by more decisions. An artist defines a problem by thinking, "I will paint a picture of that bowl of fruit on the table. Now I must decide from what angle or perspective to draw it. Shall it have a sketchy or sharp look, muted or bright colors, or be bold or gentle in design? Should component parts be realistic or simplified abstractly? What parts should be emphasized, what parts should be contrasted?

In making these decisions, the artist not only carefully scrutinizes the subject, but also identifies his or her own point of view. During this process, the artist arranges and rearranges the parts of the composition, constantly evaluating decisions and refining concepts.

In the creation process, an artist (1) selects personally significant objects, (2) examines relationships between and within them, and (3) attempts an arrangement of visual forms that has a logical order according to the individual's point of view. When complete, the painting may state: "This is a bowl of fruit, boldly stated in geometric patterns, painted flatly in broad areas of bright color, and expressive of my interest in the variety of shapes and patterns as they appear on a flat surface."

Children making art engage in much the same process. They (1) select objects from their surroundings that are important to them ("My mother and me and the sun."), (2) begin to explore the relationships among them ("My face and my eyes are round like the sun. Mommy's face is round, too."), and (3) arrange them according to a personally meaningful system, that is, translating their selected subject matter into visual forms of their

Even young artists reveal their own points of view. To a small child, a grown-up appears as tall as the sky itself.

own design ("Mommy is smiling at me. The sun is smiling at us. Mommy is almost as big as the sky.").

In their first drawings, young children draw what are, to them, significant objects in the environment, putting them in an order which makes sense to them. At the same time, they fit themselves into this scheme of things. While reconstructing experiences in an imaginative way in paint, clay, or other media, children reveal their thoughts and shape new ones. Experimenting with media involves curiosity and heightened sensitivity. As children become aware of their power to change and reorder the shapes they have created, they develop self-confidence and an appreciation of their own possibilities and assertiveness. These are by-products of the art process. They are also the goals of every educator.

CHILD ART AND FINE ART— HOW THEY DIFFER

Children produce art in a spontaneous and natural way, yet all children do not become great artists, or even artists at all, when they mature. In part this is because other expressive techniques, such as verbal language, are perfected, while the skills necessary to the arts are permitted to atrophy. But it is also true that adults have different standards for child art and fine art, and each is expected to fulfill different functions.

Young children practice art to express ideas, to explore art media, and to assert themselves. These concerns are so engrossing that they show small interest in perfecting techniques or mastering form. They are more absorbed in what the *process* has to offer than in how their *products* will be evaluated. They seem to respond to internal rather than externally imposed criteria.

By contrast, the fine arts are very much concerned with form and technique. Technical mastery may be achieved with beauty and perfection, and most fine artists are very much concerned with external criteria, such as their previous achievements and what their future impact will be.

In child art, adults look for revelations about patterns of thought and feeling that may help them to understand a child and to communicate with her or him. We value the spontaneity of children's artistic expressions and appreciate the energy, thought, and joy that went into their production.

Our expectations of the fine arts are quite different. Here unique visions, technical excellence, profound and challenging experiences, and aesthetic pleasures are valued. Great art uplifts, jolts, inspires, or affirms essential truths; it sharpens and enlarges our perceptions. Child art may achieve these results at times, but we do not have these expectations for it. In analyzing child art, the primary approach should be on gaining insight into the child and her or his spontaneity. In fine art, the approach is on gaining insight into the physical world and the human condition within it. Both child art and fine art create bonds of human understanding and are manifestations of individual creativity and power.

WHAT WE MEAN BY THE TERM "ART EDUCATION"

Art education is concerned with the production of both child art at the early stages and fine art as children become more adult. The former is facilitated by providing suitable materials and opportunities for self-expression. The latter is enhanced by technical instruction and extending frames of reference, that is, broadening awareness of the range of human experience and of the possibilities open to individuals. This includes exposure to possible viewpoints, possible uses of materials, possible goals. Extending frames of reference is one of the most critical functions of the arts. Through art, people can observe many ways of looking at the world and can accept differences as natural rather than threatening. Learning to respond to other people and ideas and recognizing that other views and tastes are valid are surely primary aims of education.

Is art education just the act of randomly working with art materials? Or does it mean organizing these materials to express ideas? Is it making art objects for the pleasure of the process? Or is it for the pleasure of having the final product? Is it learning how to look at art objects in order to enjoy them? Is it understanding an art object as a product of a particular social, cultural, or political setting or as a visual expression of one's personal feelings?

Art created in school can be any or all of these things, depending upon the age of the student and the skill and point of view of the teacher. An educator comparing art and poetry instruction noted that, "in schools all over America, children are excited when the art teacher comes in; and a look at children's art in recent years shows that something really happens in those art classes."[3]

In quality art experiences, which need not be confined to an art room, analysis shows that children are learning:

- to observe carefully and to record their observations
- to organize ideas and to express feelings
- to work with purpose
- to solve problems individually through trial-and-error methods
- to respect themselves through their own achievements
- to communicate
- to discover their own points of view
- to appreciate different viewpoints and cultures
- to create change in their environment using a wide range of media
- to make aesthetic discoveries and judgments

All these learnings may occur if children are given opportunities to work with art materials in ways that challenge their own ideas rather than dictate 1-2-3-type procedures. Recipes that result in identical finished products may improve skill in taking directions but not in creating art. Everyone needs technical instruction about how to proceed with a task, but in art for children, techniques should be determined after significant goals have been defined. This approach is more meaningful and is easier for teachers in the long run.

Compiling recipes may seem simple, but it usually requires a frantic search for the latest gimmick. Teachers should be reassured that they do not need to come up with a new idea for an art lesson every week. Instead of an endless succession of superficially explored materials, basic media and the time to use it should be readily available. Encouraging repeated use of crayons, paint, and clay does not limit students to prosaic tasks. Rather, it guarantees children the basic right described by Pearl Greenberg—"the chance to improve."[4]

This is not to say that innovative uses of unconventional materials should never be suggested; it is simply that desperate searching for novel art experiences is neither necessary nor desirable. Frequently the simplest and most accessible materials can

---

[3] John Gardner. "They Clapped When He Entered the Classroom," *New York Times Book Review*, December 23, 1973, p. 1.
[4] *Children's Experiences in Art* (New York: Van Nostrand Reinhold Co., 1966), pp. 48–9.

provide the deepest experiences if they are handled with intelligence and sensitivity. It is not the styrofoam or even the crayon in the hands of children that makes art. Rather, it is what children *do* with media that counts—what they say about themselves and about nature and how they experiment with color, form, or texture.

Children can also be taught how to evaluate their work and that of others. Evaluation should take place in both an individual and group context. Individual children six years old and up can advance their understanding of their own growth when their work is placed before them for this purpose. A teacher might suggest, for example, "Let's look at this painting by placing it beside the one that you did last week. Which one do you like better? Let's think about why you think it's better." If children observe that they have not only used more colors but have also mixed some new ones, it can easily be pointed out that real improvement has been made. Adult approval as well as their own recognition will encourage further mixing of colors and thus more individualization of their paintings. If children do not notice differences by themselves, they should be pointed out to them.

Another change might involve spacial relationships. If children make their main figures very small and place them down in a corner of the page, they can be commended for making a new figure larger and placing it in a more dominant position.

In this type of interchange, teachers are both evaluating and setting standards of taste as they point out the strengths of each child's work. For more talented children, more sophisticated comments may be made, for instance about the quality of line or solidity of form.

At the group level, evaluation may be handled by a coming together at the end of every art session. (This only refers to group art activities, of course.) As the work is spread out, the group could be asked, "What was our objective when we started today? Do you think we achieved what we set out to do? Which of these pictures does it well, and why do you think it has been successful?" Verbalizing opinions and observations establishes standards of quality in the minds of children. It is extremely valuable and adds dignity to their art efforts.

*　　*　　*

When asked why art education is needed in school, several third-graders furnished their own answers:

Sylvia, emotional and volatile: "When you feel bad, it makes you feel better to make a painting—and then you're not so mad at everybody."

Noel, thoughtful and analytical: "Art lets you see inside of somebody."

Mary, practical and down-to-earth: "You need art because you want to make your school look pretty."

Bobby, dreamer of the future: "Who knows, someday you may want to design a rocket or something. . . ."

GENERAL GUIDELINES FOR TEACHERS

When introducing art activities the following techniques will help implement the approaches proposed in this book:

- Plan new subject areas with open-ended lessons.
- Encourage individual choices of subjects, forms, and colors.
- Treat every child with respect and be sensitive to his or her sense of personal dignity.
- Encourage children to express their own feelings and opinions. Differences of opinion need not threaten your sense of authority.
- Handle children's work with care. Mount selected pictures and have the children make portfolios in which to keep their own artwork.
- Look for something positive to say about each piece of work, but train yourself, through discussions with the children, to distinguish between serious efforts and thoughtless scribbling.
- When children express frustration, gently suggest techniques or alternative ideas. Relate the assignment to their own interests and experiences. Help them to create an abstraction of their mental images by emphasizing essential components and eliminating unnecessary details. Give recognition to what is attained and praise perseverance.

3. The Nature of Children's Art

Children's art was far from my mind when I visited the ancient walled city of Acre in Israel some time ago. Dark, narrow passageways framed by Moorish arches, sunny courtyards encircled by tiered galleries and the aroma of tamarindi, a pungent drink made from dates combined to make the setting exotic. While walking in a courtyard, I suddenly noticed a sheet of paper on the ground. Imagine my surprise when I picked it up and found a most familiar picture. Two simple and identical flowers were standing on each side of a smiling person who was drawn in geometric shapes. The figure was perpendicular to a straight line near the bottom of the page. Another straight line near the top signified the sky.

The artist identified herself as an Arab girl by drawing her conical hat. But the emphasis on the central person, the bright sky, and the symmetrical flowers arranged with stability on the horizontal groundline revealed her affinity with the children I taught in the United States, who repeatedly drew the same images. I was not so different from the people of this strange place as I had thought! If I could have met Ohmima (I had the name on the paper translated later), I could have communicated with her using paper and crayons, although I couldn't speak her language.

Young children everywhere use geometrical shapes to represent people and horizontal lines to represent the sky and the earth. This happy drawing was made by a small Arab girl living in Israel.

From infancy most parents complain proudly about a child who is "into everything." Active children demand alert attendants, and their busy behavior indicates vital curiosity that should be encouraged. Children not only "get into" places, but they do things with the objects they find there. They stack blocks, bang pots, and rearrange the boxes or shoes or cans or spools of thread without regard for the order of their elders. These pursuits engross youngsters for long periods because they not only discover new objects, they can make their own arrangements of them. The creative impulse is a companion to the discovery drive in all people. Individuals experience curiosity and creativity in different degrees, but everyone has these impulses. We learn about the world and our roles and possibilities in it through these drives. Retaining their vitality is one of the primary goals of modern educators.

Children's art collected from almost every country reveals that no matter what their culture or location, children begin to draw at about the same time and their drawings show similar arrangements of forms and sequential patterns of development.[1] Just as the first sounds that babies make are the same around the world, children's first scribbles are also the same. Linguists hypothesize that there may be biological structures for language patterns.[2] Perhaps there are similar structures for aesthetic development. This will be an exciting area of study in the future.

"Aesthetics" is a word commonly associated with an appreciation of the beautiful, but each person's perception of beauty is different. The term itself derives from the Greek word pertaining to sense perception, the ways individuals perceive and critically evaluate their surroundings.

Aesthetic experience begins even before children come in contact with crayons and paints. When they express preferences for colors, shapes, sounds, tastes and textures, they are making aesthetic choices. They are also learning to choose between alternatives and to develop personal values. An aesthetic re-

---

[1] Rhoda Kellogg, *Analyzing Children's Art* (Palo Alto, Calif.: National Press Books, 1969), and Dale B. Harris, *Children's Drawings as Measures of Intellectual Maturity: A Revision and Extension of the Goodenough Draw-a-Man Test* (New York: Harcourt Brace Jovanovich, 1963).
[2] Noam Chomsky, *Language and Mind* (New York: Harcourt Brace Jovanovich, 1972).

sponse is a requisite for this development; it has been called "the beginning and model of other types of judgment."[3]

When infants make an aesthetic response, whether through an eager clutching of a silky blanket, or a delighted thrashing at a bright object or a shuddering rejection of an objectionable taste, they are beginning to assert their unique identities. Their reactions express their preferences and communicate them. Long before children can speak, their responses to the shapes, sounds, and other sensory phenomena around them establish their special personalities and their styles of interacting with the world. These aesthetic responses to sensory stimuli are the beginning of self-expression. They provide the bases for "individualized" learning for all children, whether in Tokyo, Chicago, or Helsinki.

The gusto and intensity with which infants register their early aesthetic choices continue to typify their contacts with the arts. When children begin to draw and paint, they appear totally absorbed in their movements. They seem to give little thought to a subject or purpose, although they are delighted when they see the marks they have made. The fact that such pleasurable movements have produced marks heightens feelings of satisfaction. The marks become a source of pride in personal achievement. The picture that remains after the experience is evidence of a child's power. Later, awareness of personal impact on the environment through such things as artistic creativity and others' recognition of it play a key role in school achievement.

AS AN EXPRESSION OF GROWTH

Children's first scribbles appear haphazard, but they soon exhibit a measure of control. Similar motions are repeated, which create designs. While kinesthetic satisfaction is the first primary motivating factor, coordinating motor and visual considerations later becomes an objective. Here again children's increasing awareness of their ability to control actions and create designs enhance their feelings of individual power.

As children grow and begin to examine the pictures they enjoy making, they begin to see images in the lines they have drawn. After pushing and pulling a light green crayon for several

---

[3] Eric Larrabee, "Arts—The One Stable Currency," *New York Times*, September 2, 1973.

minutes, a three-year-old was startled at "the grasshopper jumping at me." As if by magic, his next picture produced "a polar bear cuddling up to a polar bear friend." This child had reached a very important stage. By perceiving images in his drawings and

DEVELOPMENTAL STAGES IN

APPROXIMATE AGES	PIAGET'S STAGES OF COGNITIVE DEVELOPMENT	LOWENFELD'S STAGES OF ART DEVELOPMENT
0–2	SENSORI-MOTOR Infant's behavior depends on reflexes. Habits form. Can't evoke absent objects. Grasping, manipulation, other tactile and kinesthetic sensations aid beginnings of thought	Art begins when the senses first contact the environment and the child reacts to these sensory experiences. Touching, feeling, seeing, manipulating, tasting, listening are essential background for the production of art

2–4	SYMBOLIC FUNCTION
	Representation of absent objects and events begins through:
	    deferred imitation—imitation after model disappears
	    symbolic play—pretending, make-believe
	    drawing—
	        enjoyment of exercise as play
	        recognition of form in what was aimless scribbling ("fortuitous realism")
	        attempts to render model from memory—parts of whole are often misplaced by adult standards ("failed realism")
	    mental imagery
	    speech
		SCRIBBLING
		Notation of imaginative self-expression begins through:
		    uncontrolled scribbling—kinesthetic experience is satisfying
		    control of repeated motions—increasing coordination of motor and visual activities
		    the beginning of naming drawn forms—showing change from kinesthetic emphasis to imaginative thinking. Child realizes that:
		        there are relationships between drawn figures and outside world
		        absent objects and events can be pictured
		Results—Drawings become a record of concepts and feelings. Drawing displays visual retention of absent objects, events, i.e., *symbolism*, which is basic to reading skills

4–7	INTUITIVE THOUGHT
	    egocentric—cannot take other viewpoints into account
	    draws what he knows not what he sees ("intellectual realism"). Conceptual attributes pictured although not perceived visually (carrots growing underground, both legs of horseback rider in profile)
	    spontaneous geometry of child and drawing observations converge (see Piaget's *Child's Conception of Space*). Relationships of proximity, separation, enclosure and other topological considerations begin to be explored
		PRESCHEMATIC
		    egocentric—self is center of spatial considerations. Symbols for people based on self-awareness
		    draws what he knows not what he sees. Transparencies or X-ray pictures indicate what is known to exist although not logically visible
		    drawings begin to show attention to relationships in the environment, such as spatial arrangements. Child begins to rely on geometric lines and shapes

[4] This chart is meant as a frame of reference that may be helpful in understanding children's growth, but it should not be rigidly interpreted. The primary sources are: Piaget and Inhelder, *The Psychology of the Child* (New York: Basic Books, 1969) and Lowenfeld and Brittain, *Creative and Mental Growth*, 4th ed. (New York: Macmillan, 1964).

naming them, he indicated that he was thinking imaginatively.

The shift from kinesthetic emphasis to an interest in mental imagery is a significant one. At this point children understand a relationship between their art and the world around them. They

CHILDREN'S THINKING AND ART[4]

APPROXIMATE AGES	PIAGET'S STAGES OF COGNITIVE DEVELOPMENT	LOWENFELD'S STAGES OF ART DEVELOPMENT

7–11	CONCRETE OPERATIONS
	symbolic representation becomes coherent through interest in classification (relating groups of objects), and generalization (inferring principles, systems)
	comprehension of reversible operations, such as joining and separating, takes place through perception of transformation processes
	intellectual realism continues
	chain of chronological events may appear in one drawing
	at about 9 *visual realism* appears in art with attention to:
	    one *specific perspective*—excludes concealed parts; profiles are accurate; background objects are smaller
	    understanding of *proportions* is attempted
	    overall plan emphasizes *relationship of parts to whole*
	sense of Euclidean metric geometry begins
	decentering begins—can conceive of other people's viewpoints
	interpersonal relations take on cooperative aspect
	socialization involves cognitive, affective, moral domains
		SCHEMATIC (7–9 YEARS APPROX.)
		symbolic formuli—individual schemas are used to show personal concepts and generalizations
		further generalization indicated by deviations from standard schemas used to exaggerate the important and omit the unimportant
		groundline, sun, sky show attention to *spatial organization*
		planned *grouping* of different episodes in same drawing, e.g. elevated groundlines to show several events in a sequence
		
		DAWNING REALISM (9–11 YEARS APPROX.)
		child focusses on one perspective—gains ability to overlap forms without revealing concealed parts. Examples: sky meets the earth; objects behind others are only partially visible
		lines become more realistic than geometric. Formula schemas and baseline format disappear
		discovery of plane
		cooperation in group work—interest in team effort—"The Gang Age"

12–15	FORMAL OPERATIONS conceives of alternate possible changes in reality. Begins to form plans for the future—interests oriented toward non-present and future values and ideals become important child can reason about hypotheses, draw conclusions from possibilities beginning deductive thought. Can deal with verbal abstractions, anticipate through deductive capacities peer influence is great. "Final fundamental decentering"	PSEUDO-NATURALISTIC (12–14 YEARS APPROX.) "Age of Reasoning" love for dramatization and imaginative action (expressing exploration of possibilities) attempts to render perspective accurately (showing diminution of egocentric viewpoint) human figure—usually caricatured, rarely individualized. Self-portraits are avoided—"Identity crisis" color used to express mood, emotion. Child is increasingly self-critical CRISIS OF ADOLESCENCE (13–17 YEARS APPROX.) critical awareness of environment naturalistic depictions of momentary impressions value relationships emphasized abstract qualities aesthetic considerations

understand that pictures can be symbols of other things. They show that they can think about things that may not be obvious at the moment. All of these nonverbal operations are essential steps in the intellectual development that will later enable children to read.

This development has fascinated many psychologists, learning theorists, and art educators. Jean Piaget has elaborately described cognitive development, while Viktor Lowenfeld has dealt with drawing development. The progressive patterns in each area have been grouped by both theorists into stages. These defined stages have been sources of great controversy when they have been rigidly interpreted, but as guides for understanding children's viewpoints and growth, they can be most helpful to teachers and are, therefore, included here. Teachers must always be wary of using any formula to label or categorize individual students. The described stages are not cubbyholes for sorting and storing youngsters; instead, they provide an interesting theory for understanding normal patterns of development.

Piaget, Lowenfeld, Montessori, and others believe that biological patterns of growth are nourished by the environment and advance in a general sequence. Their shared approach does not deny or minimize the importance of individual differences. They argue that an understanding of normal development is the necessary starting point for appreciating differences between individuals.

As can be seen from the chart, there are striking correlations between Piaget's theory of cognitive development and Lowenfeld's descriptions of drawing development. The obvious parallels attest to the validity of using children's drawings as indicators of their thinking.

Both Piaget and Lowenfeld discuss the egocentric behavior of children in the "intuitive thought" and "preschematic" stages. At these stages, children's drawings are often large representations of the self at the center of the paper with other elements revolving around the self-image. When children enter the "concrete operational" and "schematic" stages, they become more objective and a new spatial organization appears. A sturdy groundline is drawn horizontally across the lower portion of the paper, which usually supports blades of green grass. In the upper area, a parallel line stands for the sky but stops short of the edges to allow a sun to shine over all. Frequently, children draw in these elements first with ritualistic fervor. Only when they have completed them are they ready to consider anything else. These basic components set the stage. The people, houses, clouds, flora, and fauna that are next added to the scene also have the appearance of formula. They are schematic representations of what they stand for. Children at this stage are not attempting to mirror reality but are using symbols to communicate.

A seven-year-old child sitting in front of six different kinds of trees will draw a row of green circles with identical brown lines beneath each one because the actual trees are cues for her or his own tree symbol. Similarly, children of this age usually develop a characteristic pattern of lines that stands for "person." Men, women, and children are drawn in the same pattern with only slight modifications. This is a type of shorthand children know can be understood. Their use of these schematic patterns indicates a need to find a logical order in the environment and a comprehension of such cognitive skills as abstraction and generalization.

AS AN EXPRESSION OF INDIVIDUALITY

Within the normative theories advanced by learning theorists, various modes of perception and styles of problem-solving are recognized. Stated simply, some children see forests, while others see trees; some create imaginary animals and fantasies of idyllic retreats, while others must examine rock, leaf, and lichen in minute detail. Educators are often asked to analyze each student's personality type and maturational level in order to "match" her or his particular configuration to the appropriate learning situation. This presents an awesome task for most teachers, especially since definitive information about the various learning styles is not known at present. The existence of different styles is undisputed, but the specific nature of the differences is still a matter of conjecture.

The emphasis must be on providing for variation. Teachers must offer a choice of avenues toward any desired goal. This is far simpler in art than elsewhere in the curriculum because in art variation is assumed and highly valued. In addition, observation of students' methods of working with various art materials may provide clues for more clearly defining their styles of learning. Is a child more comfortable with two- or three-dimensional media? Does a child depict precise details or boldly simplified forms? Does she concentrate on particular subject matter? Does he

Seven-year-olds utilize many symbols to portray scenes in the world around them. In this crayon drawing, for example, the row of trees in a formula design represent a dense forest of many different kinds of trees. Perhaps the fish being caught by the fisherman was inspired by Jaws. The young artist included himself at the top of the bank of the canal.

confine himself to a limited area on the page or does he expand beyond its borders? What relationship do these tendencies have to the child's general demeanor? Considerations such as these may further illuminate knowledge of personality types and learning styles.

In addition, children regulate their activities in art to a much greater degree than in other subject areas. Given materials, they proceed at an individual rate and produce according to individual interests and capabilities. External demands such as group levels of instruction are less influential in art than in other curricula. The teacher need not be concerned about assignments that may be too advanced or too limited because each child performs art tasks on his or her own terms and develops them individually. They are able to refine concepts through observation and practice. Art activities are truly self-pacing!

These qualities of the art process greatly reduce the danger of frustration. The trial-and-error method of problem-solving is completely acceptable in art. In fact, it is the preferred method. Art has been called "the subject no one fails" because students are encouraged to keep trying new solutions. There is a much more relaxed attitude about experimentation, acceptance of errors, and new attempts. There is no single right answer to be memorized and spewed forth. Children are willing, even determined, to persist because of the intrinsic enjoyment of their own activities. Making art is the prototype of the play-learning and learning-by-doing situations favored by Piaget, Dewey, Montessori, and others.

*   *   *

One day when four weeks' worth of drawings and paintings of thirty-three children had piled up around me, I decided that the accumulation would have to be returned. Although many of the first-graders had neglected to sign their names, distribution was not a problem. Almost before owners could look up from admiring their last pictures to claiming their new ones, others were advising, "That's Michael's," "That's Lynn's," or "That's David's." The subject matter of the artwork did not have a very wide range. Houses and flower gardens, children and pets, birds and airplanes, whales and ships abounded. Still, the children were able to recognize the distinct personal styles of their classmates.

As often as I have carried out this task, I always find it exciting. Children's art has so many universal characteristics in which so much seems typical of all children, and yet it has so many unique qualities that each child's work retains its individuality. When children look at their own artwork and that of their friends, I think that they too experience a thrill in sensing both shared and distinctive characteristics.

AS COMMUNICATION

Historically, art has served to communicate the values, beliefs, myths, and traditions of a culture to its people. This communication has been of particular importance in societies where most individuals were illiterate. Similarly, among children who have not attained literacy, art functions as a potent force for transmitting information to them and for yielding information about them. Art symbols are more powerful than verbal ones because they have obvious references to visible realities. They are not as arbitrary as alphabets. In fact, the symbols of written alphabets were derived from pictures such as those seen in hieroglyphics. Some languages retain a closer relationship to picture-writing than others; for example, Chinese uses ideograms as symbols.

As noted, the production of ideograms, which Lowenfeld refers to as "schemas," are a natural development of children's drawings. These are abstract graphics which children use to stand for person, tree, house, sun, bird, and the like. After producing their own meaningful symbols, children can then understand others' symbols in reading.

At first, children are able to describe real experiences and imaginary adventures with greater facility, complexity, and intensity in drawings than in writing or even in speaking.

*   *   *

Susan was extremely reticent. Her kindergarten had been in the same room, but everything was different now. Children from other schools, many of them older than Susan, had joined us for a summer art program. All the kindergarten furniture had been moved out, and large tables for artwork were everywhere. Instead of the doll corner and the sandbox, there were collage and sculpture centers. And strange adults kept coming and looking around. I knew that Susan was confused and upset at the changes. She looked sad, moved slowly, and spoke only in barely audible monosyllables.

One day everyone came in excited about the thunderstorms

during the previous night. It was impossible for the youngsters to listen to each other because so many urgently wanted to speak. Those who shouted above the rest sounded incoherent because they tried to rush out so much information. I suggested that everyone draw their experiences of the night before. Even Susan, who had shown no excitement, proceeded cooperatively to the task. Her picture contained a wealth of detail.

"I see someone with a broken umbrella," I noted.

"That's my father; the wind made his umbrella break," Susan contributed.

"Is that person holding a big key?" I asked.

Susan beamed, "My mother is running to close the windows of the car."

"And there is the lightning flashing in the sky," I observed.

"Yes," Susan added, "it is scaring me. See, I'm in my night-gown."

And there she was, conversing for the first time.

I wrote down Susan's story about her picture on a separate piece of paper and mounted them together. Her request to take the large sheet home showed more enthusiasm than any of her responses during the previous three weeks. After that, Susan made many story pictures, which she held up under a smiling face at "Sharing Time." At first, the other children deciphered the stories while Susan nodded or shook her head to indicate if their interpretations were correct. Two weeks later, Susan was explaining her pictures to visiting teachers. At the end of the summer session, Susan compiled a number of the drawings she had been inserting daily in her folder and wrote a story in a first-grader's uneven script to accompany them.

"I like sunny days. I like to walk my dog Pepsi. I like Jodi to go with me. I like caterpillars. I didn't like our room before but now I do."

Then Susan made a cover for her book and wrote, "Summer School is good. I like to color," on the outside.

AS AN EXPRESSION OF EMOTIONS

Jeffrey was in the second grade when Dr. Martin Luther King died. He came into class the next day extremely agitated. He had many fights with classmates, some of whom were very close friends although they were black and he was white. I tried to

The day after the assassination of Dr. Martin Luther King, a second-grade white boy drew this strong portrait of the civil rights leader.

talk to Jeffrey, but he only pouted sullenly and seemed on the verge of tears. Since he wouldn't participate appropriately, I finally had to isolate him. Later I found a print of Murillo's *A Girl and Her Duenna*, which he had taken off the bulletin board. On the back he had drawn the powerful crayon portrait illustrated here. The dignified man doesn't look exactly like Dr. King, but I knew who it was.

As with complicated ideas, youngsters often find it easier and more satisfying to create a picture of an emotionally laden subject than to describe it in words. Children communicate with themselves in this way and are freed from explaining details to make another person understand. Observing children at work on art projects, one frequently finds them exclaiming, humming, grunting, sighing, laughing, or talking to themselves while they concentrate intently.

All children's art defies realistic proportions and colors can be considered "expressionist." Expressionist artists distort for the sake of psychological impact, while children depict relative sizes of things according to the aspects that are important to them. They choose colors on the basis of personal significance or appeal. Frequently their choices distort reality. While mature artists may choose to be realists depicting outward appearances, or expressionists probing inner sensations, or formalists concentrating on intellectual problems, children do not have these choices. Their art combines ideas and feelings inextricably. The concentration characteristic of children's artistic production releases emotions as well as satisfies the need to communicate. Fulfilling these needs is one of the reasons children find art activities so satisfying. The end product is fine and highly significant, but it is of secondary importance to the contacts with ideas and feelings that were enjoyed during its production.

Many psychiatrists, including Dr. Robert Coles, often provide crayons and paper as "ice breakers" at the start of their sessions. While serving this function, the drawings produced also yield many insights into the concerns of the youngsters and provide obvious subject matter for discussions. Teachers can also use drawings to gain insight into student interests and to initiate discussions. Some children who appear to be struck dumb when asked to discuss simple occurrences, such as a weekend's events, become highly articulate when given a picture to describe, whether their own drawing, that of a classmate, or a dramatic photograph. Teachers can use drawings and paintings created in an art period in many ways to encourage children to write and talk about subjects that are important to them.

*   *   *

Eric was a shy and extremely quiet but physically active six-year-old. He told this story after he drew a picture of a tearful boy:

THE BIG BULLIES

This little boy was walking down the street. Some big bullies threw snowballs at him. His mother told the big bullies to stop. Then the boy went to sleep. He dreamed a mosquito bit him and he jumped up. He saw the bullies out the window. Then he saw his father coming home from work. He fell asleep again.

Calvin described his picture of a man and a whale:

A STRONG SWIMMER

One day a man swam underwater. He found a big shark. The shark had many sharp teeth. The shark jumped and jumped. The man took a shortcut but he landed in a dark whales' cage; the whales were not sleeping, either. The man was trapped. He saw a whale walk on its tail. . . .

Some men saw the trouble and jumped out of their boat and worked hard. Finally the man got home by steamboat.

I posted these stories next to their pictures and frequently observed the boys and their friends identifying words to each other.

Children who are petrified of certain situations are sometimes relieved by picturing them in detail. One boy was able to articulate his terror of returning to a dentist's office after painting a highly expressionist version of the scene complete with glaring lights and harsh colors. He was noticeably more relaxed about the necessary return visit after making his painting.

Some children's ardor for producing nightmare scenes of war or horrifying assemblies of monsters may be their attempts to define and conquer their fears. This would be similar to children's delight in violent fairy tales. Paintings or drawings seem to translate vague anxieties into clearly labeled objects that thus become less menacing. "Don't worry, Jimmy," I once heard a five-year-old assure his imaginary friend, "I put the monster on the paper where we can see him all the time and he can't bother us anymore."

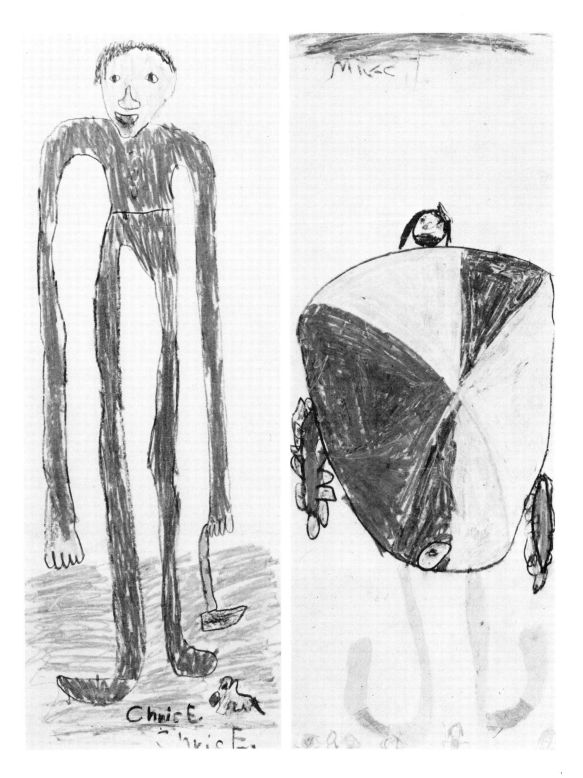

These two very different perceptions of John Henry are examples of the ways children distort size and shape to emphasize the important reality. Note the tiny people and the small animal at the bottom of the drawings.

Children's responses affirm art as a natural mode of expression and communication. If teachers recognize children's art as a powerful means of experimenting with ideas and expressing feelings, they can help to keep these valuable channels for learning open.

ART AND LEARNING

4. Learning About One's Self

CHRIS, WHO COULDN'T READ

I first met Chris when he was in first grade in a small private school. A not too well-coordinated, short blonde child, he held his head at a slight angle and generally wore a questioning look. Chris was especially noticeable because of the maturity of his drawings and paintings. As early as first grade, his paintings were clearly well composed, with thought given to the negative as well as the positive spaces. (Positive space is that occupied by a house, or tree, or main shape; negative space is the area around it.) Many young children tend to leave large empty spaces when they paint, but Chris never did this. His work was always rich in detail and color, indicating high intelligence according to some psychologists. Therefore, it was with some surprise that I learned that he was thought to be a poor student by his classroom teacher; his first-grade reading level was below average, and his work in arithmetic was decidedly poor. His classroom teacher, slightly irritated, classified him as an unresponsive student, a slow learner. She recommended that he repeat the first grade.

In this school, subject to parental consent, a child with learning problems was usually given a battery of tests in an effort to locate the source of the difficulty. The art teacher is not given the test scores but is simply notified, as I was, that Chris would repeat first grade. Earlier, I had put a comment on his report card saying that his artwork was excellent for his age; now I decided to put a special note in his cumulative file to that effect.

During the next two years he stumbled along, not doing too well with either his classmates or his teachers. He was considered to be a "sweet child" but was not treated with much respect. His art ability continued to develop. As Chris and I evaluated his efforts together, we talked about color quality, his use of line, the placement of shapes on the page, and the like.

"Did you use this color for a special reason Chris?" I might ask.

"Yes, because I was mad."

"I'm glad you thought about it. I'd like to suggest that you try mixing your colors more—you'll have more to choose from."

"Hm-mm— Never thought of that."

His critical sense was sharpened and as he observed his own growth (we kept portfolios of the work), he began to see his own strengths. But it was in third grade, when his class was taken to see an exhibition of contemporary art, that Chris especially came to my attention in a new way.

We stood as a group before a large nonfigurative piece of wood sculpture. It was a beautifully carved group of forms set in subtle relationships to one another, some close, some touching, and some set farther apart. The children and I stood looking at it quietly for a few minutes. I was trying to understand it without looking at the title, and I urged the children to do the same. "If art is a language," I said, "the piece should speak for itself."

"Well, what do you think the artist is trying to tell us?" I finally asked, not too sure about this piece myself.

Silence.

Then, from the back of the group, Chris volunteered, "It's a family, of course. Everybody is sort of separate, and yet they sort of lean on each other, sort of." His voice had a happy, confident tone that was rare for him.

"Ah," I was taken aback, "what do the rest of you think?"

"He's right," said one child, leaning down to read the label, "the name of the piece is *Family*."

"Wow."

"Not bad."

"Hey, Chris, that's good!"

The children, appreciative of his insight, turned to him in admiration and someone slapped him approvingly on the shoulder. He smiled happily and threw out his small chest, delighted.

As for myself, I was a little incredulous. *Family* was a very sophisticated piece of sculpture, and Chris was a third-grader. Later, casually, I asked whether he had ever seen this piece before.

"Oh no," he replied, "I just thought about it."

We passed on to other pieces in the exhibition, and from time to time one of us would ask Chris's opinion of something. He always had an answer, and he absolutely glowed at the general acceptance of his responses.

By the end of the visit I knew that this child required some special attention and help. He must not be permitted to go through his school days labeled a poor student. As his art teacher, I was probably the only one who was really aware of his special talents and insights. The joyful and somewhat surprised look on his face when he received the approval of his classmates was something I had never seen before. I suddenly knew what the term "self-concept" meant. This child had been convinced that he couldn't do anything well and wasn't worth much, and he rarely, if ever, claimed the attention of the important "others" in his small world. (I knew little about his family except that he was the oldest of three boys.)

What was to be done?

First I related the incident to his classroom teacher. "Very nice, but a quirk," she said, firm in her negative evaluation of him.

"If you look at Chris's file," I protested, "you'll see that even in first grade he was outstanding in art."

"Well, dear, I love art, of course, but what is important is that he be able to read and write, and he's not really very smart." Furious, I was convinced that her attitude reinforced the boy's negative evaluation of himself. (At a later date we discussed using books about art to stimulate his interest in reading. Eventually he wrote and illustrated his own book; see chapter 8 for more on this subject.)

If that teacher had no real respect for or knowledge about art, it would take something drastic to shake her. What Chris needed was a one-man show, even though it necessitated staying after school to set it up. With the principal's approval, Chris's exhibit was placed in the school's main hallway to demonstrate his special ability to the whole school community. A note went to all teachers announcing that the event would be scheduled to coincide with a parents' meeting and asking them to call it to the attention of their students.

But the reminder to the children was not necessary. Many of them were interested and excited and most admiring of the twenty paintings that made up the show. Chris and I selected the work together, and a parents' committee helped to mat the final choices. Chris was, of course, proud and delighted and also very modest. "Do you really think it's good enough?" he would ask, as I held up one piece or another. The "yes" was emphatic.

After the parents' meeting, Chris's teacher came to the art room. "He really is very good, isn't he?" she admitted, impressed by the overwhelmingly favorable reaction to the show. "Do you have something of his that could go up on the wall in my room?"

His parents, delighted and somewhat amazed, commented, "We knew that he liked to draw, but we never took his interest very seriously." (Meetings with his parents had taken place when Chris's academic problems were of concern to his teacher, but, needless to say, his art teacher was never invited.)

Gradually it became clear that Chris was somebody, even to himself. ("Maybe I'll be an artist when I grow up," he mused.) His teacher treated him with more respect, as did his classmates. When he made a mistake in reading, the teacher would say, "Come now, Chris, just try. I know that you can do it." (What a difference from her former deprecatory attitude!) And he did try. His reading and writing showed decided improvement. He was even ready to tackle arithmetic, which had previously been agony for him.

When the class was preparing a play for an assembly program and some stage sets were needed, the children said, "Chris should do it. He's good at that." And he was. In fact, he became better and better.

This story should end with "and they all lived happily ever after," which in some sense is true but, of course, not entirely. Chris's academic work generally hovered at about average, and he had to work hard to keep it up to that level. However, despite periodic academic slumps, Chris's growing art ability helped him to develop enough confidence in himself to struggle his way through rather than give up in despair. He did complete high school and went on to an art college, confident that he would find an art area in which he could develop professional competence (When last heard from, Chris had graduated with honors from a prominent art school.)

*　　*　　*

A psychologist would be better equipped than I to describe all the factors that influenced Chris's change in self-concept; however, a teacher's primary concern must be how such changes can help the learning process. My view from the art room makes it clear that children are not all the same and their school activities cannot be evaluated in exactly the same way. There are children who are verbally oriented; others are body and movement oriented; still others are visually oriented. Richard M. Jones says this in another way.

> A credible psychology of instruction must at the very least be suggestive in respect to three types of students: those who are predisposed to lead with their thoughts; those who are predisposed to lead with their feelings; and those who are predisposed to lead with their fantasies.[1]

Ignoring these differences makes for poor teaching and can injure the self-concepts of the students involved.

Many educational researchers have alerted teachers to the dangers of the "self-fulfilling prophesy." Experimental manipulation of teachers' expectations has shown the astonishing degree that children's intellectual growth is affected by the attitudes and expectations of their teachers.[2] Chris's story is eloquent testimony to the validity of this data. When his teacher saw him as a competent art student, there was a marked change in her attitude and expectations regarding Chris's other work. This tended to improve Chris's own attitude in a similar way. The manner in which he was treated by the school community also changed as there was a growing recognition of his artistic intelligence and skill. The total effect was a positive improvement in Chris's self-concept, which sustained him through his schooling and must have affected other areas of his life as well.

---

[1] *Fantasy and Feeling in Education* (New York: Harper & Row, 1970), p. 197.
[2] Robert Rosenthal and Lenore Jacobson, *Pygmalion in the Classroom: Teacher Expectations and Pupil's Intellectual Development* (New York: Holt, Rinehart & Winston, 1968) and A. B. Wilson, "Social Stratification and Academic Achievement," *Education in Depressed Areas*, A. H. Passow, ed. (New York: Teachers College Press, 1963), pp. 217–36.

An interest in the learning problems of black children in an inner-city school led me naturally to the Follow-Through Program, which continues the work of Head Start. Poor self-concept is thought by many educators to be more of a problem for black children growing up in a white society than it is for white children. It is dangerous to generalize, but if this is true for even a few black children, teachers might well ask, "What kinds of art experiences can help inner-city black children feel more comfortable with themselves as they try to cope with the demands of a predominantly white educational community?"

MAKING MASKS[3]   In an effort to answer this question, we started making masks in a first grade Follow-Through classroom. One day when the children came to class, they found African masks made of wood, some reproductions of Greek masks, and some contemporary sculptured masks. But, most important, they found a large mirror, the height of a tall first-grade child.

As we looked at the masks, the reaction was one of squeals and laughter. "They're funny!" or "They're scary," the children said. We talked a little about where these masks had come from, why they looked the way they did, and about their use and magical powers.

"When do we wear masks in our country?"

"Halloween." The answer was unanimous.

"But these masks were made for other purposes," I said.

They were most interested in the African masks, some of which were made for tribal rites, some as death masks, and some for ornamental purposes. The children volunteered small bits of information regarding Africa itself. The teacher's respectful references to these fine African artists was in itself important for the self-concept of these black children, according to many black writers on this subject.

After looking at the masks, we looked into the mirror to see ourselves. To make a mask, a child must be made conscious of all the features that make up a face. The children loved that. Many

---

[3] This section extracted from Elaine Pear Cohen, "Does Art Matter in the Education of the Black Ghetto Child?" *Young Children*, vol. XXIX, no. 3, March 1974, p. 177.

of them had never seen themselves from head to toe. They were very excited, dancing around in front of the mirror.

"Do we all look the same?" I asked. No. We all have eyes, noses, mouths, but we are not the same. The sizes and shapes of the features are different. The color of the skin varies. The shapes of the heads are different.

"I like those differences," I said, "because that's what makes each of us a special person. Life would be very dull if everyone looked exactly the same as everyone else." They thought that one over. Not so sure about that.

The children began to make their own masks, using the time-honored method of cutting and pasting paper bags and using bits of fabric and other collage materials for the features. The first step was to cut out space for the shoulders and holes for the eyes. For many of them the skill involved in using scissors proved to be the greatest problem. I had to plead with one little boy, Nathaniel, to get him to try. He kept saying, "I can't do it." He expected failure, which was a common occurrence when he tried to do something new.

Finally I said, "Look, Nathaniel, even if you don't get it exactly right, the world won't come to an end. I'll even give you another bag if this one doesn't work. Just try. Besides, if you make a mistake, the clock will go on turning. You will still go to bed tonight and wake up in the morning. (He smiled.) And I will still arrive here next Wednesday. Come on, just try."

At that point he was laughing a little, and he did try. He didn't do a magnificent job, but he was able to cut out something resembling spaces for eyes after he figured out how to hold the scissors. His own eyes were shining, and he was very pleased with himself. Was it because I, the "significant other," approved of what he did? Was it because he found out for himself that he had the needed skill? Or was it because for one moment he forgot to be terrified that his lack of experience and skill might once again be a source of embarrassment? Perhaps the answer involves some elements of all of these factors.

Another child, Kim, remarked as she worked, "Now my mother won't have to buy me a mask for Halloween. I can make it myself." She was very pleased with her newfound competence.

When everyone had finished, the children put on their masks, and photographs were taken of the group. They proudly paraded down the hall to the administrative offices of the school. After everyone had been duly admired, the parade returned to the classroom. The children were happy, feeling very pleased with themselves.

*   *   *

How did all of this relate to self-concept? First of all, the children were given an opportunity to see themselves, perhaps for the first time, and to enjoy the process. The individual child saw his or her own eyes, nose, and other features and yet felt part of a group, each of whom had similar characteristics. We didn't just look—we looked with approval and appreciation. Then, having made some new observations, we used the new knowledge as we made the masks. Each child created a mask having the same features, but each mask was very different. The children were free to make them as they liked, and, after a while, some even discarded the paper bags and used collage materials alone. But they were helped with problems of technique (how to hold the scissors, how to make use of the differences in the textures, how to spread paste efficiently, and the like), and then encouraged to work, each in her or his own way. "Mine will have a big mouth," one child would say. "Not mine, I like big eyes," another would respond. "My man is a square," laughed one, "he has a square head." "Mine is long, long, long," another commented. They made these personal choices with pride, enjoying their freedom to select and the complete power each had over his or her own product.

The parade and the response it evoked from important adults also added to their feeling of self-importance.

*   *   *

Studies regarding self-image among young black and white children indicate that as early as four years old, many black children already have negative self-images because they are black.[4] Clearly any school activity, such as an art experience, which has the potential to alter this tragic state of affairs in any positive way, should be given serious consideration. It should be added that white children as well as black ghetto children can benefit from the same experiences. Creating masks can help the self-concept of *all* children. Further, white children should be famil-

---

[4] B. R. Brown. *The Assessment of Self-Concept Among Four-year-old Negro and White Children, A Comparative Study* (New York: Institute for Developmental Studies, New York University, 1966), and K. B. Clark and M. Clark, "Racial Identification and Preference in Negro Children, *Readings in Social Psychology*, E. Macomby and Others, eds. (New York: Holt, Rinehart & Winston, 1958).

iar with the imaginative work of black African artists as part of their general education.

USING AND BEING CAMERAS   I had been taking photographs of the first-graders discussed previously over a period of weeks, and many of the pictures were quite good. A photographer's decisions about what to photograph and from what point of view are basically aesthetic and philosophical. If I could select an aspect of a child to photograph, why couldn't the children do the same and photograph each other? I borrowed cameras from other classes and from friends and, with the help of the Follow-Through teacher aide, gave each child a chance to take a few pictures. They needed help on how to use the cameras and where to stand in relation to the light. It was agreed that each child could take five pictures of whatever she or he liked. "Why not pick someone or something that you especially like," I suggested, wanting them to give serious thought to their selections. The children practiced first, using a camera without film, and then proceeded to look around very carefully. Finally, each child snapped some shots. They were excited and interested, but they seemed unsure about what the final product would be.

The next week a slide projector and the developed slides were brought to class. As the pictures appeared on the screen, the response was overwhelming. The children screamed with pleasure! They had all chosen to photograph one another. The pictures varied in quality, but very few had to be eliminated entirely. One was a photograph of feet. The children laughingly examined everyone's shoes until they found the right pair. The feet belonged to Vanessa. As this was going on there was such an explosion of enthusiasm that the office personnel came running out of the offices to see what was wrong. But nothing was wrong. On the contrary, it was all very right. The children, who saw themselves on the screen, were beside themselves with delight. As I review my notes for that day I see the following comment: "I kept saying, 'Doesn't he look great!' or 'What a lovely smile she has,' or 'Wasn't that a great shot.' No one responded directly, but I could see from their faces and from the occasional shy smiles that they heard and relished every compliment."

The slides had to be shown twice. After that the children begged for more cameras and a chance to photograph again. Since the program was funded with a very meager budget, it was impossible to repeat the procedure. However, the school district's photography department was persuaded to enlarge enough slides so that each child was included in some picture. The classroom teacher put the enlarged prints all around the room, and each child wrote her or his own name under her or his picture. The sense of importance and pleasure that the children derived from this activity was impossible to measure in quantitative terms. Did it elevate the self-concept of these children? The results cannot be proven in absolute terms, but a partial answer may be suggested by an incident involving a boy named Aaron.

Aaron, age seven, was a wiggler. He found it very difficult to sit, or to listen, or to become deeply involved in anything. His academic work was poor, and he was one of the few children who did not particularly care for art activities. However, the photography experience must have hit a sensitive spot. After his picture was shown (and it happened to be a nice smiling one), some of his behavior changed, at least in his relationship to me. He became my shadow, following me around and watching for opportunities to be helpful. Almost every time I asked the group a question he would volunteer an answer, whether he really had one or not. It was as if no one had ever paid any particular attention to him in school before, and he was pathetically grateful.

Several months following this episode, after I had bid the class good-bye and was working with another group, I drove up to the school one day with some large pieces of sculpture, boxes, and other supplies. As I debated with myself about how to carry the load, I looked up and saw Aaron and another little boy running eagerly toward my car.

"Need help? Need help?" he called.

"Yes. . . ." I paused for a moment, looking at him thoughtfully, trying to estimate his strength.

"You remember me, I'm Aaron," he said urgently and then whispered to his friend in a confidential tone, "She took my picture, so sure she knows me."

*　　*　　*

The week after the slide presentation, we pretended that we were cameras, holding our hands up to our eyes in telescope fashion and focusing upon one person or one area of the room. Then we drew with colored chalk on bogus paper whatever we had selected. "Choose something that you like, or something you don't like," I suggested as before. This was to give them further experience in expressing a personal choice and having this choice treated with dignity. All this was important, but it was a prelude to something else that might give the children a clearer picture of themselves.

LOOKING INSIDE OURSELVES[5]   The next time that we were together I said, "Last week we were cameras, looking out at the world. This week let's look inside of ourselves and think about how we feel. Art has a great deal to do with people's feelings." I held up some reproductions of paintings by Matisse, in particular a woman painted in bright colors. Was this a happy picture? The children's opinions were divided. Some thought the colors were happy, but several commented that "her face isn't happy." They were quite right about that. Then we looked at a painting in sombre colors of a storm by Courbet. No, they thought, that this was not a happy picture. It was "scary," some said. Then, confidently, I showed them van Gogh's *Sunflowers*. Surely this was a happy picture. "Not all happy," said Gail, "because those flowers are droopy and tired. Happy colors but droopy flowers." Again the others agreed.

Then I showed them a Kathe Kollwitz print, the famous war poster showing children holding up empty bowls for food. They got the point immediately. "They are hungry," the children said. "They are not happy at all."

I changed direction. "Let's think of a time when you were very happy. Can you tell me about it?"

Lots of hands waving. "My birthday party," "At Christmas," "At the zoo."

"These are the times you felt happy. But think about the feelings inside of you. Perhaps you can't describe it in words but try to think about *how* you felt at those times." Thoughtful silence. After a few minutes, a change in direction again. "When I have to say good-bye to someone I love very much, I feel bad inside of me. Have you ever felt that way? Can you think of a time when you felt very sad?"

Quiet. Then Gail, a very tiny child, said seriously, "When someone bigger than me gives me a whippin'."

Several children laughed. I chided them. "Don't laugh. I bet you feel that way sometimes too. You wouldn't like it if she laughed at you."

Heads shook. "Yes."

---

[5] Cohen, *op. cit.*, pp. 178, 179.

"When I'm sick, I feel bad," offered Vanessa, who had recently been in the hospital.

"All right. Don't tell me any more in words. Let's put it all in a colored chalk drawing, the way the artists did in their paintings. Those pictures we saw were all telling us about the artists' feelings. They had feelings just as you do. Think about when you were feeling especially happy, or sad, or whatever feeling you want to express. Just be sure that the picture is really about you." They were reminded that colors express feelings and then they were on their own. As they worked, they commented:

"I'm happy because I'm playing cowboy with my friend."

"I'm sad because I'm hungry—look." The drawing was an attempt to copy the Kollwitz picture.

"I'm happy. Here are my Christmas presents."

For a first try at this sort of thing, the results were really quite good. Although there were no "guts" pictures, I think the children did understand the words used, and they certainly reacted to the paintings that had been shown.

Another time we worked more directly on using color to express feelings, experimenting with paint as well as colored chalks. Clearly first-grade children can handle more sophisticated ideas than we give them credit for. At the end of the session they were asked if they preferred to draw feelings or if they liked being cameras better. The vote was about half and half, until one child remarked, "I like to draw about us," and then they all chorused, "Yes, yes."

THEORIES OF SELF-CONCEPT IN ART EDUCATION

Bonaro W. Overstreet describes the affect of self-image as follows:

> Every person's primary life-relationship is to himself. The first creative venture he undertakes—long before he realizes its significance—is the building of the self-image. . . . By and large, his approach to situations will, all of his life, reflect the image of himself he builds in his earliest years; the image of himself as wanted or unwanted, worthy or unworthy, strong or weak.[6]

---

[6] *Understanding Fear in Ourselves and Others* (New York: Harper & Row, 1950), pp. 41–2.

Children's approach to the school situation, if colored by poor self-image, predisposes them to failure. For this reason many educators express an enormous concern with the problems of self-concept.

In the literature on self-concept, there are many different points of view about how a negative self-concept can be altered. Many contend that self-concept is based upon the evaluation of the "significant others" in a child's life, such as parents, peers, or teachers. Wilbur B. Brookover considers parents the most important significant others.[7] His extensive study suggests that it is essential to change parents' expectations regarding their children if academic improvement is desired. When discussing high school students, James S. Coleman considers peers to be the most important significant others.[8] Both theories have gained wide acceptance. However, both ignore studies by psychologists in the field of person perception, who stress the many different styles of perception.[9] Even if educators were able to change parents' or teachers' expectations, children's perception of themselves might still be distorted as a result of their particular "hang-ups." Their reading of parent expectations could be quite different from that of parents themselves. Therefore, self-concept should be defined not only in terms of significant others, but also in terms of the particular personality characteristics that determine a child's perception of the world.

There are still other approaches to understanding how self-concept is established and how it can be changed. Much of the literature indicates that the degree of competence is directly related to personality strengths or defects that have developed as a function of the socialization process. Psychologists differ in their views about which elements in the socialization process are crucial. The "cultural conflict" people, when discussing poor children, stress the differences between the standards of the white middle-class culture and the survival standards of the ghetto. The "educational deprivation" writers stress the importance of teachers' expectations and, in the case of minority group

---

[7] *Improving Academic Achievement Through Student's Self-concept Enhancement* (East Lansing: Michigan State University Publication Services, 1965).

[8] *Equality of Educational Opportunity* (Washington, D.C.: U.S. Department of Health, Education, and Welfare, Government Printing Office, 1966).

[9] Gordon Allport, *Pattern and Growth in Personality,* (New York: Holt, Rinehart & Winston, 1961).

children, the effects of school segregation. Writers with a psychoanalytical bias stress early emotional deprivation, such as frequent father absence. Another interesting area of study has been that which J. Rotter, M. Seeman, and S. Liverant call "the sense of personal control of environment."[10] This involves whether children feel that they can or cannot effect changes in their environment or whether they are dominated by a feeling of helplessness and dependence upon chance. However, the crucial point for educators is that they recognize the complicated nature of self-concept and that they be willing to at least consider suggestions that may offer some potential for influencing it in positive ways. Kenneth R. Beittel, an art education researcher, wrote:

> One of the goals of learning in art is the development of the capacity for creative action, as indicated by changes in one's personality or self-concept.[11]

Why should the making of art objects alter one's self-concept? What is there about this process that makes it particularly pertinent to this discussion? My own answer to this question is:

> Art represents the individual's perception of his world. He perceives; he identifies his perception; he restates this perception in some objective form, whether it be in paint, clay, film, sound, movement, or words. In the process, the artist is not only communicating his personal insights to others, but is first clarifying them for himself. This is what I see, or think, or feel, he says. To do this he must face himself as a separate thinking entity.[12]

The art process can help young people (or anyone) to discover, in another dimension, who they are. This is especially true of dark-skinned persons trying to find their way in a white-dominated society. They produce an art object, a product of their own hands and minds, something that is unique and personal. They see it as an extension of themselves—and thus learn to know themselves better.

---

[10] "Internal vs. External Control: A Major Variable in Behavior Theory," *Decisions, Values and Groups*, vol. 2, N. F. Washburne, ed. (London: Pergamon Press, 1962).
[11] *Research in Art Education* (Washington, D.C.: Report of the Commission on Art Education, NAEA, 1965).
[12] Elaine Pear Cohen, "Color Me Black," *Art Education*, vol. 22, no. 45, April 1969, pp. 7–9.

A third-grade boy is proud of the dragon he molded and painted as part of a class study about the art and life of Japan.

Within the classroom there are many other ways in which art experiences can affect self-concept. Good art education embodies all the qualities necessary for good general education. In art, for example, the imaginative or individual quality that shows up in a child's work is valued. There is no right or wrong way of making a painting or a piece of sculpture. In arithmetic, 2 plus 2 equals 4—there is no room for interpretation. But in art there is no limit to the many different ways a child can paint a tree, or a person, or a design—or anything. Differences in outlook revealed in art products are precious. They fertilize our minds and give insights into other people's thought processes. These differences are valued because they enrich our view of the world. Teachers' expression of this appreciation can affect children's self-concept. Think of how a girl or boy feels when she or he discovers that her or his shape of a tree has just as much validity as the next child's. Think of their reactions when they learn that their emphasis upon a heavy solid trunk is considered by the teacher and other children to be of equal interest to someone else's emphasis upon the lacy quality of the leaves.

Another example is the use of color. Many different greens can be produced by mixing yellow and blue paint (see chapter 6), but an entirely personal choice dictates the particular green a youngster uses in a painting. This is an independent decision. And children make many such decisions in the course of making a painting, or piece of sculpture, or collage, or other artwork.

The experiences described earlier point up some of the other ways in which art activities can affect self-concept. Chris is only one of many children whose strengths are visual rather than verbal. Nathaniel, who can gather courage to attempt a manipulatory activity but is fearful of other new situations, is another. And Aaron, who finds a new view of himself in photography, is still another.

Self-knowledge is an active ingredient in creating a piece of art. Teachers who are truly concerned about the growth of their young students will take advantage of this fact.

Suggested Related Activities

Play a "Me" Game   Ask the children to look at their bodies and think of words and movements that describe what they see. Some may suggest words such as round, long, flat, tall, short, or solid. Next, encourage them to think about times when they have had strong feelings. Mirror-play will show them how their facial expressions change in different situations. Some may suggest that they have been smiling or serious, mad or happy, or scared, worried, hopeful, or wishing for something. Suggest dramatic situations or movements that will help them develop ideas. Then let them put these impressions on paper using paint, chalk, felt-tip markers, crayons, or wax-resist. Learning words that describe these experiences may also be useful. Be sure to make this open-ended so that the children will provide words and ideas from their own experiences.

Be a Telescope   Children should be asked to look *outside* of themselves. What do they see when they look around the room? Out of the window? Whom do they see? Holding hands telescope-fashion, they can pretend to focus in on friends or on anything else that interests them, noticing how the telescope frames a limited space. The image can then be recorded on paper, using the media suggested above.

It's also fun for them to look *inside* themselves at their bodies, minds, and feelings by pretending they are microscopes. As in the "Me" game, they may wish to express ideas about their own bodies. The "microscope" idea is simply a device to help them to look a little deeper to learn about themselves.

Make Portfolios   Children can make large folders from heavy paper or cardboard in which to store their work neatly. Encourage them to decorate these with a picture or symbol that identifies it as theirs. Ask, "Do you like football, or flowers, or colors, or cats, or food?" Decorative work on the portfolio should be expressive of each child's interests and preferences.

Pictures of Themselves   It's best for children to make their own decisions about self-portraits. The following subjects should be used only with children who need help in getting started and should never be rigidly imposed. Possible topics to suggest are: "Me, in My Favorite Place," "Me, When I Grow Up," "Wearing My Favorite Dress/ Shirt," "Me, with My Family," "What I Like to Do Best at Home," "What I Like to Do Best with My Friends," or "One Night When I Was Dreaming. . . ." Once a child indicates understanding, stop making suggestions and encourage deviation from these subjects, if desired.

Class Album   After each child does a self-portrait on paper, names and personal comments can be added to adjoining sheets. When all of these have been completed and bound together, the children can take turns taking the album home to introduce the class to their families.

Ideas about One's Self in Clay As indicated above, the following ideas for self-portraits should be only used as starters, when needed: "Reading a Book," "Watching TV," "Lying on the Beach," "My Pet" (the one I have or the one I wish I had), "If I Could Invent an Animal No One Had Ever Seen, It Would Look Like This," or "Members of My Family" (singly or gathered together).

Dressing Up for Dramatic Play A variety of materials, lengths of fabric, feathers and assorted trimmings can be combined to create costumes. With the help of a mirror, children can create different roles for themselves. Their views of themselves and their aspirations are often revealed in this sort of activity, which can produce many surprises. Posing behind a shadow screen offers further possibilities and delights for dramatic play.

5. Learning to Think

The lesson I had given on "Changing Points of View" had gone exceptionally well, I thought. Thirty-five fourth-graders had concentrated for over an hour on sketching a still-life arrangement from different positions in the room. I felt that this was an important step toward gaining the understanding that people with different perspectives see things differently. Noticing that their own views differed when their physical locations changed might help children to accept the different views of others.

Still, when I met Ms. Donovan in the hall later the same day, her greeting was reserved, even chilly. Although I had been excited to see nine-year-olds recognize the validity of different viewpoints, apparently their teacher was unimpressed.

"What did you think of this morning's lesson?" I asked eagerly.

"I was grading papers and couldn't give it much attention."

She hesitated, knitted her brows, and then blurted out, "Frankly, neither I nor the children have so much time to spend on art. The parents of my students tell me that they're glad their children had creative experiences in nursery school and kindergarten, but once they enter the grades, it is time to unplug the creativity and plug in the skills!"

I stood rooted to the spot stunned, but I remember thinking that Ms. Donovan was honestly revealing her own feelings, not just those of the parents of her students.

"And besides," she continued, "I just received this huge reading manual from the county office. How am I supposed to get through all this material *and* math, *and* science, *and* social studies if you are going to keep the children drawing for an hour and a half every week?"

She hurried off, saving me the trouble of organizing my counterattack instantly.

I had attended the Board of Education meeting where the new reading manual was presented. It had seemed to me that there were many implications for art activities in the pages of the large volume entitled *Comprehension, Critical Reading/ Thinking Skills, K–12.*[1] The speaker introduced the book by citing significant statistics:

> Ninety-five percent of the serious reading done in our country is done by only five percent of the population, and that is largely because they have to for professional reasons. Of the pleasurable reading, ninety percent is done by only ten percent of the population. Obviously, we have trained people to recognize words but not to become readers.[2]

Mr. O'Connor went on to discuss changes in instruction necessary to produce readers—people who will continue to read for pleasure and information. Comprehension and retention of what is read, as well as personal satisfaction in reading, depend on strengthening many cognitive skills beyond word recognition. Instructional programs should provide many opportunities to exercise emerging cognitive skills in varied contexts.

ART AND COGNITION

It became increasingly clear to me that art activities can meet these requirements. While children create art, they also organize their thoughts and actions in patterns necessary for skill in reading. While drawing the still life, Ms. Donovan's fourth-graders were creating symbols by translating objects into a different visual form. By observing the changes in their own viewpoints when their physical positions changed, the children gained an understanding of certain transformations. They also

---

[1] Bulletin No. 246, *Teaching Reading Skills*, vol. II (Rockville, Md.: Montgomery County Public Schools, 1974).
[2] James O'Connor, Reading Specialist, Montgomery County Public Schools, Rockville, Maryland.

learned something about objectivity because they became less attached to one self-centered viewpoint. These experiences relate directly to cognitive skills identified as basic to skill in reading. Far from distracting students from basic subjects, art provides opportunities to reinforce and clarify the concepts necessary for learning "the basics." Ms. Donovan should become aware that art can strengthen her reading program by providing her students with varied contexts in which to exercise developing cognitive skills.

Practice in different contexts is considered essential for skill mastery. Applying skills to new situations demands thought and tests basic understanding. Besides offering these challenges, art activities have additional advantages of providing both learners and teachers with tangible records of thinking.

These records and the process of making them are of great importance even before reading skills are taught. They are evidence of the mental imagery that must precede reading comprehension. Art media invite children to manipulate objects, to derive tactual and kinesthetic reinforcement in the development of perception, to organize their perceptions, and to form images. These media also provide the responsive environment that learning theorists, including Piaget, Hebb, Hunt, Montessori, and Bruner, have held essential to the development of linguistic skills. While drawing, children are inventing visual symbols. Usually they depict objects and events that are not physically present. If they are drawing things they see in front of them, they are still obliged to solve many problems in translating the seen objects into drawn forms. Accomplishing these tasks exhibits the understanding of symbols required by reading.

Those who do not understand the role of children's art tend to dismiss typical children's drawings as ordinary and uninteresting. However, the simple pictures commonly produced by all youngsters often contain great significance. For instance, one picture was accompanied by these words:

> May there always be sunshine,
> May there always be blue skies,
> May there always be Mama,
> May there always be me.

This poem by a six-year-old Russian boy was his description for the painting he contributed to a Moscow exhibition of children's art. So universally familiar and appealing was his expression,

This drawing of "Mama and me in the sunshine" could have been made by a six-year-old in France or Sweden or South Africa or Brazil for its symbols of familiar objects are common to children everywhere.

both visual and verbal, that the poem became a popular song around the globe. Reproductions of the original painting were unnecessary because six-year-olds everywhere produce their own "originals" of the same theme. In most of them, a blue sky appears across the top inch of the upper edge of the paper, a spiked-ball sun is sharply defined without a trace of atmospheric effects, and a horizontal groundline supports flowers and figures drawn totally out of proportion. Yet we know that much more is right than wrong with our six-year-olds' versions of the important things in life.

Children of six or seven who repeat a formula representation of a familiar object, such as the ubiquitous lollipop tree, are not bereft of creativity, perceptivity, or intelligence; instead, they are organizing the world around them and trying to give some logic to its arrangement. They are thinking. The formulas or *schemas* they develop are not meant to mirror specific objects. They are symbols of a child's ideas or concepts about the objects. Whether they reside in sprawling mansions or crowded tenements, most children draw a gabled cottage when they mean HOUSE. The people who live in the house are usually too big to fit in the door, but then, the people are more important.

According to Susanne Langer, "The material furnished by the senses is constantly wrought into symbols which are our elementary ideas. Some of these ideas can be combined and manipulated in the manner we call 'reasoning'." Thinking individuals, children or adults, constantly create symbols of their experiences in order to think about them. Symbolization is necessary for thought to take place.

The reasoning that occurs when children combine and manipulate symbols on paper is part of cognition. Drawing activity for young children is really "thinking out loud"—it is an easier method than the verbal style favored by adults. Writing would be impossible and articulating the words too tedious. But while words may form hesitantly, lines flow in gay abandon from the crayons and brushes of children from two to adolescence. These lines disclose much about their creators' thought processes.

> The essential functions of intelligence consist in understanding and inventing, in other words in building up structures by structuring reality.[3]

---

[3] *Science of Education and the Psychology of the Child* (New York: Orion Press, 1970), p. 27.

These words of Jean Piaget have profound implications for the role of art in cognition. Through art, children build structures by structuring reality according to their own designs; they learn to understand through their own inventions. Piaget's suggestions for learning situations that include the active involvement of students because knowledge must be internally constructed, that involve social communication, and that allow the development of representation are clearly met by classroom art activities.

Growth and new situations force individuals to continually adjust their perspectives, organize their responses, and adapt to their surroundings. These efforts to define and regulate individuals' realtionships to the world express cognitive development. They rely on processes described by Piaget as *assimilation* and *accommodation*. Learners first absorb meaningful aspects of new findings, integrating them with existing concepts and modifying those concepts, and later the combined information is called upon to fit personal needs. "Watch this!" Steven commanded after making a row of blue strokes on his painting, "I am going to turn these lines into grass." Then he carefully mixed a brushful of yellow paint into each blue blade. He had recalled previous color mixing experiments and was now able to predict what could happen and use his information to produce what he needed—green grass for his picture and attention from his classmates, some of whom were puzzling over how to get green when they were given only red, yellow, and blue paints.

Cognition includes the complex mental processes of perceiving, conceptualizing, reasoning, and, finally, knowing. As cognition develops, one uses increasingly complex symbol systems. Symbol systems enable individuals to deal with situations that are remote in time or place. The level of concept formation individuals have attained governs their handling of new situations. Any new situation can be overwhelming unless individuals can select and organize the aspects of it that are important to them. Crucial to the concept formation that controls this process are abilities to perceive likenesses and differences, to classify objects according to their similarities and differences, and to generalize by assigning objects to their proper class. The qualities and relations of objects must be identified, compared, abstracted, and generalized. Only after performing these mental operations can individuals evaluate and handle new situations meaningfully and independently.

Piaget describes two major aspects of cognition. The first is the *operative* aspect that involves actions that cause changes in individuals or their environment. The second is the *figurative* aspect that involves descriptions of reality based on perception, imitation, or mental imagery. When real situations are not immediately present, an individual can think about them by evoking a mental "copy" rendered by the figurative aspect of cognition. The copies also reflect individuals' interpretations and understandings. Because art activities involve both transformations of reality (the operative aspect) and individually made "copies" of reality (the figurative aspect), they can have tremendous impact on the development and revelation of cognitive processes. This obvious but neglected fact is one educators should explore in developing art activities to strengthen cognitive structures.

Most people look for meaning in art and seek the message of the artist, but child artists are not only communicating with the public, they are primarily communicating with themselves. When children use art materials, they can see ideas take form. They can achieve a sense of order as the symbols of their experiences are carefully arranged. This in turn gives a sense of control over elements in the environment and an awareness that one's own reactions have power. In this way, children shape new thoughts and learn what they really look like in concrete form. The effect is comparable to that of a writer setting down her or his ideas in words. The "physical" existence of the words and/or shapes clarifies the ideas so that they can be defined, enlarged, and organized. The processes of selection and arrangement that are part of all art activities are also crucial aspects of organizing experience. Thought, cognition, and intellect all rely on the ability to organize experience. Learning to think is really learning to organize one's experiences logically.

In discussing thinking and drawing phenomena, both Piaget and Lowenfeld deal with children's egocentric attitudes, difficulty in understanding abstractions, importance of manipulation, and the great significance of repetitive behaviors. Commonly held views associate repetition with tedious "busy work," that is boring, purposeless, unimaginative tasks akin to rote learning. Many teachers, and adults in general, want children to always move ahead to something new, but Piaget, Montessori, and Lowenfeld consider repetitive behavior as characteristic of emerging mental abilities and the need to realize them through action.

"Use is the aliment of a schema," states Piaget. Lowenfeld believes repetition reflects the need for finding order within the environment, self-assurance, and mastery. He considers the repetitive schemas in drawing important to the development of abstract thinking. People working with children should recognize that the drawing formulas (schemas) employed repeatedly by children should not be disparaged as symptoms of creative poverty or laziness; rather they should be valued for their contribution to cognitive development. Schemas express to Lowenfeld

TABLE OF

TERM	DEFINITION	EXAMPLES IN ART ACTIVITIES
Perception	Direct knowledge of things through the senses. The mental product acquired through complex sensations chiefly of the kinesthetic and visual sort (see chapter 6).	Manipulation of sea shells and study of their shapes and contours followed by translation into art forms, widens the child's perception of form and texture.
Discrimination and Differentiation	Observation of resemblances and differences and indication of those differences (preparatory to classification and other complex processes).	The child who sees different shapes among an assortment of green leaves has powers of discrimination. As he selects particular shapes, he differentiates between them.
Identification	Recognition and designation (labeling) of what something is.	A child who can draw, or select from pictures, a "triangle," "square," and "circle" has identified those shapes.
Symbolization	Ability to make something stand for or represent something else. The capacity to form and use substitutions for the real thing: mental images, words, or pictures.	Rendering ideas and objects in art relies on symbolization. The child who understands that 𝗤𝗣 means tree, ⚹ means sun, ⌂ means house is using symbols. The picture of an apple ♂ is as much a symbol for the actual fruit as is the word "apple."
Imagery	Mental evocation of absent objects and events. Internal "pictures," which are necessary auxiliaries to thinking.	Recalling a day at the beach, where a sandcastle was built, a starfish found, or a lost toy last seen, requires mental imagery. Art activities act as reinforcement.
Classification	Putting together like objects or facts under a common designation. It may involve gathering similar things into a class or groups into more specific divisions.	In design activities in which children are confronted with an array of geometric shapes, children who can sort them according to shape, color, and/or size possess classification skills.
Generalization	Thinking in terms of schematized ideas or systematizing experiences to derive principles that can be applied to new situations.	Although children know that flowers come in different sizes, shapes and colors, they form a schematized representation, or general model of a flower: ✿

a striving for orderly relationships, and this indicates readiness for a meaningful reading program.

Piaget's contributions to our present knowledge of the development of cognitive skills are numerous and complex. We have extracted those elements essential to the subject matter of art for the accompanying table. All the skills listed operate as ways of organizing experience so that learning may take place. Abilities to organize experience according to the enumerated skills depend on the maturational level of individuals as well as on the nature of their experiences.

COGNITIVE SKILLS

TERM	DEFINITION	EXAMPLES IN ART ACTIVITIES
Socialization	Social interaction in which ideas are exchanged and concepts are enlarged and clarified through joint experiences. Through this process children learn about different views and thus become less egocentric.	When a group of children create a mural, they share ideas, plans, symbols, space, and materials in its execution and the rewards and reinforcements upon its completion.
Abstraction	Forming a concept by epitomizing, summarizing, and/or separating essences from their concrete embodiment to conceive a general meaning.	A child who carefully makes a painting symmetrical shows concern for the abstract concept of balance.
Orientation in Space and Time	Determining one's own position in relation to spatial and temporal considerations.	Concepts of "here-there," "on-under," "near-far," and the like are essential to space orientation, while such notions as "before-after," "first, second," "if-then," and "because" relate to temporal reasoning. Landscapes require assessment of positions in space; seasonal pictures require placement in time.
Quantification	Determining characteristics subject to measurement: size, amount, mass, capacity, degree, content, magnitude, number, and the like.	Composition of a painting involves consideration of relative sizes of forms; the making of sculpture necessitates estimations of relative volume; construction of assemblages requires evaluation of relative weights in questions of balance.
Seriation	Placing one thing after another according to some order of succession in space, time, or thought.	The child who can arrange a series of pictures recapitulating the events of a story in proper order exhibits this skill.
Transformational Imagery	Understanding of sequential changes. While young children focus on initial and final stages of events, older children can understand changes that occur between the two states. Concepts of causality (the relation between cause and effect) and conservation (the maintenance of certain essential properties in spite of irrelevant changes) are aspects of this development.	Children who are aware that equal balls of clay can be modeled into different shapes and yet continue to have the same amounts of substance, weight, and volume, despite their varied forms, understand conservation.

Mont Ste. Victoire was painted many times by Cézanne, odalisques interested Matisse, sunflowers entranced van Gogh, and circus figures captivated Picasso. The treatment of each subject is remarkably similar, but fine distinctions can be made between the various works. The small changes tell a great deal about the artist's way of thinking at a particular time. Art activities, such as those that follow, can be explored with different media, different sizes or colors, slightly different arrangements, and different numbers of participants, or they can simply be repeated if the children wish. The satisfaction resulting from repetition expresses many basic needs, including those for thorough understanding and good performance.

Of course, teachers should analyze the type and function of repetitions being made. Children who master reproducing cartoon characters such as Snoopy and repeat them endlessly are not thinking. Facile and hasty copies of other's work are very different from the engrossing pursuit of a personal subject.

A teacher's goal should be to stimulate more thinking and to widen frames of reference so that children's own themes become more accurate and more complex. This is not done by giving technical instruction in how to draw in a mechanical fashion but rather by offering many opportunities for careful observation, by providing the vocabulary necessary for labeling and refining discriminations, and by questioning in ways that will prompt new ideas and perceptions. Ellen illustrated many of these processes.

*   *   *

Ellen loved flowers. She brought small bouquets for the classroom and drew many pictures of herself picking and smelling flowers. But she had very little information about flowers and her pictures of them were always the same, although the types in her bouquets differed. After a while, I thought that she might like to know more about flowers. I asked her to bring a large one from that morning's bouquet to our "sharing circle" so that everyone could look closely at it. "How many petals does this flower have?" I asked, and the children counted out "six." In response to a question about color, the children observed that the center was white with deep pink spots, that a light pink was in the middle of each petal, and that a narrow band of white fringed each petal. Many other facts about the form of the flower were noted. We borrowed a book on flowers from the library and carefully searched its pictures until we found one similar to Ellen's flower. We learned that it was a type of lily that came from China long ago.

After our discussion, Ellen went immediately to the easel. There she selected a sheet of black paper and painted one very large flower. Its overall shape was very much like her favorite design, but this time there were six carefully made petals, each of them pink rimmed by white. In the white center, deep pink dots were arranged in a lively pattern. After school I looked through the pictures in Ellen's folder. Every flower made before today's discussion had a single dot for its center and at least ten petals, each a different solid color. Ellen's concepts about flowers were changing.

The next day Ellen brought in a tiger lily and eagerly announced her intention to paint it. "This flower is like the pink lily but it has two colors of orange and has brown spots. Its leaves are different too." The new painting reflected Ellen's observations. Just a few questions about color and form had focused Ellen's interest and enabled her to refine her perceptions. Her paintings now showed a much richer assortment of flowers and a clearer understanding of their parts. She also became interested in looking at books to find out more about the flowers she collected—what their names were, what other flowers they were related to, and where they came from. Soon the backgrounds of Ellen's paintings began to contain more details than the flat groundline and beaming sun that had been the only accompaniments previously. Those elements remained, but they were now joined by birds, insects, rocks, streams, and other characteristics of the habitats of the varied flowers.

From the start, painting was both the motivation for and expression of Ellen's interest. By very deliberately incorporating new information while retaining certain favorite aspects of her own style, Ellen reflected in her paintings the assimilation and accommodation of new knowledge that Piaget describes. Her paintings helped to form a deep interest, which may well remain with Ellen all her life; they also recorded the growth of that interest.

I have seen other children become similarly absorbed in painting, drawing, or sculpting prehistoric animals, fish, ships, outer-space, American Indian and Eskimo life, and Civil War history. In each case, the opportunity to produce art gave an impetus to gather more information and make individual interpretations.

MAKING A COLLAGE MURAL   After reading the poem "City" by Langston Hughes, a first-grade class decided to make its own pictorial versions of the city by day and by night. First they made small individual drawings in order to compile a list of ingredients. Next the children identified important elements in their drawings and listed them on a long chart. Many classifications were made, including different sorts of vehicles (cars, trucks, bicycles, trains, boats, planes), sizes of buildings, life forms, and types of people. Next, they compared the day and night charts. They decided the day picture must have more people, especially children outside, more cars on the highway, the sun shining, lighter colors, and shadows on the street. The night picture should have lights on in some windows and shades down in others, stars in a dark sky, maybe the Big Dipper, and colored lights to indicate airplanes. Many objects would be repeated in both pictures, but darkness and neon lights would make them look different.

It was agreed that everything should be bigger and more plentiful in the murals than in the small preparatory drawings. Two lengths of brown wrapping paper six by three feet were measured and cut. Construction and tissue paper in assorted colors and sizes, crayons, scissors, and paste were made available. The general layout decided upon included a river in the foreground, a highway parallel to it, and a park in the middle distance. As children created, decorated, and cut out their contributions, they brought them to the mural paper and discussed their placement. Where should big shapes go? Where would smaller ones fit? Which would appear close? Which farther away? We considered the shape and design of buildings and the ways their structures related to their functions and their arrangement in the neighborhood. Even young children can begin to think about architecture as an art form.

When almost every inch of the two murals was covered with boats, bridges, taxis, towering skyscrapers, apartment houses (drawn in cross-section so that their inhabitants were seen in varied aspects of family life), construction workers, policemen, dogs, birds, stars, and even a spouting whale, the children surveyed their work. "It's true," they agreed, "we've never seen a spouting whale in the river, but he looks so good there and Calvin had so much fun remembering the story about him and

A collage mural of the harbor of New York City, complete with a spouting whale, lighthouse, and boats, was created by first-graders after they had heard Langston Hughes' poem "The City."

making his big shape, that we want to include him in our city. Who knows, perhaps he once swam there or will appear again someday. And the little red lighthouse doesn't really have eyes and a mouth, but giving personality to the structure was Jaime's way of showing the lighthouse's function of warning the boats." Acceptance of these details, though they may be logically "incorrect" to an adult, shows the teacher's openness to the children's points of view. This is what is meant by keeping activities open-ended. It imparts an attitude more important than the accumulation of specific facts. After all, the class created a symbol of the city, not a mirror of it.

"A big, busy, beautiful city—day and night, indoors and out," was the satisfied pronouncement of the first-grade artists.

DRAWING FROM MODELS   The goals of this project were to look for many details and to discover relationships between parts of the body. Piaget suggests that children develop spatial concepts as a result of visual and motor action. Drawing from nature combines visual and motor action and can facilitate conceptual development. But children at different ages (and stages) have different capabilities for using what they see in their pictures. It is common to note that young children draw what they know rather than what they see. An example of this is clear in the story of the teacher who thought it was time for an eight-year-old to learn that the sky does not stop one inch below the top of the paper. She took the child to the window and pointed toward the distance. "Look Tom, can you see that the sky comes down to meet the horizon and the trees stand straight up in front of it?" Tom seemed to acquiese, but the next day he produced another familiar picture in which the sky ended with a hard edge in the upper part of the paper.

"Tom!" exclaimed the teacher. "You saw that the sky comes down to meet the ground!"

"Yes," said Tom, "but I live over there, and it really doesn't."

Tom wanted his picture to be sensible according to his own concepts rather than visually accurate. Many children his age share this preference. They should not be forced to change their styles of drawing, but they can be guided to revise their concepts through careful observation.

Whatever their capabilities and preferences, children should be encouraged to manipulate art materials to express their points of view. The actions themselves build competence and confidence. Inactivity fosters the inhibitions so many feel about drawing, particularly about drawing the human figure. This inhibition is unfortunate because children and all people are naturally fascinated by the human form. Children throughout the elementary school enjoy drawing classmates and their teachers. Crayons are suitable for this task because of the detail sought, and clay is also an excellent medium.

According to art education researchers, drawing from a model encourages children to look more carefully, and a drawing itself reinforces the looking. Most children develop a favorite form or schema of the human figure. They repeat the basic shape whenever people are required. No matter how varied the actual people may appear, the standard shape suffices because it means *person*. However, children can be encouraged to enlarge their schemas. Young children will continue to prefer their basic forms, but even the inclusion of a few new details will reveal increased perception and the awareness of new relationships.

To begin this project, portraits by Picasso, Kollwitz, Gauguin, Kirchner, and other well-known artists were displayed to provide reassurance that photographic likenesses were not required. Students were urged to concentrate on their own points of view: "Your viewpoint is what you see, what you know, what you imagine, what you prefer."

Several models in different poses were placed at different positions in the room, and each child chose the model he or she wished to draw. Everyone was asked not only to study the poses carefully but also to imitate them. They were asked to touch parts of their own bodies, noting the location of the neck, shoulders, elbows, wrists, and eyebrows. More importantly, the large forms of the body were observed and felt through movement. The teacher made suggestions such as the following: "Bend at the waist. How much of you goes down? Pretend to throw a ball. What parts move? What happens to your hips when you do the hokey pokey? Where is your left foot, when your right foot steps forward? Do your feet look different when you change their direction? Can other parts of your body go in different directions?" After moving about, the relationship of artist to model was discussed with emphasis given to the fact that each artist, having a different position, would have a different viewpoint.

As the children moved around the room, bending down or standing on perches for different views of their subjects, the teacher urged them to think about the shapes they were going to draw. "Everything visible has a shape, and all shapes have size, color, texture, volume, and relationships to each other." Sample questions were, "How do the shapes look from above in an airplane? How do they look from below to an ant? How do we organize the shapes we see? Which ones are simple? Which complex? Which have symmetry or asymmetry? What is repeated? What has pattern (systematic repetition of shapes)? Look for arrangements of shapes, positions in space, repetitions of lines, variations in direction, simple or complicated shapes, similar or different shapes. Then you will understand what you see and discover your own point of view. That is a wonderful discovery to make!"

The seated figure by Len shows careful observation of his subject. A verbal description by the boy would probably be cursory, but his visual representation exhibits keen powers of observation and intelligence. It is clear also that problems of handling the anatomy and clothing in detail caused him to shape his concept with care and precision.

A kindergartener drew a view of his teacher as a towering figure with a glaring expression. "This is Miss Schwartz when she is mad!" Benjy announced.

As I looked at Miss Schwartz's portrait, I noticed that her hands had more than the usual complement of fingers. I thought that the young artist did not understand that there are five fingers on each hand. In their zeal to include precisely the right number, children frequently draw the fingers larger and more prominent than the rest of the hand and even the arm, but the exact number is almost always there. I sat down next to Benjy, asking, "How many fingers does your teacher have?"

"Oh, she has only five on each hand but she was so mad at me that she was shaking!" he explained.

Multiplying elements to show motion is a characteristic technique of young children. It is seen in drawings of apparently ten apples in a vertical line between a branch of the tree and the ground; instead a single apple in each stage of its fall is being depicted.

PAINTING POETRY   It is unnecessary for teachers to be reluctant to read or teach poetry to young children because of the abstract symbolism, sophisticated imagery, or uncommon language frequently used. When poems are suggested as subject matter for painting, children listen with keen interest. The pro-

A realistic seated figure such as this one made by an eleven-year-old required a knowledge of proportion, spatial relations, and anatomy as well as the ability to observe and reproduce details carefully.

Miss Schwartz
when she is mad!

Multiplying elements is a common way young children indicate motion. One five-year-old artist knew his kindergarten teacher really had only five fingers on each hand, but, he explained, "She was so mad at me, she was shaking."

posed painting gives children a reason for relating a poet's words to their own actions.

An invitation to imagine and depict fantasy is also a challenge to solve many problems independently. When imagining, no authorities can dictate precise answers, and no one can declare that a child's interpretation is wrong. With freedom thus assured, children can experiment with symbols and ideas that are truly their own. As images are invented and given form, they can be related to ideas raised in the poem or compared with the pictures of other class members for their unique viewpoints and contributions.

The language of poetry may present some problems for young listeners, but by painting their own images, the symbolism of a poem can be changed into concrete forms children can handle. The imagery of paintings reveals children's interpretations of new concepts. According to Piaget, thought requires representations (mental symbols, visual images) and operations (internalized actions). Producing paintings in response to poems links the elements of thought (representations, operations, and language). Personal responses to specific verbal imagery encourage independent thinking. Moreover, poetry highlights the unique vision of the poet, an emphasis shared by all the arts.

The following poems by Amy Lowell offer intriguing subject matter for elementary school painters. Comparing the two poems would be interesting for upper graders, since one is in free verse and the other in rhyme. Comparison of the techniques used to visualize each poem would logically follow.

Sea Shell

Sea Shell, Sea Shell,
   Sing me a song, O please!
A song of ships, and sailor men,
   Of parrots and tropical trees;
Of islands lost in the Spanish Main
Which no man ever may find again,
Of fishes and corals under the waves,
And sea-horses stabled in great
   green caves.
Sea Shell, Sea Shell,
Sing of the things you know so well.

Reading or listening to poetry can stimulate many forms of creative expression. This colorful mural of underwater life and movement captures the lyrical feelings of the sea poem that inspired it and also depicts the children's knowledge of the sea environment.

Hey! Cracker jack—jump!
Blue water,
Pink water,
Swirl, flick, flitter;
Snout into a wave-trough,
Plunge, curl.
Bow over,
Under,
Razor-cut and tumble.
Roll, turn—
Straight—and shoot at the sky,
All rose-flame drippings
Down ring,
Drop,
Nose under,
Hoop,
Tail,
Dive,
And gone;
With Smooth over-swirlings of blue water,
Oil-smooth cobalt,
Slipping, liquid lapis lazuli,
Emerald shadings,
Tintings of pink and ochre.
Prismatic slidings
Underneath a windy sky.

CREATING IMAGINARY ANIMALS AND PLACES The
Churkendoose has the head of a chicken, the legs of a duck, the
body of a turkey, and the bill of a goose. Is he ugly? No—just
different. In the story *What Am I*[4] the Churkendoose explains
that everything depends on how one looks at things. He helps
the barnyard animals to see things more clearly and to accept
differences from the norm.

The Churkendoose is not a chicken, not a turkey, not a duck,
and not a goose, yet he has characteristics of all those animals.
Creating an imaginary animal by combining different parts from
real animals is an exercise that challenges many thought processes. The attributes of real animals must be identified, selected,

---

[4] Ben Ross Berenberg, New York: Wonder Books, 1946.

and represented (an elephant's trunk, giraffe's neck, porcupine's quills, or beaver's tail). Then the parts must be related to the whole by adjusting proportions and including connecting segments that may have been overlooked.

Are all the parts the animal needs there? Can he move, eat, see, hear, and smell? Does he have protection from the weather and from possible attack by other animals? What are the essential parts of all animals? What do some have that others lack? What might be forgotten—hair, feathers, fur, scales, nails, claws, shells, or antlers?

When animals that satisfy their creators have been put together through cutting, pasting, and coloring construction paper, the final shape can be cut out and pasted to a contrasting colored sheet, making a bold, unifying silhouette. Clear contours delineate an overall shape and also define various parts sharply. This method facilitates the observation of clues by classmates who may wish to guess how the imaginary animal was composed. A name combining letters from the real animals that inspired the creation can also be invented. Lists of the specific parts and the animals from which they were derived should be written on the backs of the finished works. If exhibited, riddles to be completed by observers can be attached to the pictures. Environments or habitats for each animal can also be created. This is a project children enjoy working on in groups.

*   *   *

I never saw a moor,
I never saw the sea;
Yet I know how the heather looks,
And what a wave must be.
—Emily Dickinson

"Everyone knows about the purple cow the poet never saw and doesn't want to be," the teacher began, "but today let's think about some serious ideas. How did Emily Dickinson know about the things she never saw?"

"Maybe she read a book about it."

"Maybe she saw a picture of it at the museum."

"Maybe it was on TV."

"Maybe her mother told her."

"I've never been to Puerto Rico, but I sure know how it looks because my whole family talks and talks and talks about it."

"Maybe she just imagined it."

A seven-year-old's conception of a "churkendoose," an animal combining characteristics of a chicken, duck, turkey, and goose. Even imaginary creatures have features based on real animals, however, and children must do some hard creative thinking to draw them.

"O.K.," continued the teacher, "let's imagine some things we've never seen but sometimes think about."

"I can imagine Puerto Rico with lots of palm trees, and there is a beautiful fountain at the airport."

"I can imagine China with many people and a big wall that's very old."

"I can imagine my great grandfather. He had a white beard and told lots of jokes. My grandfather tells me good stories about him."

"I'll imagine the jungle. Someday I am going to see it for real!"

"I'll imagine the bottom of the ocean. I want to be an under-water photographer."

The teacher resumed: "Close your eyes and imagine. Think about the shapes that appear as you concentrate on your subject. Many people are thinking about Puerto Rico. Some children who don't come from there have heard about it from friends and think a lot about it. What colors do you see in your mind's eye? How tall are those trees? What grows on them? What shapes are the leaves? How does the bark feel? If you are thinking of your great grandfather, how big was he? What kinds of clothes did he wear? What did he like to do? Everyone can think about the shapes, colors, sizes, and textures of his or her imagined subject. When you have a good idea, you are all set to begin a painting of things you never really saw. You may get more ideas while you are painting. Let your imagination and your brush explore your ideas. Someday you may see the real thing. Then you may laugh at your old ideas, or you may be proud of how close to reality you were—or of how imaginative you were."

Some paintings executed under these stimuli are so vivid that they seem to capture intensely real experiences. Although the subjects are imaginary, the act of painting them crystallizes the children's essential concepts about them so that a deeper under-standing is gleaned—both by the children and their teacher. If real objects can be viewed afterward, concepts can be refined by comparing reality with the imagined representations. This is the reverse of drawing from nature, but it can promote observation of nature in a highly personal and meaningful way.

MAPS IN TWO AND THREE DIMENSIONS Recounting trips is a familiar assignment in most schools. The class that visited a zoo might produce several variations of the theme:

PEOPLE

Tall people, short people,
Thin people, fat,
Lady so dainty
Wearing a hat,
Straight people, dumpy people,
Man dressed in brown;
Baby in a buggy—
These make a town.

Lois Lenski

"We went to the zoo and saw lions and tigers and bears. Then we came home." A picture of a lion behind bars usually accompanies this verbal account.

Another approach was taken by a second-grade class who wanted to work as a group. They created a three-dimensional map of their trip through the zoo on a tabletop. Pipe cleaners were used to model a facsimile of the ornate entry gate. Colored strips of paper, likened to the yellow brick road Dorothy followed through Oz, were laid out to reproduce the route taken. Everyone concentrated hard to recall the order in which each animal was seen, and then clay or papier-mache animals were stationed at the appropriate points.

Other landmarks, such as refreshment stands, ponds, parking lots, hills and wooded areas, were also constructed and placed at their approximated positions along the route. Arrows and directional signs with small pictures of the animals were placed strategically as they had been encountered.

This activity permitted students to retrace their steps in a more complete manner than is usually characteristic of the verbal account by this age group. The three-dimensional reconstruction widened the focus to include intervening landmarks. It made visible the sequence of events that took place as the class proceeded through the zoo. Older children might tackle the relative scales of the animals seen and the distances traversed. The second-graders noticed that paths branching off in different directions were inviting prospects for future trips, and they realized that the zoo's area was larger than what they could see in one day.

*   *   *

The success of this group map, which was scrutinized repeatedly by its creators, led the teacher to another map-making project. She began by recalling the path of crumbs that Hansel and Gretel dropped through the forest in hopes that their father would track them down by following it. This can be acted out with paper confetti. She asked the students to visualize what the closely spaced crumbs might have looked like to a bird flying overhead.

"A feast!" piped up one youngster, to everyone's delight.

"A dotted line," someone else responded.

"Supposing you carried colored chalks with you and drew a long, long line from door to door when you traveled to school this morning. What would that line look like?" the teacher queried. The children were asked to close their eyes and recall the trips they made each morning, step by step. Several were asked to act out their habitual journeys. The children panto-mimed going down stairs, out doors, across streets, around corners, and through crowds. They were asked to recall the direction of turns taken and the significant landmarks passed en route.

The group decided on some basic symbols to indicate doors, steps, curbs, and the like. Using colored chalk and large sheets of paper, each child then worked at his or her own diagrammatic representation of the trip to school. Home's front door was the starting point. Turns were indicated by changes in direction of the line. Landmarks, such as a friend's house, a store, a traffic light, or an ever-present barking dog, were inserted near the chalk line at a place corresponding to the one where they ap-peared during the trip. The line stopped at the pictorial desig-nation of the school's entrance.

This exercise requires many cognitive skills. It is also fun to make and is decorative in its finished form. The teacher showed the class reproductions of paintings by Stuart Davis and Piet Mondrian so that they might see other artists' conceptions of movement through city spaces. The children agreed that whether journeying through outer space or city streets, whether interpreting a map or enjoying a painting, an understanding of the arrangement of forms in space is crucial.

CONCLUSION

Nevertheless the sign as such, conventional (arbitrary) and ready-made, is not an adequate medium of expression for the young child's thought; he is not satisfied with speaking, he must "play out" what he thinks and symbolize his ideas by means of gestures or objects, and represent things by imitation, drawing and construction.[5]

The foregoing activities illustrate the use of art to develop and strengthen cognitive skills basic to logical thinking. According to Piaget and other learning theorists, the acquisition of cognitive skills relies on the nonverbal operations of manipulating, sorting, constructing, interpreting shapes and symbols, and appreciating

[5] Jean Piaget, *The Psychology of Intelligence* (New York: Harcourt, Brace, 1950) p. 159.

different points of view. The essential component of cognition is action on the part of a child. Children must learn by physically manipulating materials and having concrete experiences so that they form their own examples of concepts—they can't just absorb someone else's ideas. No matter how well a teacher has organized those ideas, they remain remote—the work of someone else. Young children must organize their own ideas because it is the practice of organizing that teaches them how to think. Retention of specific facts is not a gauge of learning. Understanding may still be lacking. Instead, it is the ways in which children order, evaluate, or put together the stimuli before them that reveal and promote their mental development. Dewey called this "learning by doing." Montessori called it "auto-instruction." Piaget calls it "play-learning." Whatever it is called, it is *the* method of art activities.

Suggested Related Activities

Sensory Stations Obtain six small cartons, such as the cut-down variety given away by gardening stores or those found near soft-drink machines. Children can paint or otherwise decorate these, covering up any advertising. Label the cartons: PLEASE TOUCH, PLEASE LISTEN, PLEASE LOOK, PLEASE SMELL, PLEASE TASTE, and PLEASE MOVE. Ask the children to bring in small objects suitable for any of the boxes and to be prepared to tell why a particular object and the possible reasons for the different responses. Individual vocabulary list next to each box. Allow small groups to examine objects together.

Ask each child to draw objects or events experienced elsewhere but having characteristics similar to those observed at school. Discuss the drawings in a group, noting the divergent associations from the same object and the possible reasons for the different responses. Individual or group notebooks may be compiled, or exhibits of mounted drawings arranged around a single object.

Possible objects include: TOUCH—tree bark, rough and smooth shells, fur, sponge, net, satin, velvet, steel wool, sandpaper; LISTEN—music box, bells, timer, large shell, Kalimba or another small instrument; LOOK—mirror, magnifying glass, opened watch, skins of molted snakes and shells of insects and butterflies; SMELL—spices, such as cloves, cardamom, vanilla, coffee, and cinnamon, leather, newsprint, soap, olive oil, freshly cut wood, pine needles, rose petals; TASTE—(keep these in covered containers and check allergies) sweet and unsweetened chocolate bits, mint leaves, lemon slices, green onion, vinegar, endive, orange peel, pretzels, pickles; MOVE—tennis ball, chiffon scarf, bean bag, aluminum foil, elastic, yarn lengths, rubber band.

Print Patterns   Beginning concepts in understanding patterns visually include: 1) Common objects have basic shapes and the shapes have relationships to one another. 2) Shapes can be combined to make new shapes. 3) Shapes can be combined so that the spaces between them become shapes (negative space). 4) Shapes can be repeated in an orderly arrangement making a pattern. 5) Patterns can have symmetry and rhythm. 6) Observation of the relationship of parts in a pattern can lead to an understanding of proportion.

Use simple geometric shapes, such as square and rectangular art gum erasers and round corks or cut simple shapes from vegetables, such as potatoes and carrots to use as printing blocks. Dip the surface to be printed in a pan of tempera, finger paint, or water-based printing ink, and then stamp it on paper. After experiments with the stamping process, ask children to create a repeated pattern in two colors by varying the stamps in a planned way. Stress that the negative space between the stamped shapes also has a shape that is part of the pattern. If stamps touch one another, this space is easier to control. The allover patterns created can serve as book covers, placemats, or gift wraps. Discuss the methods that were used and what techniques produced successful patterns.

Classification Collages   Children may cut out animal shapes from felt or other fabric scraps. They then sort the animals according to habitat—land, sea, air, or swamp, jungle, or desert. The animals should then be arranged and glued to panels of burlap that have been color coded according to categories. Environmental details may be added. Colored paper may be used if fabric is unavailable.

Mobiles   Look at works of Alexander Calder, who invented moving sculpture. String a clothes line across the room slightly above the children's heads, and attach to it thin string, suspend dowels, pipe cleaners, straws, or strips of reed or wire. Children may work in twos, tying lightweight found objects (pine cones, shells, buttons) or colored paper or cardboard shapes to the structures, adding new arms as needed for balance or design. Or they may begin at their tables and raise combined objects working from the bottom up. In either case, they will have to continually adjust for balance. Point out that mobiles should move through space in response to air currents and so should not be too heavy or so crowded they will tangle. While working, children should observe that placement as well as weight affect balance. When finished, they should note changes in appearance of the mobiles as they move.

Motion Pictures   Give children strips of paper marked with six empty frames of identical size. Ask them to depict a bird flying across a cloud, or a flower gradually opening, or some other change taking place in stages. Place the strips in a cylinder with a peep hole, and spin to create illusion of motion.

Funny Pages for the Class Newspaper   Ask children to draw detailed pictures in which one thing is awry and then challenge classmates to discuss, "What's funny about this?"

Comparisons   Ask children to paint equivalents for some of the following phrases from an old nursery rhyme, or situations in which they felt like them: As cool as a cucumber—as warm as toast;
As heavy as lead—as light as a feather;
As steady as time—uncertain as weather;
As hot as an oven—as cold as a frog;
As gay as a lark—as sick as a dog;
As flat as a flounder—as round as a ball;
As blunt as a hammer—as sharp as an awl;
As brittle as glass—as tough as gristle;
As neat as a pin—as clean as a whistle.

6. Learning to See

*The more a child has seen and heard,
the more he wants to see and hear.*[1]

*The greater the awareness of all the
senses, the greater will be the
opportunity for learning.*[2]

Imagine a Ms. Jones opening the door of an apartment house, walking down the steps, and turning right down the street to a bus stop. A neighbor across the street may observe to herself, "There goes Ms. Jones," and turn away. A boy riding by on his bicycle may say to himself, "Ms. Jones is wearing a new red coat to work this morning. It looks bright and cheerful against that gray stone building and the black leafless trees."

Obviously the boy is noticing more and accumulating more information about Ms. Jones's simple act. He is not only making more accurate observations but he is also probably obtaining aesthetic pleasure from his observations. It is very probable that

---

[1] Jean Piaget, *The Origins of Intelligence in Children*, translation by Margaret Cook (New York: International University Press, 1952).
[2] Viktor Lowenfeld and Lamber W. Brittain, *Creative and Mental Growth*, 5th ed. (New York: The Macmillan Company, 1970).

the youngster on the bike is living more fully and having more fun in the process than Ms. Jones's neighbor.

TEN CHILDREN PAINT TREES

"I can't draw a good tree. Do it for me."

"Do it for you!" I replied in a shocked tone.

"Yes—show us," the other children in the fifth-grade class pleaded.

"But if I draw a tree," I objected, "it will be *my* tree—the way I see a tree. We don't just draw trees with lines. We draw with our eyes, our hands, our brains, and with all of the experience we have each had with trees all of our lives. So how can I show you *one* way to do it?"

"Well . . . maybe," responded one skeptic, "but a tree is a tree. It doesn't change when different people look at it."

"That is probably true, but people *do* notice different things. When we look and when we draw, each of us selects from the general image called a 'tree' what he or she thinks is important. What is important for one person is not necessarily important for another. And drawing or painting is not just a matter of skillful hands. It's a question of what one does with what one sees." The children were not sure. . . .

"Would you like to conduct an experiment to see whether this is true or not?"

"Yes—let's do it," they grinned.

"Each of you close your eyes and think about what you like best about trees." Quiet . . . "Now what about the large tree just outside our window. Shall we go and take a look at it?"

They crowded around the window.

"I like the big fat trunk."

"I like the way the leaves move when the wind blows."

"The strong branches."

The answers came in a rush.

"I'd like to touch it," remarked Mary.

"Good idea," I replied, "but do you think it's possible for all twenty-two of us to go down and do that without disturbing the rest of the school?"

The children promised to be very quiet and in a few minutes they were reaching out to the tree. Some merely touched the trunk with their fingertips; others embraced it, reaching around it as far as their short arms could go. A few children also picked up small branches that had fallen to the ground nearby, examining both the wood and the leaves.

After everyone had had a turn, I said, "Good . . . now you have some ideas. But let's not say any more with words. Let's go back to our room and each of us can make a picture. Decide whether you think you can tell more about your tree with line, using chalk, ink, or pencils, or whether you'd prefer to say it with paint. Think hard as we go upstairs, and remember that in your drawing or painting you are going to tell what it is that you feel about that tree. And just to make it a real experiment, try not to look at your neighbor's work."

Everyone chose paint. The room became very quiet as each child began this exercise in careful observation.

Surely every teacher and every parent recognizes this situation—"Do it for me. . . ." "Show me how so I can copy it. . . ." "I can't draw it. . . ." Both teachers and children need to realize that everyone with two eyes and a brain can learn to look for her or himself. After further experimentation and work (and with varying degrees of success, of course), individuals can draw something of what they see. The famous refuge of inexperienced persons, "I can't even draw a straight line," is nonsense. It only means that they haven't given themselves a chance to really look and to try to put down what they see. Chapter 5 discussed some techniques for drawing from a model. Although in the early stages children may draw somewhat standardized forms, the pace of their later development varies considerably and individual differences emerge more clearly.

As the children completed their paintings, they set them down to dry in the drying corner and cleaned their tools as they waited for the others. When most of the children had finished, the group looked at the work together.

"Wow—they sure are different!"

"Look how rough the trunk of Bob's tree is. It makes me want to touch it."

"That's a good picture," nodded several others approvingly.

"Sylvia made her leaves yellow and blue. What a dumb idea."

"Nobody's idea is dumb," I protested. "The ideas are just different. You wouldn't like it if someone called your idea dumb, would you? I'm sure you wouldn't. Now—why not look at the tree again and see whether you can see how she got the idea." (Sylvia sat pleased and smiling to herself, as if she had a secret.)

Several rushed to the window and looked hard at the tree. "I

By the time they become ten or eleven, children who have had opportunities to observe and record their impressions of nature no longer draw the lollipop trees that are universally made by younger children. Here are two completely different renditions of a tree painted by children who had observed the same tree in their schoolyard. The teacher encouraged each student to think, to "tell what it is that you feel about that tree," and to experiment with forms and colors.

guess the color does change when the wind blows the leaves around, but it still doesn't look like blue to me." Jack shook his head vigorously.

Claudine added defensively, "Well, she has the right to make her leaves any color she wants to, doesn't she, teacher?"

Sylvia, her chest thrown out proudly, added, "Anyway, blue and yellow make green."

"Yes, it's her tree," I answered Claudine, "and she can make it any way she wishes. I wonder whether our eyes do the mixing for us. But," I continued, "Jack also has the right to disagree. Maybe he doesn't care for blue leaves. As long as he makes some effort to understand why Sylvia, or any other artist, made them that way, it's fair enough for him to disagree. But let's look at Jack's painting to see what he thinks is important about trees."

"I like . . .," but we stopped him.

"Jack, let the painting speak for you. You don't need words."

Jack's tree stood black, solid, stark, and dramatic, branches extended symmetrically, no leaves. His idea of "tree" was indeed very different from Sylvia's lacy creation. (I couldn't help thinking that each tree was very much like the child who created it—Sylvia, whimsical and a dreamer, and Jack, a stolid, tough little character.) His choice was obvious.

"He likes branches," volunteered his friend approvingly, "and so do I." True enough. Turning to Danny's picture, we saw quite a different branch-dominated tree, with a few leaves, but not many.

And so it went. No two trees were alike. They varied in shape, size, color, and emphasis.

Several different things happened as we worked that day. First, the children were asked to think selectively about what they saw. When they did, they interpreted what they saw differently. Their paintings reflected those differences. They looked with their eyes, brains, and emotional makeups; they integrated their observations through the interaction of their hands with the paint. No two trees could have been exactly alike, even if they had tried to make them so, but when encouraged *not* to make them alike and to make them personal, the children painted with more confidence, identifying for themselves what they saw and felt.

What happened when the children looked at one another's work? Seeing another's concept of "tree" challenged them enough to make them go back to look again, thus extending

One girl in the same fifth-grade class painted still another kind of tree and added a sun and two horses to her picture.

their visual experiences. By looking at someone else's painting, they saw new aspects of "tree" that they may not have noticed before. Each time they looked at trees after that, they would look more carefully, more searchingly, since they then knew that there were many possible visual interpretations of "tree."

As was to be expected, some children were more stimulated by this experience than others and wanted to paint more trees. I spent some time discussing techniques with these youngsters. We discussed the differences in texture that could be obtained by varying the pressure and position of the brush on paper; we talked about the importance of mixing colors carefully; they considered the placement of the tree on the page. Each of these considerations was important to the statement that each child would make about "tree."

*　　*　　*

Many writers agree that responses to this sort of experience would vary as a function of a child's personality. As described by Richard M. Jones in chapter 4, some children are influenced by their emotions, some by their fantasies, and some by their thoughts.[3] Art educator Viktor Lowenfeld offers another theoretical position that identifies children as tending to see the world as spectators and viewing things in a literal sort of way or tending to react to experiences in a highly affective way and viewing things on a more emotional level.[4] The "tree" experience was meant to counter the general feeling that drawings must be photographic representations of a subject. The children were asked to stress the elements they preferred in a tree because experience has shown that they would have expressed that preference anyway, as shall be seen in the incident with the Soviet children. By discussing preference openly at the beginning, we help children bring their own ideas to a more conscious level.

"But," someone may say, "perhaps there were differences in the paintings because the children varied in their ability to draw, because of talent, or the development of their eye-hand coordination, not because they interpreted what they saw differently." It seems questionable to this writer that eye-hand coordination

---

[3] *Fantasy and Feeling in Education* (New York: Harper & Row, 1970), p. 197.
[4] *Op cit.*

exists as a mechanical operation separate from the selective activity of an individual. Children make choices, consciously or not, on the basis of their needs and experience. For example, when drawing a hand they consciously or unconsciously decide whether they see it as a clenched fist, or a relaxed caressing friend, as a punishing bony structure, or as a capable tool for doing things they want to do. Having chosen a point of view, they then transfer their knowledge into abstract shapes that say "hand" and "fingers," what Rudolf Arnheim calls "construction."[5] This is surely a more complicated operation than the mechanical, repetitious activity generally implied in the term "eye-hand coordination," which is cited by teachers as justification for endless exercises in penmanship.

What is called talent or ability is certainly related to genetic differences in art aptitude. Of course ability varies from person to person, but I am quite irritated when individuals say, "I don't have any talent in art," and then quickly relate how they have hardly ever tried to work at it. Experience is also a large component of ability. According to J. P. Guilford, experimental evidence indicates that, "Exercise devoted to certain skills involved in creative thinking is followed by increased ability."[6] When a six-year-old child came to my class drawing extraordinary pictures of football players (as one did), his ability could not be separated from the fact that his father played professional football, and the child often watched, while his mother, a sensitive, intelligent young woman, provided him with space, materials, and encouragement. By contrast, so much of children's latent talent is stifled by lack of experience and lack of confidence that this writer is unwilling to accept generalizations about children's "ability." Give them all years of rich experiences and consistently good teaching, and perhaps more talent will be revealed than is apparent at present.

RUSSIAN SIX-YEAR-OLDS PAINT A TRUCK

A visit to a crèche, a day nursery for children of working mothers, just outside of Moscow provided another insight into the ques-

---

[5] *Art and Visual Perception* (Berkeley and Los Angeles: University of California Press, 1954).
[6] *Intelligence, Creativity, and Their Educational Implications* (San Diego, Calif.: Robert R. Knapp, 1968).

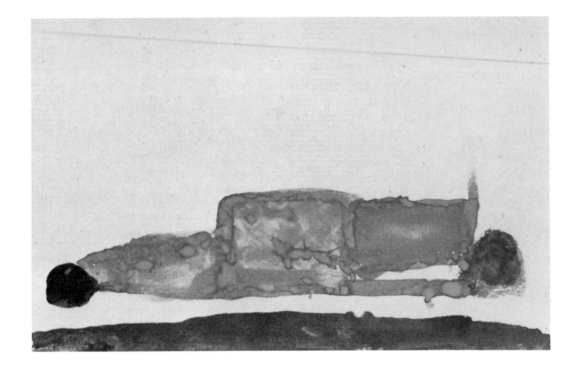

Individual differences are perceptible even among six- and seven-year-olds. The Russian children who painted these very different pictures had been instructed to copy the same drawing of a truck carrying sand.

tion of whether children observe things differently from each other.

As a visiting art teacher, I requested permission to see some of the children's artwork. The teacher brought out about twenty small paintings done by six- and seven-year-olds and entitled "Truck Carrying Sand." Clearly the teacher had drawn a truck for the children and had instructed them to copy its shape and color. But as the paintings were placed side by side, the differences between them were most apparent. One child made a big bold truck, almost filling the page, another made a small timid truck, on the side and bottom of the page, and another did a long sleek truck, which could have been designed by General Motors. And still another couldn't stand the empty space around her or his truck, so had filled it with spots, perhaps rain or snow. (No conclusions should be drawn from the fact that these were Soviet children. They did free drawings as well as copies, but their teacher was proudest of the copied truck drawings, which were in the same category as the Easter baskets, pumpkins, and Christmas wreaths one sees all over the United States at holidays.)

The very obvious differences in the truck paintings could be interpreted in many different ways. Did they express the personality of each child or did the children actually see the teacher's drawing differently? What about the child who made a mirror image, as so many children do when they begin to write? Physiologists, psychologists, and anthropologists all contribute answers to these questions. Are some teachers' attitudes based upon an unconscious acceptance of one point of view or another? What are some of the differences?

DIFFERENCES IN SEEING

In the area of visual perception, studies have shown that "seeing" is not a simple operation. Biologists Roderick A. Suthers and Roy A. Gallant refer to the eye as a "light-gathering device."[7] However, our eyes don't just gather in all light indiscriminately. Since it is impossible to notice every detail of everything that our eyes see, for example, each leaf on a tree, we tend to see what we are looking for. What we see, these biolo-

---

[7] *Biology: The Behavioral View* (Lexington, Mass.: Xerox College Publishing, 1973).

gists say, depends upon "whether we have a particular search image in mind."

It may be said then that the children mentioned earlier all saw a tree when they looked together, but their "search images" were different. In psychologist's terms, they "processed" the information differently.

Art educator Fred Schwartz relates this phenomenon to the field of art by writing:

> *Physiology has helped us to understand how the eye receives light. . . . Perceptual psychologists have . . . indicated the subjectiveness of response to vision and how the human organism . . . applies psychological filters to what is visually perceived. . . . Studies in all of these fields . . . have produced underlying bases for understanding works of art.*[8]

And, one might add, for understanding the process by which artworks are produced.

The "psychological filters" referred to by Schwartz have been described in detail by workers in such fields as Gestalt psychology, psychoanalysis, behaviorism, and others. When people make art, the ways in which these filters function can be very clearly seen. Why, for example, do some individuals draw a man and others draw a woman when asked to draw a "person"? Why do some draw this "person" from a front view, some from the back, and some from the side? Why do some include many details, while others omit some of the most obvious parts of the body? It has been observed that some subjects of the "draw a man" test[9] draw a large figure and place it smack in the middle of the page; by contrast, others draw a tiny figure and place it down in a corner. All this can only mean that although everyone understands what a person is, the psychological filtering or processing varies greatly from one individual to another.

M. H. Segall and his colleagues state:

> *The normal observer naively assumes that the world is exactly as he sees it. He accepts the evidence of perception uncritically. He does not recognize that his visual percep-*

---

[8] *Structure and Potential in Art Education* (Waltham, Mass.: Ginn-Blaisdell, 1970).
[9] Karen Machover. *Personality Projection in the Drawing of the Human Figure: A Method of Personality Investigation* (Springfield, Ill.: Charles C. Thomas, 1974).

tion is mediated by indirect inference systems. . . . Socially, one important aspect [of this attitude] is the observer's assumption that all other observers perceive the situation as he does, and that if they respond differently, it is because of some perverse willfulness rather than because they act on different perceptual content.[10]

This would explain the shocked reaction to some works of art by observers who find them completely outside of their frames of reference. The phrase "perverse willfulness" may also sound familiar to some teachers who may have characterized students this way in some situations.

It is also worth noting briefly the view of the cultural anthropologists who ask, "Do we perceive only what a culture teaches us to perceive?" They describe cultures with very different perceptions from ours. As long ago as 1923 Malinowski reported that among the Trobriand Islanders, in a matrilineal society that regarded mother and child as blood relatives, but not father and child, children were perceived as resembling their fathers in appearance but never looking like their mothers. Although Malinowski and his team pointed out resemblances that seemed very apparent to them, the Islanders were unable to perceive them and were in fact embarrassed by the suggestions. Also, a cultural taboo prevented any discussion that implied that children of the same father might look like one another, although many such resemblances were also observed by the team. The Islanders' perception was tied to a value system imposed by their culture, which was very different from ours.[11]

Another revealing instance was reported by M. J. Herskovitz who wrote from Africa about "a Negro Bush woman who turned a photograph of her own son this way and that, in attempting to make sense out of the shadings of greys on the piece of paper she held. It was only when the details of the photograph were pointed out to her that she was able to perceive the subject."[12] Apparently she saw first the white edge around the photo. The photograph as we know it seems to be an "arbitrary linguistic convention not shared by all peoples."

---

[10] *The Influence of Culture on Visual Perception* (Indianapolis: Bobbs-Merrill Co., 1966), p. 5.
[11] *Ibid.*, pp. 26–7.
[12] "Art and Value," *Aspects of Primitive Art* (New York: The Museum of Primitive Art, 1959), p. 56.

Other differences involve perceptions of color. During one hundred years of study there has been disagreement among researchers as to whether there are genuine differences in perception of color or whether there are only differences in color vocabulary. Early studies showed that many ancient languages (Hindu, biblical Hebrew, Norse Eddas, ancient Chinese, and ancient Greek) lacked a single word for blue, and some lacked words for green and yellow. It was also reported that Filipinos have no native words for green, blue, and violet, although individuals tested seem able to distinguish between these colors.[13]

There are numerous theoretical positions regarding the relationship between children's drawings and paintings and their levels of perception. Is the quality of perception unalterably determined by genetics, or can its development be enhanced by education? Do children draw what they know or what they see? There is considerable literature on these subjects (see bibliography). Studies by social psychologists indicate that, "It is recognized that after a series of rewarding events, one perceives the object and the total field differently, and correspondingly responds differently."[14]

In this same vein, Lowenfeld says, "Through direct experience with tactile, visual, and audial phenomena, the child's imagination and perception powers are developed." This idea is compatible with Herbert Read's thought that, "The child should learn through the cultivation of his sensibilities." It also sits comfortably with Dewey's "learning by doing"; nor does it contradict Arnheim's Gestalt approach, which notes that perception develops from "wholes to particulars," raising further questions about the particular route that increased perception follows.

The interested reader will find much food for thought in the work of all of these and other writers. For our purposes we must note that almost all writers agree on the usefulness of heightened perception, not only for learning but also for living. The accounts that follow are intended to suggest ways of stimulating young students in ways to whet their appetites for constantly expanding perceptions of the world. A useful definition of what we mean by perceptual training has been provided by R. A. Salome, who says, "Perceptual training is instruction which

---

[13] R. S. Woodworth, "Color Sense in Different Races of Mankind," *Proceedings of the Society for Experimental Biology and Medicine*, vol. 3, 1905–6, pp. 25–6.
[14] M. H. Segall et al., *op. cit.*

develops the ability to observe and respond selectively to visual stimuli."

WHAT COLOR IS THE SKY? A small boy in a third-grade classroom was working on a painting. His friend, Paolo, working beside him, suddenly looked up and said loudly, "Look! Robert made his sky red."

"It's when there's a sunset, stupid," Robert blurted, embarrassed.

"I didn't say it was bad," Paolo replied, indignantly. "I was just surprised."

"What color do you think of as sky color, Paolo?" I asked.

He looked out of the window for a moment and then answered, "I think the sky is sort of gray."

"Gray!!" interjected another child, "It's supposed to be blue."

"I know what it's supposed to be, but the sky outside that window now—it's gray."

Rose, at the other side of the room, protested too. "Blue! Why I've seen it when it's a pretty orange, and that's how I really like it."

Everyone was talking excitedly now. "Well," I suggested, "maybe we think of the sky differently. Does anyone else have another idea? We now have red, blue, gray, and orange—four colors."

Eve put up her hand. "Teacher, when it rains it's black, and sometimes even purple. I get scared when it's like that."

"But when it's snowing and cold, it's all white," called out another child.

"Seven colors now."

"But on a foggy day, near the big factory on our street, it sometimes looks yellow," volunteered another girl.

"Eight colors now," I smiled.

"But blue, what's blue?" remarked Robert. "I've seen at least three different blues at different times."

"Yes," everyone agreed, "that's true."

"So—we now say the sky can be eight different colors, and three different blues. Do you think, after this talk, that we all think of the sky in the same way?"

"NO!!" they responded.

"And now that you know that other people think of sky differently from you, will you always say that it's only blue?"

"No" again as they returned to what they had been doing.

A few minutes later Robert tugged at my smock and asked me to bend down. "I still like red," he whispered in my ear.

MY MOMMA—A FIVE-YEAR-OLD VIEW   A group of kindergarten children were drawing with crayons. Many of them were doing simple figurative pictures, similar to what most five-year-olds do.

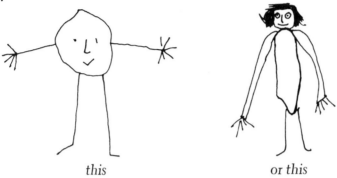

this   or this

Suddenly I noticed one that looked like this:

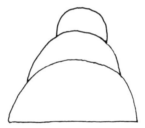

"An igloo?" I wondered privately. "Tell me, Leila," I asked approaching the child, "tell me about your picture."

"That's my momma," said Leila proudly.

"Oh," a bit surprised, "what a nice momma."

The drawing was forgotten until a few weeks later when Leila's mother was visiting the school. As we stood chatting, I dropped my pencil and bent down to pick it up. I looked up at Leila's mother as I rose and saw a buxom lady with a large stomach who from down below looked exactly like her daughter's drawing. Leila was apparently an extremely observant child, and her drawing defied the usual developmental patterns of young children. I had benefited from a new and important insight as a result of a child's drawing and a dropped pencil. The world must indeed look very different from down there.

COLOR AWARENESS   A first-grade class gathered around me as I placed a tray with paints, a brush, a jar of water, and a sponge on a table. The paints were the primary colors (blue, red, and yellow) and black and white.

"Here we have only the primary colors because all other colors are made from these. The black and white can be used to make these colors darker or lighter, but they don't change the basic color. Let's be careful to notice which ones are primary so that we won't forget," I announced.

The word "primary" was written on the board, as were the names of the three colors, which the children spelled and repeated as I wrote. (Some of these first-graders were just beginning to read.)

"Now, what would happen if we were to mix some of these?" I asked. "Shall we try it?'

As we agreed, David reached for the brush. "I want to mix blue and yellow," he said.

"Fine! Go to it."

He gingerly placed some yellow on the tray and then lifted the brush to put it into the blue paint.

"Oh," I exclaimed, "what will happen if he puts that brush in the blue paint?"

"He'll dirty it up," said Mary.

"Right. What would you suggest, Mary?"

"Wash it." The jar of clean water suddenly became yellow, much to their delight.

"Let me make a suggestion," I said. "If you want to keep your colors clear and bright, in case you need a beautiful clean yellow later on, it's always good to wash the brush between colors. Also, remember that your sponge is your best friend. It does many things for you, but between colors, if you wipe your drippy brush on the sponge, it helps to get rid of the extra water, making it all ready for the next color."

David proceeded as suggested, and as the blue paint met the yellow there were "ohs" and "ahs" from the group. It was exciting to see the two colors blend, suddenly producing a new color.

"Do you like that green, David?" I asked.

"Yes," he smiled.

"Then let's put a blob of it on this large sheet of paper." As he did this, the other children were asked, "Do you all like this? . . . What is it?"

"Green," they answered.

From the back of the group came a voice, "I don't like it so much."

"Well, come and change it. How can you change it anyway?"

"More blue," this youngster suggested. She tried and indeed made a quite different green.

"A blob on our paper, please," I requested. "How many other children like this green better?" A few hands were raised. "Can we change it still more?"

"Yes! Yes!" came the answers.

"How?"

"By using the black or the white," someone said.

The children mixed, and mixed, and mixed, taking turns and expressing preferences as they went along. The green changed many times, and soon a large paper was covered with blobs— each different.

"Now," I said, holding up the paper for all to see, "what is the name of this color?"

"GREEN."

"But are these all alike?"

"No."

"This tells us that there is only one word 'green' for every- thing you see here. But obviously there are many different greens, and each of us seems to like some better than others. This is a very important thing to remember. Words have limita- tions. There are times when colors speak more clearly than words, and that is why paintings—and art in general—are so important. Art can often say things that words don't say ade- quately. The reason we are painting with only the primary colors, and black and white, is to help you to be able to mix your own green, when you need green, instead of just using some- thing that comes out of a bottle, which someone else calls green. Does that make sense to you?"

"Yes, yes." The children were enthusiastic.

We put the sheet of green blobs up on the wall. Then they separated into small groups and proceeded to mix other possible combinations, the red and yellow producing many oranges, and the blue and red producing many variations of purple. They found that a little of each of the three primary colors mixed together could make brown, although this was more tricky because the proportions were very important. As we went along, the children made a mixing chart to help them to remember the various combinations. It looked like this:

Red   Yellow   Orange

They decided to include the name of the color under the blob even though they understood its limitations. "To help us remember the words," some said. (This was also good for reading.)

Having done this in groups, with the children taking turns, many were itching to do it by themselves. They were told to feel free to play around with mixing colors if they wished, before starting a painting. There was an absorbed silence in the room, except for an occasional, "Oh boy—look at this."

*   *   *

This school was lucky in being located close to a wooded area. The color experience was reinforced soon after by taking a "seeing walk." We looked to see how many different greens we could see—and browns—and reds—and so on.

Some teachers or parents might question the validity of discussing with first-graders such a serious matter as the importance of art as a means of communication, but the writers feel strongly that it is precisely when children are young and ready for new ideas that these questions should be raised. Indeed they should be discussed at whatever level seems appropriate and the concepts repeated frequently.

FORMS OR SHAPES   One day my third-grade class went on a "seeing walk." As we looked around us, we concentrated on noticing differences in the forms of familiar things. For example, were all cars the same shape? Clearly not. Houses? Flowers? Trees? People? Everything we saw along the way was observed carefully from the point of view of form.

When the class returned to the school, the children found colored construction paper, scissors, and paste on the supply table. There was also a bucket of clay and some tongue depressors, which make good clay tools.

As a rule, when classes had an outing, the children were asked to select something they saw and make a picture of it. This surely sounds very familiar to most teachers. However, in this case I wished to focus upon a particular idea that I thought would broaden their understanding of what they themselves see. The discussion began as follows: "We have been using the words "form" and "shape" very freely. But actually they can be thought of in several different ways. There may be a shape on a flat surface, which we call a "two-dimensional form." That's a big word. Let's all say it together."

"TWO-DIMENSIONAL," they repeated.

"Any idea of what it means?" I asked.

No response.

"Well, a 'dimension' can be thought of as a 'direction.' If something is two-dimensional, it goes up in height, and sidewise in width, like this—

Two directions—two dimensions. If this is so, how will it feel when you run your hand over it?"

"Flat," responded Billy.

I drew a circle on the board and asked, "How would you describe this?"

"It's a round shape and it's flat," Billy spoke up again.

"Does everyone agree?" I asked, knowing that Billy was often ahead of the others. They all nodded their heads. "It's a circle," someone volunteered.

"Good! Now what is the difference between that circle and this?" I reached into a box nearby and took out a baseball.

"That's a circle too, but it's not flat," remarked Dora, and grinned. "It's also John's baseball." We laughed.

"How many directions does it have?"

"It goes up, and sidewise . . . and back!!" someone announced firmly.

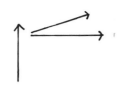

"How many directions is that?"

"Three."

"Ah!" I was delighted, "then you know another big word to try out on your parents. *Three*-dimensional! Let's say that one all together."

"THREE-DIMENSIONAL!" It was loud and clear.

"But how can you explain that to your parents, if they want to know more?" I asked.

There was quiet for a few moments. Then Jane held up her hand. "*It's three-dimensional if you can put your hand around it,*" she said. (That was really a very useful definition, I found. It was simple and clear, and I actually used it for many years after Jane offered it.)

"Thank you, Jane," I said. "Sometimes we know and feel the answers to these questions about forms, but it's not always easy to put the answers into words. You have helped us by giving a nice simple definition."

"But let's be sure we understand. What would you call this?"

"A square," someone offered, "it's two-dimensional."

"But what would you call it if it became three-dimensional?" Silence.

"Shall I draw it for you?"

"Yes, yes."

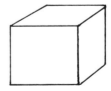

"Now, what would you call that if you felt it?"

"A box." "A cube."

(I sighed, thinking what a joy it would be if their classroom teacher had been there at that moment. We were well on our way into a geometry lesson, except that this time was set aside for "art," and my job had to do with exposing them to ideas related to form. Although I don't know much about geometry, this was too good to miss, so I urged the children to try out their new knowledge about two- and three-dimensional forms on their classroom teacher later on in the day. I said I would do the same.)

"Good. Now I just wanted to point this out to you—that the word 'form' can mean a solid or flat thing, either two-dimensional or three-dimensional. That's why we have both construction paper and clay here. I thought that today you might like to start with one form—either solid or flat—and see how many ways you can change or vary it. We can put the form and its variations together to make a design, and you can use any colors or textures you like. If, for example, you decide on a triangle, why not make many triangles—large ones, small ones, lopsided ones, bumpy ones, smooth ones—and then put them together to make a design. In the same way, one can make a sculpture of clay by making one form and then playing with variations of that same form. Any questions? If so, come to the worktable, and we'll try out these ideas. The others go ahead and get started."

Most of the children got busy, but a few who did not understand the instructions came to the worktable with me.

"Let's look at it this way," I suggested. "Think of a familiar object such as a car, or an animal, or a hot dog. Or, better yet, does anyone have a pet at home?"

"I have a turtle," Louise answered.

"Well, think about the shell of that turtle. If you put your hand on top of the shell, how does your hand look?"

"Yes," she was nodding, "I hold my hand rounded, it's like this," and she demonstrated.

"Would you prefer to make that turtle shell form in clay or in colored paper?"

"Well," she said thoughtfully, "if I cut it out of paper, it will look sort of like an egg, but if I make it solid, it will look like you cut off a piece of the egg, the long way."

"Great! Now you decide how you want to make it and go to it," I exclaimed. "When it's flat, there's even a name for it— 'oval' but I'm not sure of the name for the solid form. I don't see why you'd need a name for every form anyway." And off she went.

This anecdote suggests one easy approach to learning how to

look at shapes and forms. There are, of course, many others that are less verbally oriented. But once children have begun to think about the subject and have learned the vocabulary, they can be encouraged to look for shapes all around them—in the classroom, at home, everywhere. They can be helped to define forms in terms of their contour or outline, their mass (either two- or three-dimensional), their directional thrust (if free forms, do they move up or down or diagonally?), or their relationship to other shapes. The mass of a form can be seen by itself or as it exists in space. Does a ball sitting alone on a table look different when it is placed in a box? How does the space around it affect the feeling of mass? When one takes one simple form and repeats it many times, creating a pattern, is the form seen differently? There are endless possibilities, all contributing to increased perception. In chapter 8 on integrating art with other subjects, the specific ways in which increased perception can help children learn to read and write will be discussed. What is a letter in the alphabet if not a linear shape?

TEXTURES   Textures are such an intimate part of the pleasures of living that it seems astonishing to me that art teachers are so frequently asked, "Why discuss textures?" Fondling a baby or a loved one, stroking a favorite pet, the comfort given by a soft blanket, or the feel of a sandy beach or a grassy lawn on bare feet—all these and many more are joys involving the sense of touch. "Let your fingertips speak to you," I have often suggested. "You don't always need words."

Do textures really communicate anything more than pleasant or unpleasant sensations or are there associations suggested by the sensations? Must one experience a precise texture physically or is it possible to enjoy a texture visually—just by looking at it?

Standing beside a box of collage materials—felt, cotton, velvet, burlap, sandpaper, wax paper, corrugated paper, and the like—a fourth-grade teacher asked, "If you wanted to make a collage picture about a princess or a dinosaur, which of these fabrics would you use to suggest 'princess' and which for 'dinosaur'?" She held in one hand a piece of lace and in the other a piece of burlap, both of which she then passed around the room for feeling. The answer was obvious—nobody would ever use lace to suggest a dinosaur. But this was a loaded question; not all textures have such clear-cut associations, and not all individuals have the same associations with all textures. However, there are some generalized experiences within our culture, and the concepts associated with "princess" and "dinosaur" are examples. Was it necessary for each child to touch each fabric before understanding the differences between the two? Clearly not.

A sensitivity initially learned by means of touch can also provide pleasure and insight when experienced visually. It may not provide the *same* pleasure, but that it can provide some is indisputable. To alert children to the subtleties of textural differences, the following experiences were provided in some Follow-Through classes.[15]

The first time I met these first-graders, I was loaded with materials. I introduced myself, said that I was an artist who liked to work with wood, and asked them if they could see anything in their room that was made of wood. We looked around and, of course, found many such things. But where does the wood come from? "Trees." "The street," they said.

I held up a large log. "Wood, wood," they shouted happily. I walked around the room with the log so that each child could touch the wood. I wrote the word on the board, asking them to tell me what the letters were as they appeared. Then I wrote "sculpture" on the board, and we looked together at a half-finished piece of my own sculpture which I had brought along. I showed them how one begins with a log, such as the one they had touched, and then uses chisels and a mallet to chop away at it. Different children came forward to try the tools, cutting small chips at places that were as yet undeveloped. I showed the class the rough model in clay from which the design was taken. The model essentially showed two stylized heads in confrontation. It is called *Dialogue* and was not a realistic piece. I have shown it to adults who did not know at first what it was meant to be. Yet when the children were asked what they thought the sculpture was about, they had some interesting responses.

"It's an elephant," said one little girl.

"NO," roared a number of children.

"It's people," declared Maurice (who has difficulty in reading).

"It's two faces," added Vanessa.

"What are they doing, I wonder?" I mused.

---

[15] This next section is extracted from Elaine Pear Cohen, "Does Art Matter in the Education of the Black Ghetto Child?", *Young Children*, vol. XXIX, no. 3, March 1974, pp. 170–81.

"They're fightin' " replied Maurice firmly, while the others nodded their heads seriously.

"How smart you are!" I said, "and you have good eyes. Now I have a surprise to show you."

I took out two West African masks carved from wood. The Dan mask had a smooth finish, while the Baule mask had a somewhat textured surface. The children knew that there was a faraway place called Africa and were very interested in learning that these masks had come from there. We talked briefly about what the masks were used for and I held each one up to my face, which they found very amusing. At this point I did not wish to focus upon the mask concept (see mask section in chapter 4) because the wood was interesting enough in itself. The children were asked how they thought the wood had been changed from this rough condition, holding up the unfinished sculpture, to this smooth condition, holding up the Dan mask. They were not too sure, so I took a small piece of wood, with a rough surface, and showed them how sandpaper could smooth the surface.

Did they think that the Africans, who lived in the forest or in small villages, went to the hardware store to buy sandpaper when they needed it? They laughed. No, they used rough earth or pebbles or sand if they could get it.

"How lucky we are that we have sandpaper," I remarked.

"Yes," they nodded their heads.

"But—and this is important—I have told you that sandpaper changes the texture of wood (We defined 'texture' and put the word on the board), but how do you know that I am right about what I say? Also, do you think that all sandpaper is the same . . . or that all wood is the same?" At this point they were all keyed up, eager to answer the question. Each child was given a small rough piece of wood (scraps from a lumber yard) and two different grades of sandpaper.

"Let's see what we can do to change the texture of the wood, just as these African artists changed their wood."

They became very busy with their pieces of wood. They soon discovered that different kinds of sandpaper produced different results. They were urged to *feel* with their fingertips. "Your fingers will tell you what is happening better than your eyes. Try them out on your own piece and on your neighbor's as well."

After several minutes of very intense activity, the children began to call out, "It's soft. It's soft." We discussed the word "soft," which I wrote on the board. I then suggested the word "smooth" as well. "Soft" was something that you could push *in*, but "smooth" was something that felt good when you ran your fingers along the surface.

The classroom teacher was delighted. This was a concrete experience that enhanced the children's understanding of textures and the words that define textures. The level of participation this activity produced from the children was amazing to her. Several individuals, such as Maurice, who had always seemed quiet and withdrawn, were now working at the wood vigorously and enthusiastically.

When they had had enough, we stopped, and I asked the children whether they wanted to take their pieces of wood home. They were very eager to do this. "Alright, take them home," I agreed, "but during the next few days will you all look for things that are made of wood and, if possible, bring them in to show everyone?"

"Yes, yes," they responded.

*   *   *

I repeated this wood experience in another first grade. Interestingly enough, in the second experience the group also called the wood "soft" rather than "smooth."

Taking wood to a kindergarten was quite a different matter. The activity was too wordy, and the children were restless and talkative until I put wood into their hands. For about three minutes they were busy with sandpaper, but then most of them lost interest. I concluded that for five-year-olds who were just starting school, I would have to find another approach.

As I began to gather up the materials, ready to leave, I made one last effort and asked the group, none of whom I thought was listening, "What do your fingertips tell you about the wood?" Most of the children did not even hear the question, but, much to my surprise, about five small voices said unanimously, "It's soft." Incredible! Someone might well do a study to learn why the word "soft" was so universally, but imprecisely, used by these children.

*   *   *

The understanding of textures was deepened through several other experiences. In one, we had five mystery bags and played a texture game. The bags contained bits of burlap, sandpaper, waxed paper, corrugated paper, velvet, aluminum foil, gauze, screening and assorted fabrics. The children closed their eyes and each took turns putting a hand in the bag to find something

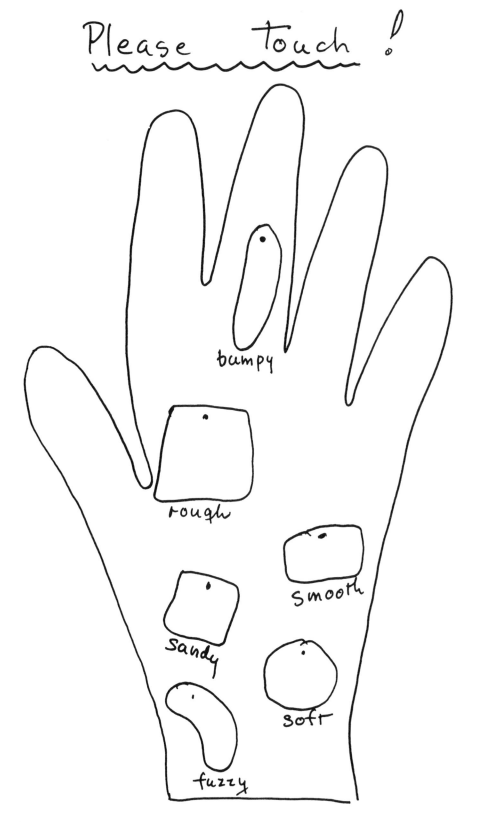

First-graders enjoyed selecting and taping a variety of textured materials onto a three-foot-high poster board hand. This concrete experience enhanced their understanding of textures and the words that define textures.

"smooth," "rough," or "soft." I had prepared a large hand, cut from colored poster board, about three feet high. As the children found their textures, they taped them to the board. We wrote a sign to put over the board. "Please touch," it said. We also attached the new words we had used.

After this, they were asked to "draw a picture of a texture." Could a crayon show a texture? Could one show a texture without using a word to describe it? Some of the children were able to understand this and drew swatches of color that were bumpy, scratchy, smooth, and the like, using the side of a crayon as well as the point. But not all of them did this. To avoid embarrassing them, they were encouraged to draw an "anything-you-like" picture or make a collage.

Another texture experience involved making paper bag masks, using textures for the features (see chapter 4 for other uses). The children closed their eyes and felt their skin, eyebrows, hair, and eyelashes. Finding appropriate textures in the collage box was fun after that.

Finally, throughout the term a conscious effort was made to use the new words that we had learned, referring to previous experiences frequently. However, it is important to note here that the method of teaching, the emphasis upon the personal quality of each child's work, and the atmosphere in the classroom all influence a child's perception as well as do the subject for the day. They probably affect self-concept as well. Human experience is often separated into its various components as if it were a deck of cards—"perception" here, and "self-concept" there. The human being is far too complex to permit this type of treatment. Many aspects of the personality function at many different levels at the same time and any separation is artificial. We have focused upon perception here for purposes of identification, realizing full well the limitations described above.

Suggested Related Activities

COLORS

Fun with an Overhead Projector   Using a flat glass dish and an eye dropper, mix drops of colored dye together. Start with a small dish of water or a flat piece of glass. Put a drop of red dye in it and then yellow. If colors don't flow, add one drop of water. By projecting the mixing actions of the color drops against a white wall or a sheet, the class can see marvelous combinations of colors. The children can take turns using the dropper and shaking the dish slightly to move the colors around.

An alternative, wet a piece of paper and let the drops mix on it while moving it in different directions.

Colored Celluloid   Provide as many pieces of colored celluloid as possible for the children to play with. Colors become more vivid if a flashlight is available to hold behind the celluloid.

Paint or Chalk on Wet Paper   Provide a bucket of water in which each child can "give the paper a bath." Colors become brighter, and mixing them is easier on wet paper. If chalk is used, suggest that the children color with the side as well as the point of the chalk.

FORMS

Modeling Clay with Shut Eyes   Suggest to the children that they close their eyes and then mold clay, turning it this way and that. The mass can be changed in any way that suits them. It can be squeezed, flattened, pounded, or whatever they wish to do. After the initial exploration, some may like to separate the mass into several forms; after poking holes into these forms, they can try to put them together. Then they should open their eyes to see what shapes they made. Ask them to consider what the new forms suggest to them—a dog? a person? an abstract shape? At this point they can be urged to shut their eyes again and to make what they saw in the clay. They should feel free to deviate from their original ideas and play with new ones as much as they like.

Modeling Animals with a Wiggle   It's fun for children to try to make an animal with a wiggle from clay. The choice of animal should be up to them; imaginary animals should always be acceptable. The value of this activity lies in the sense of the movement and rhythm of forms that the word "wiggle" suggests.

Looking for Natural Forms at Home   Wherever children live they can search for forms such as stones, pebbles, small branches, shells, bottle caps, or even scrap lumber. These are just suggestions—they will think of others. Then, using good strong glue (epoxy or Elmer's), make a design or a "something," whatever appeals to each child. It can be a three-dimensional sculpture or, if placed on a flat surface, it can become a relief sculpture.

TEXTURES

Texture Books   Each child can make a texture book by finding at home small items with different textures. As starters suggest such things as waxed paper, steel wool, gauze, sandpaper, satin, cotton pads, or screening. Ask the children to arrange the textures on the pages so that they will be pleasant to look at as well as to touch. This involves thinking about contrasting colors and shapes as well as the textures themselves.

Collages   Using bits of cloth, make a collage person, doll, animal, or design. The children should be encouraged to think about whether they wish their creations to be "prickly," "soft," "rough," or any combinations of these. They should make their own decisions but should be urged to think about them in the process.

7. Learning About Feelings

Love is a word that I like,
It is a word of friends.
We have friends and love them
So love is a nice word for us to know.
Mommy and Daddy love us.
Our brothers and sisters love us.
Even our friends love us.
So like that word called Love.

A tiny seven-year-old girl with dark sparkling eyes continued to write after composing the above poem. Her mother reported that she occasionally asked how to spell a word but did not indicate what she was working at.

When I told a story about love, I was
thinking about LIKE too,
Like is a kind of love. But is
not all the way Love, but knows about friends.
I have frends,
You have frends,
everyone has friends. If
you and your friend have a fight,
oh that can hurt someone and, you
will never be friends again!

Were you ever shy?
I was.
Being shy is when you are afraid of
something, it gets you so you
never want to do that thing again.
But I mean
afraid of going in front of
the room, when you want to make
a announcement.
But, you think everyone will
laugh at you.
But when you do it, not
one will laugh.
That is being shy.

The child who wrote the above was thinking seriously about her own feelings. Although she may have been more verbal than many of her peers, she was no doubt expressing some concerns that were as important to them as these were to her. However, many young children are not fortunate enough to be so articulate. They are locked into their own feelings and need a way to express them, but do not know what tools are available to help.

PERSONAL TROUBLES REVEALED IN ART

As noted earlier in chapter 3, a child often finds it easier and more satisfying to create a picture of an emotionally laden subject than to describe it in words. Remember Jeffrey, whose strong reaction to the killing of Dr. King was expressed in a crayon portrait. And then there was Suzy.

Suzy was thin, blonde, athletic, and very quiet in class. I was the only art teacher in her small elementary school. I taught all the children from the time that they were in first grade until they reached sixth grade. This put me in the unique position of being a constant presence throughout their elementary school years, a position shared only with the music teacher and the physical educators. Thus when Susan, generally called Suzy, came to my third-grade art class, I had already known her for two years.

At the beginning of the term, I looked around and noticed that there were quite a few new children in the class, which was somewhat unusual. Suzy was sitting off in a corner, not particularly interested in the newcomers. This was also somewhat unusual, but I was too busy distributing supplies to think about it. I welcomed the new children and then proposed the following:

"I don't know you all very well, although there are many old friends here. I wish that it were possible for me to go home with each one of you, to meet your family, see where you sleep, where you read and do your homework, get acquainted with your pet, or your favorite game, or toy, and so on. But since this isn't possible, how about allowing me to visit you at home through a painting? Think about what you would like to tell me about yourself at home, and I will be very happy to be able to visit with each one of you in this way. What do you think? Is this a good idea?"

They liked it. Many nodding heads assured me that I was on the right track. I asked the children who had been with me last year to explain the painting procedures to their new classmates. Various children showed them where to get the paint, brushes, sponges, and water. They discussed the clean-up procedure and showed them the color-mixing chart, explaining that anyone could add any new discoveries to the chart at any time. Then everyone got busy painting, and the room became very still.

Suzy sat quietly, somewhat withdrawn during all this discussion. However, since that was her usual demeanor, and since a quiet child provokes less concern in a classroom than a noisy one, I attended to my business and left Suzy to her own devices. At the end of the session, when all the paintings were set out on the floor to dry, I realized what a mistake I had made. There, pushed into the corner, away from all of the others, was a shocking painting! For the most part the children had done cheerful pictures of rooms with beds, or toys, and sometimes a television set. Quite a few included people, obviously the family group. But Suzy had painted a black room with dark brown furniture; the only bright spot was a blue cover on her bed. There were no people, no toys, no happiness. It was the painting of a miserable child. We were about to have our usual discussion about our paintings, when I looked up shocked—and saw that she was watching me with a wary expression. I had known her for two years and she had known me; she was taking a chance.

"Should this painting be discussed? Isn't it too personal?" I was asking myself, when a most improbable thing happened.

Children's paintings often mirror their inner feelings of anxiety, happiness, or sorrow. When a third-grade class was asked to paint pictures of their homes, one little girl produced this gloomy, dark picture. Realizing she was sad and upset, her sensitive teacher discovered that her parents were about to be divorced.

The bell rang for a fire drill! "Saved!" I thought, but not really.

After the fire drill, the children went back to their classroom instead of returning to the art room. I stood alone, looking at Suzy's painting, surely a most poignant cry for help. If art was ever a form of communication, this was it. If Suzy thought of home as such a dismal place, she was in trouble. I remembered her more than usual quiet withdrawal and realized something was on her mind.

Ten minutes remained until lunch time. I rushed up to Suzy's classroom. The children were getting ready for the lunchroom, and their teacher was busy at her desk.

"Look," I said to her, "what would you think about a child who paints this as a picture of home? I am not a psychologist, but as a human being—Wow!" She agreed, and we both looked up to see Suzy watching us intently.

The teacher motioned her to come up to us. Gently, with her hand on Suzy's shoulder, she asked, "What's wrong, dear?" Suzy glanced at the other children and said not a word. The teacher, a sensitive person, got the message. She assigned a leader to the group and sent everyone down to the lunchroom. We remained behind.

"My parents . . . " she started and then broke into tears. The poor child sobbed and sobbed, as if she would never stop. Gradually the story came out. Her parents had been fighting for a long time, and now—TODAY—her father was moving out. They were going to be divorced. "He says that he'll come to see me," she wept, "but maybe he won't. Maybe I'll never see him again."

The teacher was kind and sympathetic. She asked me to go down to be with her class during the lunch period, while she stayed to try to comfort the girl. Later in the day she contacted the school psychologist, who talked with Suzy and called her mother. They discussed how to help the child through this crisis. Apparently her mother had no idea how upset Suzy was. "She's so quiet," she said. "I did not realize how worried she was."

*   *   *

It's often the quiet ones who need a nonverbal instrument for communication, although they are not the only ones. In Suzy's case a young child wanted to tell someone about her personal troubles but found them too painful to talk about until the floodgates were opened. It was possible for her to express with paint what she found difficult to say with words. Real communication, however, requires not only a communicator, but also a receiver who is responsive to the messages being sent. All teachers are in a unique position to assume that role since they are with children for so many of their waking hours.

The personal, private life of each child will determine the manner in which she or he approaches the learning offered in school. I once heard the principal of an elementary school in a ghetto area explain this very well to some new practice teachers. She asked, "How do you know where they slept the night before? Perhaps it was in a bed with three other children. Perhaps the television was blaring, and they did not fall asleep until very, very late. Do these little ones come to school sometimes smelling of urine? Perhaps there was no adult to help them bathe before they left home. Perhaps the mother has to leave for work very early in order to get someone else's child off to school clean and well fed. Oh yes, and how do you know whether they had any breakfast at all before coming to school? Or was it a handful of potato chips? These are the little children whom you are approaching with problems of arithmetic and reading."

Suzy's problems were not in this category. Her feelings did not derive from urgent physical need as do the feelings of the children just described. What she did have in common with them was the necessity of expressing what was bothering her in a way that she could find help in dealing with it.

*   *   *

A ten-year-old boy who came to my ceramics class in a neighborhood settlement house in a slum area is a good example of unsuccessful coping. He loved to work with clay and enjoyed the relaxed atmosphere in the class. We became friends. One day he came in looking very glum.

"Won't be here anymore," he mumbled.

"Why?" I was astonished.

"I'm in trouble in school, and they gonna' send me to reform school. It's real bad."

"But why? What for?"

He sulked a little and then, seeming to be embarrassed, turned and walked out.

Feeling very upset, I went immediately to the secretary of the settlement house who knew everyone and everything and asked what was going on.

"Yes," she said, "the school says he steals. They have given him several chances, but he continues to do it, and now they are going to bring him up on charges."

I was aghast. He had been in my class for several months, and nothing was ever missing.

"What does he steal?" I asked.

"Don't know," she replied, "but I guess we could find out."

She phoned the school, chatted a bit with the secretary, and then asked our question. She was told that he was constantly found in the kitchen stealing food. If they put out cookies for the kindergarten children's snack, they always had to watch, because he knew the schedule and would often be there to take some. He would stuff them in his pocket and run.

"Has anyone bothered to ask him why he does this?" my settlement house friend asked.

"Don't know," was the answer.

"I'll go there tomorrow and find out about this," she said to me, looking a bit grim as she put down the phone. "Thank you for asking the question."

What she discovered was that the boy was hungry but was ashamed to say so. He felt that it would reflect upon his father who worked hard to bring home the pittance on which they lived. Not having the means to communicate his distress and to ask for help, he had dealt with it by stealing, which was hardly a satisfactory solution. He would eat some of the cookies and then save some for his sister. At the after-school class I was teaching, a modest snack was available. He was given an apple, or a container of milk with a cookie, or something similar. No wonder that he came to class so regularly and enthusiastically.

With horror I suddenly remembered that when he first came he used clay to make piles and piles of "cookies." Unfortunately I was not alert enough to ask questions about those cookies. It was my first acquaintance with a hungry child.

I must end by reporting that the settlement house followed up on our new knowledge and intervened on his behalf. He did not go to reform school; it was finally understood that punishment was not the answer to his problem behavior.

FEELINGS, THEIR IMPORTANCE IN ALL EDUCATION

Frequently educators adopt the position that "feelings" or "emotions" are "bad," are "anti-intellectual," or interfere with learning. They focus upon the subject matter to be taught with little regard for the state of mind of either teacher or student. (Is one feeling sullen while the other feels joyful?) Nor do they consider the way feelings have influenced events in such areas as history. (What feelings impelled people to keep going when they faced the incredible physical difficulties involved in crossing the wilderness that was America?) Harold Taylor has written:

> I wish to present the view that teaching people to think is not merely a question of training their intellects through the study of organized bodies of fact. . . . The intellect is not a separate faculty. It is an activity of the whole organism, an activity which begins in the senses with direct experience of facts, events, and ideas, and it involves the emotions [my emphasis].[1]

Psychologist Richard M. Jones has continued this train of thought by suggesting:

> Normally, the human mind and the human heart go together. If not normally, may we say optimally? We are witnessing a revolution in pedagogy which is committed to honest dealings with the minds of children. It follows, therefore, that we may also enjoy more honest dealings with the hearts of children. Admittedly, there are times for dispassion in schoolrooms; but teachers need no reminding of this. They do, however, need reminding that there are also times for·passion in schoolrooms.[2]

It is not a question of whether or not teachers should let "passion" in the classroom—it is already there. Passion, when defined as feeling, emotion, or fervor at an intense level, is present in the life of every human being—every child, every teacher, every parent. A small boy may *love* football, *hate* arithmetic, *detest* his baby sister, and *adore* his best friend. A teacher may *love* literature, *hate* her job (some of the time), *resent* deeply the piles of paperwork foisted upon her, and *love* her church with deep fervor. These are clearly examples of "passion" at very

---

[1] *Art and the Intellect* (New York: Museum of Modern Art, 1960), pp. 12–3.
[2] *Fantasy and Feeling in Education* (New York: Harper & Row, 1970), p. 24.

different levels—and, of course, there is sexual passion, which certainly is present in every class of adolescents.

Passion is there then. The question is, What do teachers do about it? Do we turn our backs and pretend that it does not exist? Do we assume that the learnings that take place in a classroom can be separated from the passions twisting the innards of both the children and the teacher? And not only the passions that twist but also the passions that enrich, that make life exciting and important! There is so much in contemporary society that makes for conformity and for numbness that were it not for these passions, we should all be robots.

What are teachers to do? First of all, we must agree that feelings exist, always have, and always will. An important part of children's growing up has to do with their understanding, not only of their own feelings (self-knowledge) but also of the feelings of the people around them. Part of this understanding will come as they learn to express and face those feelings. Another part will come from learning that other people experience them too. This is the key for teachers. Since all nonverbal art forms (plastic arts, dance, music, mime) are involved in one way or another with human feelings, they provide teachers with ideal instruments with which to work.

USING ART TO DEAL WITH ANGER   Holly is a very angry, upset eight-year-old. A classroom teacher or an art teacher may attempt to help her channel her feelings by painting a picture. She might paint a wild and violent composition full of reds and purples, or she may make a picture of the person who is the object of her anger and then destroy that person with harsh black lines. The teacher's reaction at this point is important. Saying, "There! you got that out of your system," and walking away, is doing only a part of what needs to be done. Rather she or he might ask, "Now what did you mean to say in that painting? Instead of just fuming, let's think of how you can use your colors to help you say it clearly and strongly. Do you want to include something in the painting to show what it was that made you so angry?" The teacher who asks such questions and respects the answers is not telling Holly what to paint. Rather, she is helping her to clarify her own ideas and to create an expression that is not just a violent striking out without direction but rather an organized statement about her own anger. This requires deep and careful soul searching as well as technical competence. It's no longer a "scribble scrabble" as my children used to say.

After a thoughtful session like this, Holly may look at her work and think, "So there!" and heave a deep sigh. This cathartic action may give her a useful sense of relief and make it possible for her to get through that day. However, important as catharsis is, it has limited value unless it can lead to a deeper understanding of oneself and a feeling of control. Holly still has to deal with the subject of her anger as well as possibly a feeling of guilt at the depth of her feelings. A little girl or boy may feel that expression of one's anger is unacceptable. "Nice little girls don't act iike that, Holly. It's not ladylike." Or "You are not being a little gentleman, Hal." The child is then beset with further confusion. But if children are taught that everyone feels anger at one point or another, and that they must try not to permit it to be destructive but rather try to understand the reason for it, then perhaps they will be better able to handle their anger. Frequently some degree of understanding can come from facing what one has put down in a painting or a piece of sculpture. In the act of producing art, one often expresses one's unconscious thoughts without realizing it until later.

It is the *uncontrolled* and *poorly directed* emotions that can obstruct learning. If Holly were so angry that her only action was to tear up the sheet of paper given her, you may be sure that such anger would also interfere with her listening to a class discussion about the causes of the American Revolution. Tearing up the paper might be a kind of catharsis but it would be of a negative kind. Thoughtful consideration of how she might clearly express her disturbing feelings in nonverbal language could better lead to the unique and valuable kind of self-knowledge that helps children to deal with their world.

USING FEELINGS IN GENERAL STUDIES Teachers may also assist in dealing with feelings by considering the ways they present subject matter to children. If teachers admit "passion" to their classrooms, children may begin to realize that anger and other strong feelings are not peculiar to themselves alone. In the study of American history, for example, a teacher perhaps can openly express an appreciation and understanding for the feelings of the people who made American history (John Adams was homesick and miserable; George Washington distrusted his own ability to be president; Dolly Madison was frightened but determined; Thomas Jefferson was angry at the Virginia legislature). The fact that anger is a human feeling common to all people may be a source of great relief to children such as Holly. In this way teachers may deal with their problems without intruding on their privacy.

Fear also strikes everyone at some time, and an acceptable way to find this out might be, for example, to look closely at the fears faced by the men on Columbus's ships as suggested in chapter 8 on the integration of subject matter. Obviously these are very simple examples that would mean nothing if used by themselves, but they suggest an approach that is applicable to many situations that arise every day in every class.

Although talking about fears will help, talk in itself is not enough. Using art media to interpret fears, process them, and transform them into shapes and colors, or dance movement, or sound so that the nonverbal aspects of an experience may be expressed and personal interpretations honored—that is learning *in depth*. This is understanding history or literature as products of human experience, made by people who felt, who suffered, and who experienced joy just as we do. The more aesthetic experiences teachers can make available to children, the more effective their teaching will be.

For instance, an appreciation of art history need not rely on the arbitrary and pedantic presentations usually associated with the painter-of-the-week format. I have often selected two paintings that relate to a current classroom theme and let the children respond to them with appropriate dramatic and art activities of their own devising. The theme of family relationships was explored through Cezanne's portrait of his father and Chardin's *Boy Blowing Bubbles*. Other themes that have been used successfully include views of circus life that contrast the gaiety of performances with the loneliness of constant travel (Seurat and Picasso), moods of parades (Crite and Lawrence), and stormy and serene seascapes (Homer and Turner).[3] The children compare the content and techniques of the artists and share their own ideas and emotional responses to each painting. A dramatic activity deepens their personal experience of a painting, while an art activity allows them to express their own

[3] These and other reproductions may be obtained from the National Gallery of Art in Washington, D.C.

conceptions of the theme. This approach combines involvement and response to children's exposure to great art.

Literature provides endless opportunities for this type of rich experience. Chapter 5 discusses the integration of the plastic arts and poetry, pointing out how the cognitive skills are used. This same integration also involves using feelings. Emotions can be visualized and expressed in paint or in other art media. The following poem works well in helping children to think in these terms.

Fireworks

You hate me and I hate you,
And we are so polite, we two!

But whenever I see you, I burst apart
And scatter the sky with my blazing heart.
It spits and sparkles in stars and balls,
Buds into roses—and flares, and falls.

Scarlet buttons, and pale green disks,
Silver spirals and asterisks,
Shoot and tremble in a mist
Peppered with mauve and amethyst.

I shine in the windows and light up the trees,
And all because I hate you, if you please.

And when you meet me, you rend asunder
And go up in a flaming wonder
Of saffron cubes, and crimson moons,
And wheels all amaranths and maroons.

Golden lozenges and spades,
Arrows of malachites and jades,
Patens of copper, azure sheaves.
As you mount, you flash in the glossy leaves.

Such fireworks as we make, we two!
Because you hate me and I hate you.

Amy Lowell

By the end of the poem, one is smiling. How can anything so beautiful really be so hateful? On the other hand, maybe the poet really is talking about serious hate. If so, the teacher who uses this poem as a stimulus for artwork is telling the children that it is human to have feelings such as hate, but that one needs to learn how to handle these feelings without being destructive either to oneself or to others. Art activities provide a channel for expressing such strong feelings, thus making it easier to examine them. Children need to learn there is a difference between expressing one's hate in words or pictures and going out with a shotgun in one's hand. Some call this a "preventive mental health activity." We are content to call it good education.

At a somewhat different level, a sixth-grade class enjoyed translating into drawings the Alfred Noyes poem about the highwayman who came riding, riding, riding. . . . The emotional tone of the story and the rhythm of the words provide excellent motivation for using art materials as part of understanding the poem.

Even physical education is utilizing feelings more and more as modern dance becomes an accepted aspect of the subject. An awareness of and ease in the use of one's body has become an objective in many physical education departments, supplementing the formerly more limited one that was simply concerned with exercises and team sports. Involving feelings and their expression through one's body using dance enriches physical education immeasurably.

A BRIEF LOOK AT FANTASY

Feelings are also frequently expressed in fantasies. The boy who sits daydreaming during an arithmetic class immediately comes to mind. He may learn nothing from the lesson that day and his fantasy may have interfered with his learning fractions, but fantasies in themselves are not always to be frowned upon. They can be a symptom of great creativity. Every inventor, scientist, writer, humanist, and artist has fantasized sometime. A scientist I know showed me a science fiction story describing an atomic bomb long before that bomb was actually invented!

The trick for teachers and parents is to channel fantasy, to enable the potential young Edison to learn enough about electricity to make his light bulb, and to enable the young Wright to learn enough about air currents to build his plane. The first way to channel fantasy is to accept the fact that it exists and to understand that it may have value. Instead of, "John, you are dreaming again! If you don't pay attention, you will be sent out of the room," a teacher might try an honest question, "What are you thinking about John? Can you share it with us?" This may not always work, but it has been known to.

Fantasies are the stuff that art is made of, and if children are too shy to talk about their dream worlds, they may be willing to draw them. Alert teachers will use children's art expressions to learn about hard-to-reach fantasies. First they must learn what the fantasies are; then, perhaps, they can use them to motivate children in the directions needed.

For children who fantasize almost constantly, there may be danger when the sharp line differentiating fantasy from reality becomes blurred. At this point professional help may be needed. But again, a therapist who understands how to read children's drawings may find them enormously helpful in pinpointing the source of the trouble.

A WORD ABOUT WRITTEN EXPRESSION

This discussion of feelings must mention still another kind of child. Although art media seem natural for most youngsters, some children, for whatever reason, do not care to work with them. Perhaps they have been taught that it's bad to get one's hands dirty, or perhaps they are afraid of messing up their clothes. In such cases, teachers must consider the ways feelings may be related to language arts. The girl who wrote about her feelings at the beginning of this chapter was not only formulating her thoughts on these matters, she was also learning how to write, how to spell, and how to select the words that would best express her ideas. Children who are encouraged in a sympathetic way to write down what they are fantasizing or feeling will be doing the same.

The manner in which children physically write may be closely related to the way in which they draw or paint. Do they write with big bold strokes, or is the writing timid, tentative, or small? Do they cover the whole page or is the writing restricted to the edge of the paper? A look at writing as an art form, that is, calligraphy, can provide teachers with a great deal of information about the state of the mind of a given child, if they are alert and look for it. This should not be interpreted as a method of prying or representing a lack of respect for a child's privacy. Rather, a sympathetic teacher needs to know how a child feels to select the best way of helping to improve his or her learning experience.

When children tell teachers about themselves, either verbally or nonverbally, they extend a hand of friendship and trust. Needless to say, this trust must be treated with respect. The following brief incidents illustrate this point.

A second-grade class wanted to paint pictures of parents. Gwen, a pert little thing, whose eyes were slightly crossed, produced something that looked like this:

"That's my pop," she said, watching me from the corner of her eye.

At first I laughed.

"No," she frowned, "it's not funny."

"I'm sorry, Gwen," I replied. "Does he know what you think?"

"No, but if you put this picture on the wall for parents' night, maybe he'll see it—if he comes. Might be good," she added, with a mischievous expression.

I did . . . he came . . . and it was good.

*   *   *

A third-grade class was discussing feelings. "Have you ever felt sad, or angry, or lonesome?" I asked. "Let's try to put down a feeling that we have known, but don't tell anyone what it is. We'll let the paintings speak for us."

Later, when we looked at the pictures, Kathy turned hers over so that no one could see it. The children were impatient.

"Aw, come on, Kathy," begged one of her friends.

She looked ready to cry but still shook her head, "No."

"O.K.," I said, "if it's private, that's her affair. Let's look at something else."

At the end of the period, Kathy was the last to leave. "You can see it, if you want to," she volunteered tentatively.

It looked like a womb, painted in swirling grays, blues, and whites, with a black background. Deep in this form, was a tiny face, a nondescript face, lacking any particular expression. The concept of the picture and its execution were most unusual.

As I looked questioningly, she offered, "It's when I feel lone-some—lots of times." I could feel what she was saying, and I realized that this was an amazing painting to have been done by a young child.

"It's a fine painting," I told her, "and since I am arranging a special exhibition, I do wish I could put it up. I think we would all learn from seeing that picture."

She thought a minute, obviously pleased with my reaction, but then she looked down at the picture, turned back to me, and declared, "No, it's private."

So "no" it was.

There have been many occasions when I thought back and wished that I had been able to exhibit that painting. An exhibit not only shows the children's work but is also a commentary upon the art teacher. I certainly would have enjoyed the glory of being told what a fine teacher I was. Many, many years later I suddenly realized that it was by *not* showing the picture that I had earned a plus mark—because it really was private.

*   *   *

Bonnie was a small black child about nine or ten years old. During class she would come up to me, a white teacher, and reach out to touch my hand. "Your skin feels nice," she said shyly.

"Well," I reached out and took her hand, "your skin feels the same way." We held hands for a minute, and then I said, smiling, "O.K. now, back to work."

Another time, when I was sitting down, she reached out to touch my hair. "Your hair is nice . . . different from mine." I thought for a moment. "Yes, but see how your little curls can curl around my finger. That's fun." She smiled and left.

One day the children were painting pictures of what they would like to be when they grew up. Bonnie painted herself as a nurse, one with blonde hair, white skin, and blue eyes. She was staring at me nervously as I looked at the painting, waiting for a criticism or some negative remark. My stomach flipped. I wanted to cry.

"Uh-huh, Bonnie," I said and gave her a big hug. This new

knowledge about Bonnie would have to be considered in any future work with her. She was reacting to a discriminatory society by deciding that it would be better to be white when she grew up. One art class will not change all of the ugly relationships that exist between blacks and whites. I could not change the basic situation that caused her unhappiness, but perhaps I could help the child deal with her own feelings about this. For now she needed acceptance and some reassurance that, "Black was indeed beautiful." I did my best, feeling how necessary but inadequate it was.

* * *

Dealing with feelings requires delicacy and sensitivity, but their existence must be faced. Children themselves can help teachers learn how to handle problems of feelings, if we really listen to what they are trying to tell us.

TEACHERS HAVE FEELINGS TOO

Whenever Linda, a second-grader, took a paintbrush in her hand, I began to tremble. Experience had taught me that the paint would surely be put on someone else's picture, or on someone else's smock, or on the table, or on fingers that would end up on faces or walls. When spoken to sharply, she would always become sullen and often nasty.

"She needs love," I told myself, but love didn't work.

"She needs attention," but attention didn't work.

"She needs to be better motivated," but even that didn't work. I would design a whole period around Linda's interests, but that didn't prevent her from spilling the water on her neighbor's work.

I was feeling frantic. One day when using colored chalks, I turned around and there she was, drawing on another child's smock as he struggled to get her off his back.

"Linda!" I shrieked, and then, almost in tears and in utter frustration, I moaned, "You make me feel so bad when you do these things."

"I do?" she responded. "I didn't know that. I don't want you to feel bad. I'll try to be better."

And, much to my astonishment, she was. Apparently, when I stopped acting the "teacher" role and just responded as a human being, I was able to reach her. She really did try.

Tissue Paper Collage   Tissue paper is available in many beautiful colors. Encourage children to select one or two colors they like best. Each girl or boy can then team up with two or three other youngsters whose colors seem to express similiar feelings. These small groups, each of which is provided with white glue mixed with some water and large sheets of newsprint, are free to make a collage or a picture by cutting the tissue paper into shapes and pasting them on the newsprint. The groups may be urged to key their compositions toward the kinds of feelings their colors suggest. When completed, it's fun to hang collages and pictures around the room and play a guessing game. What feeling does each suggest?

Clay   Give two fistsful of clay to each child. They will doubtless begin to play with it immediately without any urging. After a period of initial exploration, suggest playing a feelings game. "What would you do with the clay," you might ask, "if you felt very angry?" The variety of responses may surprise you. Some children will pound, others may slash, jab, cut, poke, or even squeeze the clay very hard. With young children you may wish to identify the verbs that describe each action.

You might also ask, "How would you handle the clay if you felt very calm or quiet? Would you just change the surface of the clay, or would you wish to change its basic shape?" Then let the children suggest feelings they might wish the clay to express. Some may make sculptures expressing a feeling; others may not. At this point they should be left alone to utilize the early motivation in any way they like.

Faces   Depending upon the materials you have available, encourage the children to make faces or three-dimensional heads expressing different feelings. These may be done in clay, papier-mache, collage, paint, chalk, wax resist, or with magic markers. A mirror should be available so that they can see what happens to their features as they change their expressions. Leave the options wide open and see what feelings the children come up with. I have had children create faces that were smiling, frowning, thinking, sneaky, and mad. They should be encouraged to work quite large, so the facial expressions will be very clear.

---

* "Suggested Related Activities" for chapters 4 and 8 also give suggestions for relating art to other subject matter.

Puppets   Following up the activity described above, children can make puppets. These may be done with paper bags, socks, or papier-mache. The bibliography lists some books on puppet-making techniques. Make a puppet stage by simply cutting out one side of a large carton so that the youngsters can hide inside and move their puppets above their heads. The children should improvise dramatic situations, making up stories as they go along. You'll be amused at their dialogues. I'll never forget the boy whose puppet said, "Mommy, here's your beer. What else do you want."

ART AND THE SCHOOL

8. Integrating Art with Other Subjects

The function of art within any type of school has been a subject of controversy among art educators. Some suggest that art should be the core of the elementary curriculum; others are opposed to any efforts to integrate art with other subjects. We believe that the natural core that can integrate work in a school is an *attitude*, not a subject area. We define that attitude as curiosity, aided by increasing perceptual awareness of and sensitivity to the world around us. The development of such an attitude is a natural by-product of a strong art program.

One must differentiate here between two closely related but different activities, namely (1) *participating* in the making of art, a studio-type procedure, and (2) *looking* at art made by others, which has endless possibilities. From an educational point of view, it is most desirable to provide opportunities for exposure to both experiences. This chapter will concentrate on the many ways in which artwork can make a major contribution to building a habit of curiosity.

AESTHETIC READINESS

When children's awareness of the sensory aspects of life have been sharpened and become a source of personal satisfaction, they are in a state of what can be called "aesthetic readiness." The term "reading readiness" is a commonplace one in teacher talk; aesthetic readiness may be just as important, but the extraordinary richness it promises is rarely understood. It can help individuals become hungry for more experiences and for the potential surprises inherent in different views of life. All this can lead to an urge for more knowledge. This desirable attitude will obviously affect the quality of a child's artwork, but how will it affect learning in other areas, such as biology, for example? The following episode illustrates several answers.

*   *   *

In a school in Oxfordshire, England, where the open classroom is the accepted style, a class of nine- to eleven-year-olds were studying owls. Why owls? Because, living in a small village in a rural area, the children were apt to see owls near their homes. (Had this school been in Philadelphia, the same approach might have been used to study the swallows living under the Girard Avenue Bridge.) From field trips, books, and pictures, the children learned about the owl's habitat, nocturnal habits, food needs, and relationships to other animals. Most of this information was strictly factual.

It so happened that one of the teachers was interested in taxidermy, and he produced a stuffed owl for the children to examine. They had worked with collage, paint, clay, and film. Such aesthetically ready youngsters had a rich learning experience as they shared with their teacher the pleasures of noticing the differences in the shape and size of the owl's wings and feathers, as well as the variety of colors, the dramatic expression of the black-circled eyes, and the soft, silky texture of the wings and body. Several children were moved to do large paintings of the bird, one child took on the task of discovering how an owl's voice would sound on tape, and another wrote a marvelous story entitled "The Owl I Met on One Dark and Dreary Night." Soon the children were asking about other birds and about flight itself. This led to a discussion of physical questions concerning the movement of air currents, atmospheric pressure, and the like. In this open classroom, aesthetic readiness was an accepted part of school life, and it led to other learning in a natural, logical way.

The purpose here is not to extol the virtues of the open classroom, which have been adequately discussed in many fine books. We have seen excellent teachers in traditionally structured schools who teach in this very same way. Regardless of the school structure, open-ended learning of this sort can lead not only to other subject areas but can also involve simultaneously a quite different kind of learning. It can further children's healthy affective growth because in an open atmosphere, there is acceptance of children's feelings about birds or owls. Perhaps one child is fearful of the night and night creatures or has fantasies about birds, and perhaps another has seen the frightening film *The Birds*. Or maybe a potential Leonardo da Vinci sits in the class, always wishing he could fly. These feelings and others can be discussed openly and without embarrassment if the teacher appreciates that learning to accept and deal with human feelings is an important part of growth. Also the relaxed personal quality that can pervade an art experience eases the way for personal disclosures and discussion.

"But," someone may say, "all this is just good teaching. I do this sort of thing in my room all the time. What does this have to do with art?" Perhaps, but is this approach really so common in schools in the United States or Europe? We have personally visited schools in many different countries, as well as dozens in the United States, where only the bare essentials of a subject were taught, ignoring completely their sensual aspects or emotional content, both of which not only give pleasure (reason enough) but also help to imprint subject matter more firmly in the minds of students. Art makes an important contribution in these areas since by its very nature it focuses upon what is sensual and emotional.

Or well-meaning teachers may say, "Now, let's all write a story about owls." But there are nonverbal observations children can make about owls that are also important. This is especially true for elementary school children who can often express more of what they see through an art media than in words. This is not to disparage children's needs to learn how to use words. We simply suggest that instead of always asking everyone to do the same thing, teachers encourage children to decide for themselves which aspect of a subject each wishes to comment upon, thus helping them to define their thoughts and feelings. Such options often produce a more appreciative use of words as well.

Perhaps a child sees the owl as a simple, beautiful shape, almost like a piece of fine pottery, and this child might prefer to make her or his statement in clay. And why not? Many elementary school classrooms have art materials available—or could have— if teachers were not so terrified about making a temporary mess.

(Happily, most children can deal with "mess" and, if left to their own devices, would make good use of the materials. They would also be happy to clean up afterward if shown how to do so in a workmanlike manner.) Or, like the child in Oxfordshire, perhaps someone would like to concentrate on the sounds related to owls. There are innumerable possibilities that children themselves will suggest if given the opportunity.

ART TEACHER OR CLASSROOM TEACHER—WHO DOES WHAT?

How does an art teacher or art supervisor share responsibilities with classroom teachers? Does the art teacher have a special function? The answer is "Yes." An art teacher who has given children repeated opportunities to work with collage, for example, has begun to sensitize them to the pleasures of textural differences. When they approach an owl they are ready to observe and enjoy the smooth feeling of the marvelous wings and the individual feathers. An art supervisor who has conducted successful collage workshops for elementary school teachers has also created an attitude of aesthetic readiness on the part of teachers, so that they too are ready to observe and enjoy and are alert to the children's responses.

Art experiences with three-dimensional media, such as clay, plaster, wood, or stone, will provide both children and teachers with a background and awareness of form, so that when they look at an owl, they are ready to observe the beauty and simplicity of the forms of its body. Again, experiences with color will prepare children to really see and open their eyes so that they are ready to notice and enjoy the intricate and subtle color variations in an owl's wings.

Does an art teacher necessarily have to be there, on the spot, when a teacher and children are ready to produce art objects? This is desirable, if it can be arranged, but it is not absolutely essential, if the art teacher has already established the aesthetic readiness discussed earlier and if he or she is available to give suggestions, encouragement, and technical advice. Given these conditions, classroom teachers can proceed on their own. Having benefited from the art teacher's leadership and technical knowledge, they can utilize visual as well as verbal means to deepen children's understanding of subject matter. It might be added that art teachers need classroom teachers as well because they provide a framework of everyday experience, common to all the children, upon which the concepts of aesthetic readiness can be built.

In helping to develop aesthetic readiness on the part of *both* teachers and children, an art specialist can contribute to learning, quite apart from providing technical know-how for project making or developing the skill of drawing so that children can "draw a picture of an owl," although that has its place too. We think skill development *plus* awareness of line, texture, color, and form can make for more complete learning in *all* subjects. Such awareness makes for more accurate learning and certainly more pleasurable learning. Surely aesthetic awareness makes for richer living, which is what we think art education is all about. Some specific applications of the above ideas in the many so-called subject areas follow. However, it must be stressed that strict separation of subjects creates artificial boundaries, which are perhaps useful to educators but do not occur in life.

SOCIAL STUDIES

WHEN COLUMBUS DISCOVERED AMERICA[1]   As two boys from a fourth-grade class walked into my art room, I heard them talking excitedly about "the parrot."

"What parrot?" I asked.

They explained that in their history class they had just finished reading a book called *I Discover Columbus* by Robert Lawson (Little, Brown). It told the tale of a parrot who was blown out to sea during a terrible storm and clung to the torn branch of a tree. As he was tossed about in the wind, he "discovered" Columbus, who was also struggling in the storm. As the two boys related the story to me, the rest of the class gathered around, listening, and frequently interrupting to clarify some detail about the voyage. I could see from their faces that this story had caught their imagination.

Suddenly I had an idea. In their last art class, I had begun to discuss the idea that color and composition in painting could express a mood or a feeling. (This was a step in the direction of aesthetic readiness.) However, because the group was so diverse in terms of personality and ability, it was difficult to talk about color so that every child would understand my meaning. But

---

[1] This section has been extracted from Elaine Pear Cohen, "Thoughts on Teaching Art," *School Arts*, Feb. 1962.

Three very different fourth-grade interpretations of the storms and dangers, imagined and real, encountered by Columbus and his men when they sailed west across the Atlantic Ocean for the first time.

now, here they all were excited about the same thing—introducing color concepts was worth a try.

"How do you think those men felt as they sailed in their ships through that dreadful storm?" I asked.

The children shivered and groaned a little in answer.

"How would you feel if you had been out in a boat all that time, never knowing whether you would see land again and with the food supplies gradually disappearing? What colors would you use in a painting to show how you felt?"

As might be expected, the answers varied. Reactions to color are always intensely personal. As one child spoke of blues and grays, another insisted upon browns and blacks.

"How would you feel when you saw that parrot? When you saw land for the first time? How would it feel to be lost out on the ocean? How would you paint a picture that would express your feelings at a moment like that? Besides thinking about the colors, what sort of brush stroke would tell your story best?"

As they discussed the answers to these and other questions, someone would say, "Oh, I have an idea for a painting."

Soon they were all hard at work putting down in paint not only the facts that they knew about the *Nina*, the *Pinta*, and the *Santa Maria*, but also how they felt about such a dramatic situation. The story was something they all shared and was also something to which each child could respond with the varying degrees of understanding and depth of feeling that one would expect to find in a group of children.

To produce the moodiness, or dread, or joy that they wanted to express, the children had to mix their colors carefully and purposefully. Everything they had ever learned about mixing colors came into play. As they painted, the quiet in the room testified to their absorption in what started as a history lesson but became a real aesthetic experience as well. To my delight, I found that every painting was very different from the others. They were truly personal expressions, which is surely the primary aim of any good art class.

The objective here, however, was different from that of the sixth-grade teacher who approached me when her class was working on a unit about the Civil War.

BRINGING REALITY TO THE CIVIL WAR "How about helping my kids do some pictures of Lincoln or of the Union and Confederate flags," she asked one day.

"Why should they make those?" I replied. "They can buy such things in the stores."

"But you are always urging us to use art in our classes," she protested, annoyed.

"Yes, but what you are asking for is not art. You want them to copy pictures that other people have made or make objects that can be made by a machine. It's only art if the children bring something of themselves and their own thoughts and feelings to what they are doing."

She looked discouraged.

"Let me suggest another approach. Why not ask them to think of some dramatic situations that might have arisen as the Civil War was being fought and then to comment on those in paint or clay."

"Like what?" she queried.

"Well, if it's alright with you, why don't I come to your room this afternoon, or you come to mine, and we'll talk with the children about it together. Let's see what they come up with."

At first there was silence when I raised the question with the class. "Dramatic situations?" To help them along I said, "I wonder how it would feel to be in a family that is split over the issues of the war. Suppose you were fighting on the Confederate side, and, as you were shooting, you suddenly realized that your own brother, who favored the Union, might be on the other side of that hill?"

They shuddered. "Bad stuff," someone said.

Then one boy spoke up. "How about if you lived in the South and knew all your slaves were going to break down your door and kill you because you weren't really nice to them?"

"Good example! That would be a really dramatic situation! Now we have begun to think. Who else has an idea?" I asked.

"If you were on the Union side," someone said, "and you even voted for Lincoln, but now you were at Gettysburg and there wasn't enough food to go around. You were hungry and you were mad. What then?"

They were off. Their imaginations were aroused, and they were ready to go.

"How would you make a painting or drawing to express the feelings you are talking about?" I asked.

"Sharp colors."

"Sharp contrast."

"I think jagged lines."

"Big stuff—nothing small."

They were beginning to think in visual as well as verbal terms. "Aesthetic readiness" was at work.

We were using an approach similar to that used in Oxfordshire. The classroom teacher had given the children basic factual information with which to work; I had then made a few suggestions to start them thinking along visual lines; then the children took off on their own. Many went directly to the paint table and started on some fine paintings. However, a few preferred to write dramatic stories and that was alright too. Others chose to illustrate the stories.

After about an hour of work, someone came up with the idea that they could make a book entitled "The Drama of the Civil War." The children liked this; the decision to do it was entirely theirs. Two boys who had recently been exposed to the ballad form in their English class decided to write a ballad. One rather meticulous child suggested that on the cover of the book there should be a time line, in bright colors, pointing up the important events of the Civil War. "Instead of putting it on the cover," another child added, "let's have a long page which can unfold out of the book like an accordion. Then you can make it as long as you like." This was a good idea and was readily accepted.

Needless to say, the teacher was delighted and remarked, as I prepared to leave, "This really is more interesting than Confederate flags—even to me."

INDIANS, PENNSYLVANIA DUTCH, AND ANCIENT GREEKS In another case a study by third-graders of the Indians of the Southwest produced a mural painted in beautifully muted colors, each carefully mixed (not just using what came out of the bottle). The pueblos had to have a "sandy" look, they said. Some weaving with strips of paper helped them to appreciate the wonderful rugs made by these same Indians.

A fifth-grade class was intrigued by the pottery made by the Pennsylvania Dutch as they studied the history and customs of this group. They asked to make such pottery, and we learned how to make coil pots, thinking about both form and function. The children also learned some general ceramic techniques, such as preparing the clay (wedging) so that it could be fired and decorating the pieces, using slip painting and scraffito. Of course each child did her or his own individual design, as did the classroom teacher, who enjoyed the work as much as the children did. (Incidentally, this helped her relationship with her class, since the girls and boys really enjoyed having her work right along with them.)

C. M. Bowra has written vividly about the Greek landscape:

> What matters above all is the quality of light. . . . Even in winter the light is unlike that of any other European country, brighter, cleaner, and stronger. It sharpens the edges of the mountains against the sky. . . . It turns the sea to opal at dawn, to sapphire at mid-day, and in succession to gold, silver and lead before nightfall; it outlines the dark green of the olive trees in contrast to the rusty or ochre soil . . . a clearness of outline and a sense of mass.[2]

A sixth-grade teacher was reading this to his class when a hand popped up.

"What does 'sapphire' mean, Mr. Faxon?" the boy asked.

"Does anyone know?" the teacher asked as he turned to the group.

"It's a kind of blue," suggested Jenny.

"Yes. Have you ever discussed the color of water, of the sea, with your art teacher?"

"Yesterday," Danny called out, "we're going to try to paint it someday."

"Why not now? Danny, let's see if you can find Ms. Cohen and see if she is busy. Maybe understanding the colors of the sea is part of understanding Greece."

This was the beginning of an experience I shall never forget. As the art teacher I was privileged to work with a most imaginative classroom teacher who understood the potential of our cooperation.

We read—and reread—this section from Bowra's book. The words that needed definition were discussed. The children put on their "word-wealth" list: "opalescent," "sapphire," "lead," and "ochre." But if the light and sharp edges were important, paint alone would not be the best medium. We finally decided to work with ink on wash (watercolor). The illustrations given on page 157, although not in color, indicate some of the results.

It is difficult to communicate the excitement and interest

---

[2] *The Greek Experience* (Cleveland: World Publishing Co., 1957), p. 11.

Bowra's idea aroused. He felt that "a people lives by its geography" and that the extraordinary physical beauty of Greece had a profound influence upon the thought and art of the early Greeks as well as upon their political and social structure. We took this idea and worked with it visually as well as verbally, and it was not only thought-provoking for all of us, it was fun!

*　　*　　*

The foregoing anecdotes suggest an *approach* as well as specific classroom activities. Each incident involved active participation of children as they made art objects related to the particular subject being studied. Even if it is impossible to include "doing" sessions as part of a social studies unit, art still has an important place in the study of history. Think of how impossible it would be to appreciate the lives of American Indians without looking at totem poles, woven rugs, decorative drums and jewelry, and beautiful feather designs. Think of how much the magnificent cathedrals in Europe tell about life in medieval times; one look at the enormous size and grandeur of the cathedral at Chartres tells us more about the dominant power of the church at that time than reams of printed pages.

One cannot imagine a study of ancient Greece without a mention of the Acropolis, the Parthenon, or Greek theater. And how much more dramatic a study of the French Revolution is after seeing the David painting of Marat lying dead in his bathtub! How much better children would understand the anger of the Parisian poor if they could see pictures of the ornate furniture and clothing of the nobility of that period. (I never understood why Marie Antoinette's "Let them eat cake" remark stirred up such hatred until I saw a painting of her, all insolence in ruffles, satins, and jewels.) And think about how inadequate a study of Africa would be without a consideration of the marvelous tribal art, wood sculpture, and fabrics.

The art objects produced by a given culture do more than enhance a study of that culture—they are that culture. To neglect them not only ignores the facts of history, but also the pleasure and excitement of the subject.

SCIENCE

At the elementary school level a course called science can mean an introduction to biology, astronomy, physics, or even simple

While studying ancient Greece, sixth-graders learned about the clarity of the light that affects the Greek landscape and produced these watercolor and ink paintings of the sea and mountains.

chemistry. Whatever the emphasis, the teacher should be aware of the possible usefulness of art techniques and understandings.

WHO AND WHAT AM I?   A group of ten- and eleven-year-olds approached the question of "Who and What Am I?" by first looking at their own hands and feeling their fingers carefully. Clearly there was something hard in each finger, namely the bones. They followed the hardness up their arms, noting the connections between bones and the different quality of hardness of their muscles. What was going on inside there? They decided that they needed an anatomy book.

After examining the drawings in a book, some children expressed a desire to make a big skeleton. I thought that the struggle to copy an exact drawing of a skeleton had very limited value at this age, but it might be useful if, in the process of making a skeleton, they could also learn to work with papier-mache and to understand in a three-dimensional sense the way in which the forms of bones are related to one another. Many books discuss methods of making papier-mache (see bibliography), so it is suffice to say that we used a long piece of flexible aluminum wire to connect the papier-mache bones. Since the bones would fall apart without the wire, it was obvious that something else held them together in nature. This discussion clearly defined the role of the tendons. As an art teacher I knew how muscles and tendons looked, but the classroom teacher's knowledge of biology helped us understand the ways they function. Our cooperative venture worked beautifully—the classroom teacher got her hands into papier-mache and I learned some biology.

Meanwhile other activities were going on. While the skeleton group did its job, other children were making large self-portraits, some using paint and some using small pieces of cut colored paper, mosaic fashion. The more verbal types wrote stories about themselves when they were small children, including photographs and making small illustrated books describing their "childhood days." (Remember we had started with the question, "Who and What Am I?") These pieces of writing were not straight objective accounts, for the children were asked to also include emotional moments that they remembered. Some were really charming, i.e., "I remember when my first-grade teacher made a birthday party for me in class. We had cupcakes.

When the children sang, I felt very hot and red, and I didn't know where to look. I liked it, but I didn't know what to do."

DARWIN'S THEORY OF EVOLUTION   When a sixth-grade class was studying Darwin's theory of evolution, the children painted a huge mural depicting how early forms of life might have looked. They painted a monstrous blue whale, marvelous birds, amoebas, and imaginary prehistoric animals. When they reached man in the process of evolution and learned that in the Paleolithic period there had been people who did paintings, as at Lascaux and Altamira, they were really intrigued. These Stone Age people painted on the walls of caves rather than on paper or canvas, but what did they use for paint? Clearly they must have found natural products that provided colors.

"Let's try that ourselves," I suggested. "When you go home tonight see what you can find in your garden, or on the street, or anywhere—something that will provide color. Then we can try to use the materials ourselves and see what the problems were like. But the color *must* come from nature." Here is a partial list of what we discovered:[3]

- Juniper berries make a light brown.
- Walnut shells make a dark reddish brown.
- Holly berries make a purple.
- Sage brush makes yellow.
- Oak bark makes a purplish brown.
- Red onion skin makes green.
- Charcoal makes black and gray.
- Soil makes dark brown and sometimes dark red.

We mashed and squeezed the plants, sometimes adding a drop of water. Some plants produced color and some did not. It was all very interesting. The children decided to make a small mural showing what they knew about life in the Stone Age period. The painting was not exceptional, but the process was very worthwhile. Although this project started in the context of science, we were soon involved in social studies, and if some of the questions had been followed up, we could have delved into biology. Had there been some interest in the nature of paint, this project

---

[3] Some of these (and more) are included in a chart, "Sources of Navajo Native Dyes," published by the Natural History Museum of Los Angeles County Foundation, 1972.

might have led us into some questions of a chemical nature. One thing is certain, however, and that is that these children acquired a depth of appreciation plus a respect for the fantastic artists who painted in the caves at Lascaux thousands of years ago.

Another opportunity presented itself when the same science class discovered that the aurora borealis would be visible on a particular night. Two interested youngsters stayed up late to see it. They came to school the next day, very sleepy, but enthusiastic about the beautiful colors. They decided, with the help of the art teacher, to put their impressions on paper in colored chalk. They worked very hard on this, and the resulting panoramic drawing was proudly displayed for all to enjoy.

*　*　*

An important element in scientific methodology is careful observation. The observation of color, rhythm, pattern, form, and line that has been discussed as an essential for aesthetic readiness is the very same kind of careful observation practiced by scientists in their work. Both children and scientists observe nature. Their words may be different, but the process is the same. Art provides both a method of observation and a method of recording observations, and it is in the means of recording and interpreting that science differs from art. Also modern scientists ask questions about what they observe and design experiments to test their ideas. But for both artists and scientists the training can be the same for learning how to make initial observations and how to detect subtle differences and changes.

LANGUAGE ARTS

THE ALPHABET[4]   The alphabet is a combination of linear forms—some round, some vertical, some horizontal, some angular. I was reminded of this when working with a first-grade class who were learning to recognize the letters *i*, *o*, and *n*. After a brief observation period, I asked the teacher if I might help. "Of course," she replied.

I asked the children to think about the shape of the letter "*i*." Did they see anything in their room that was this shape?

"Let's play a game," I suggested. "When you see something that looks like an *i*, put your hand up but don't say a word."

---

[4] Parts of this section have been extracted from Elaine Pear Cohen, "Does Art Matter in the Education of the Black Ghetto Child?" *Young Children,* vol. XXIX, no. 3, March 1974, p. 175.

They perked up, looked around, and the hands began to go up. When called upon, they pointed out the frames in the windows, the edges of the doors, the sides of the blackboard, and many other items. One observant child pointed to the straws lying next to the milk cartons. We discussed their ideas, laughed together, admired each other's ingenuity, and had a good time.

After the *i*, we switched to the *o*. That was easy—the clock, a dish, and even our heads were round, although we agreed that no one had a really o-shaped head. This brought up the question of whether being round like an egg was the same as being round like an *o*. Here we were getting into generalizations and we were also practicing careful observation. Of course the children could not see any objects that looked like *n*, but they decided that *n* was round like an egg cut in half across its middle, with a straight *i* on one side.

The emphasis was on the shapes—really seeing them and observing the changes in direction they took. By giving each child a few pipe cleaners to work with, these observations can be put to use on the spot. It is not necessary to be an art teacher to think in these terms; all one needs is a visual awareness. This can and should be developed as part of any teacher training experience if it has not been done earlier.

READING AND WRITING READINESS Among those alarmed at the poor reading performance in our schools are people who would cut out all other subject matter and "just teach them to read!" But immediately others would ask, "Why bother to read under those circumstances? What would anyone be interested in reading?"

While working in widely disparate elementary schools, many art teachers have noticed that children's drawings are very similar, although their achievement levels are as divergent as their communities. Some, like Washington, D.C. art teacher Penny Platt, have formulated reading programs using children's drawings.[5] Instead of imposing a system on the children, she hypothesized, why not use the communication system they already had—their pictures, which are more powerful in the early years than their rudimentary oral language. "What a waste it is to ignore this system—this glowing, constantly growing graphic equipment!"

---

[5] *Platt Early Reading Program* (Menlo Park, Calif.: Addison-Wesley Publishing Co., 1971).

Ms. Platt concurs with many psychologists in believing that, "When a child draws an object, you can be certain he knows a lot about it—except how it looks as a word picture." Children who make a skyline at the top of the paper and a groundline at the bottom exhibit a desire for orderly arrangement and an ability to see objects in relation to one another. At this stage children are ready for reading. When they produce a picture of a tree, they can be commended and told that there is another way to make a picture that means "tree." Writing the word as closely as possible to the picture enables a child to use his or her own symbol as a clue to learning the new one. This method is truly child-centered! When specific objects in drawings are labeled, children begin reading words that stand for obvious concrete concepts: house, bird, girl, boy, and the like. The abstractions that often cause difficulty in the front sections of basal readers— oh, stop, when, they, come, and so on—are not in evidence and therefore do not pose the usual problems. Nursery rhymes or shared experiences acted out in class furnish good source material for drawings to be labeled because they utilize a common vocabulary.

Another first-grade teacher produces picture albums with her classes. Each child makes a picture of herself or himself engaged in a favorite activity and dictates a label for it: "I am Belinda, I like to dance," "I am Carlos, I like to color." Children who like to jump, hop, draw, read, or play ball appear frequently to the delight of the young readers and their teacher who finds the repetition good reinforcement for important new words. The pictures are placed in scrapbooks accompanied by their labels. The teacher's picture also appears with the legend:

> I am Ms. Gainer.
> I like to see you read.
> I like to see you jump.
> I like to see you dance.
> I like to see you draw.
> I like to see you!

The children enjoy learning about their classmates by reading their picture albums. They especially like taking turns at carrying the album home to introduce their school friends to their families.

Picture dictionaries are another device for combining words and pictures. A Halloween dictionary made by one class listed

Early childhood educators have found that children's own art is a means of teaching reading. Labeling the main figures and details of their drawings teaches youngsters the written words for objects with which they are already very familiar.

witch, ghost, haunted house, spook, spider, owl, bat, moon, black cat, and jack-o'-lantern, and on each page, a picture and its word label appeared prominently. Students were encouraged to look up the words they needed for story writing and picture labeling.

Dictionaries on a wide variety of subjects were kept with the picture albums in the class library. Here class versions of favorite picture books and other stories were also assembled. When favorite stories were read aloud, many children asked to illustrate them. Following the reading, significant events in the story were identified and listed in sequential order. Acting out the story was fun and helpful. Each child chose or was assigned a topic to illustrate in an agreed-upon medium on uniform sheets of paper. The completed pictures were sorted and arranged in order. Problems of sequence, transformation, and causality were related to the story line by discussing the reasons for the placement of each picture. Sometimes, several versions of the same story were assembled and bound. Similar events and differences in interpretation of those events in the different versions were compared.

Remembering to return favorite books to the library was not a problem when personal editions of the books had been amassed in the class's private collection. During free time, the children often gathered around a book and exclaimed delightedly, "Diane, we're reading your page now!"

Chris, the boy discussed in chapter 5, was taught to read by using his interest in art as motivation. He wanted to learn about the great artists whose pictures and sculpture he found so intriguing. His teacher located books on a subject meaningful to him, just as another teacher might use books about baseball players to motivate another child to learn to read. Chris soon began to write imaginary stories about artists and illustrated them as well. If teachers can discover what really interests a child, they can surely teach him or her to read.

MATHEMATICS

As art teachers we certainly have not had experience with all the intricacies of teaching mathematics, but as citizens of the modern world, we have observed that people are using mathematical concepts all the time. Thus we have tried in our teaching to point out the connections between math and art.

Mathematics is basically concerned with *relationships* for which symbols have been devised as a means of identification. Strangely enough these symbols seem to have achieved an existence of their own. Thus we speak of numbers or geometric shapes or algebraic units, but when using these words, we are still speaking about relationships, some of which are absolute and some relative. It is relationships that give one a sense of the order or disorder of the world. In chapter 2 we discussed art as being concerned with relationships and a quest for order. While certainly not exactly the same, there are places where these types of order do converge.

Edith Briggs suggests that there are three general objectives in teaching mathematics to young children: (1) encouraging children to think for themselves; (2) enabling them to appreciate the order, patterns and relationships of math as a natural presence in their lives; and (3) giving them knowledge and skills in computation.[6] A good design experience can give children some experience with all of these, with aesthetic pleasure thrown in as well. The term "design" can be best understood if described in operational terms. Therefore consider design as it might relate to the study of symmetry in a first-grade classroom.

SYMMETRY AND DESIGN   A first-grade teacher was introducing symmetry to children in a Follow-Through class. They were having a little trouble understanding the idea.

"There should be a simple way for them to see it and work with the idea," she muttered. "What do you have to suggest?" she asked as I came into her room.

"Try getting them to look at their faces in the mirror and then to draw what they see," I replied. "If they draw a line down the middle of the head and see what is the same on each side, they will begin to understand. I'll return soon with something else."

These children had just finished learning to identify geometric shapes—squares, triangles, and spheres. I returned with a large box of gaily colored *square* shapes—different colors and different sizes but all squares. I also brought a package of assorted colors of 9×12-inch construction paper.

"Let's use some paste and squares to create a beautiful design

---

[6] *Mathematics for Older Children* (New York: Citation Press, 1972).

that is symmetrical," I proposed to the children. "You can play around with the squares and arrange them on your paper in any way that you like, just so long as you make something symmetrical that you think is nice to look at."

"I don't know how to do it," frowned Lewis.

"Let's help Lewis by making some suggestions. We all know what a design is, don't we?"

"Yes, when it isn't a picture of a real thing, it can be a design," called out Beatrice.

"That's a pretty good definition," I nodded, "but let's try looking at this."

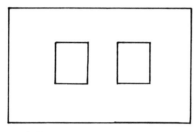

"Is this symmetrical?"

"Yes," they nodded.

"But do you like to look at it?"

"Not so much."

"What can we do to still keep it symmetrical but make it more fun to look at?"

The suggestions that followed looked like this:

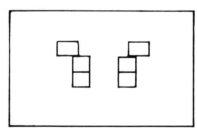

or this:

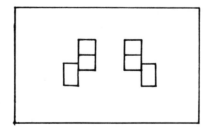

"Can they overlap—sit on top of each other—and still be symmetrical?

The answers were these designs:

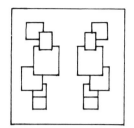 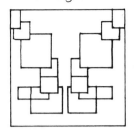 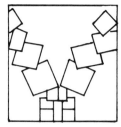

Now the children sat up and became more interested. This was fun! We thought about the placement of contrasting and closely related colors as well as the placement of squares but kept our eyes on the objective—symmetry. The use of the word became commonplace. One six-year-old looked at his friend's design and said, "That's nice, but it ain't symmetrical."

Clearly this activity had many dimensions. The children were learning a mathematical concept; they were experiencing the pleasure of making a design; and they were learning the verbal symbol that identified a particular mathematical relationship.

This activity could be repeated using other forms. Or it could be followed by making an asymmetric design, using triangles instead of squares. (Triangles are by their very nature more amenable to asymmetric design.)

There are many other concepts that can be taught in the course of making pleasing designs, for instance, patterns. There are geometric patterns on bathroom floors, on the linoleum in kitchens, on the fabrics from which clothing is made; pattern is everywhere. It is easy for children to understand pattern after they have made a design, using repetition and variation of shapes and forms. Once they have the idea, they can better understand pattern in equations and in fractions, and they will recognize patterns on flash cards, dominoes, and in sets.

Then there is enclosed space—wide, narrow, thick, thin, tall, short, deep, and shallow. All these concepts, which are expressions of mathematical relationships, can be pleasantly experienced and learned in the course of making a carefully thought-out design with a clearly defined, limited objective. It must be noted that this is a very different design concept from what children often call "scribble-scrabble," which utilizes accidental combinations that occur in a free, open-ended playing with forms. Such combinations are sometimes pleasant to look at, and a mature artist will often take advantage of the lucky accidents in which they occur, but basically a design is a carefully constructed set of mathematical relationships. Braque, Picasso, Mondrian, and others were definitely not depending exclusively upon scribble-scrabble as sources for their abstract paintings.

A sculptor, adult or child, who creates a piece of clay sculpture is thinking about the relationship of volumes. When creating a portrait, how large should the volume called "nose" be in relationship to the volume called "head"? How large should the volume called "ear" be in relationship to the volume of the nose? How far from the back of the head should volume "ear" be placed, and where does it sit with reference to the volume called "jaw"? All this decision-making involves quantitative judgments (see chapter 6).

The experience of constructing a piece of sculpture teaches about balance in an unforgettable way—if the piece is not balanced, it will topple over. Equestrian sculptures one sees in the streets of some cities give the impression that leaping horses can exist as balanced structures, but it's all a fake. There are heavy pieces of pipe inside those horses' legs holding them up. Any small child who has attempted to sculpt a jumping horse will realize that the public sculptures have some kind of help inside. These children have experienced balance and if they have tried to make a mobile using the wire of coat hangers, they know still more.

* * *

Summing up, it is clear that in the course of making art objects, many mathematical concepts and procedures are utilized. In painting, we are concerned with the *quantity* of any given color, the *size* of a given space, the *balance* of the forms, the relationships between *positive* and *negative* space. Sculpture involves thinking about *weight* (heavy or light) and *proportion* (relative size of each form). Work in design involves the *sorting* of shapes and the creation of *pattern*. The artist is constantly *matching* and *fitting* forms into one another or into a limited space. In the early years it is possible to use these concepts without naming them, but as children develop, evaluation and criticism of their artwork becomes impossible without using the vocabulary of mathematical relationships. An art teacher uses these terms all the time. All the words italicized above pop up when listening to an art critique in an art school or reading art criticism in a newspaper.

As we have said many times, art experiences help people to see relationships. Visual symbols, such as rods, can explain frac-

A large class-made mobile gave third-grade boys a firsthand experience of learning about spatial relationships and balance.

tions, proportions, or squares and are also symbols of relationships that exist in the real world. Visual symbols make it easier to discuss these relationships mathematically.

An elementary school math teacher puts it this way: "I see math as a way of describing the real world. Math is an ordering. We use the language of elementary math to describe relationships more precisely, but we can experience those relationships visually and discuss them from what we see as well."

Suggested Related Activities

From Signals to Signs to Designs   While studying modes of communication among the American Indians (smoke signals, hand signs, pictographs), children can invent their own sign languages by transcribing gestures that have a meaning understood by the group into line dawings. If a rocking motion signifies baby, it might become ⤳ in visual terms. Sunrise might be ⟿ or friendship ⤲ .

Children can convert these symbols into design patterns by doodling with them, repeating them, making them larger, or emphasizing certain parts. After experimenting with black crayons on paper and producing at least four designs from different sign words, each child should select the design he or she considers strongest. A large piece of white fabric, i.e., part of an old sheet, can be stretched over a table and rectangles of varying sizes blocked out on it. Each child then chooses an area in which to transfer her or his selected design using a wide black marking pen. When all the areas are filled, the class will have a handsome wall hanging. It can be accompanied by a key of a smaller size, but having the same proportions and block areas. In the box corresponding to that on the large hanging, each child can sign his or her name and the word that prompted the design.

After this activity, children may wish to study some black and white fabric designs from Africa which have code meaning.

Make a Story Cloth   Study the appliquéd banners of Dahomey and note that they tell the history of a people. Each colorful motif has a long story behind it, which families must tell to each other. Ask each child to select an aspect (a figure or object) of a favorite story from folklore or history and to re-create it using fabric or construction paper scraps on a black backing. The scraps can be stitched or glued.

Children can then group their individual contributions and mount them on a large black background. They can further compile written stories or tape recordings so that the story cloth can be shared throughout the school.

Spin Yarns   Study the process of spinning and the derivation of this phrase. In the past while people (many of them children) worked (teased, combed, and carded the wool), they entertained each other by telling stories. When the stories were retold, they were stretched and exaggerated.

Read Carl Sandburg's "Yarns," tall tales, or fish stories, or sing additive songs such as "I Know an Old Lady (a Scholastic book/record combination) or repetitive story-songs such as "The Foolish Frog" (Pete and Charles Seeger, Macmillan, 1973; also available as a film from Loom Productions, Inc.). What parts of these stories might actually have happened? What is an exaggeration? Stretch the children's imaginations by having them add their own versions of these yarns. They can depict with crayons or paint a further adventure of a tall-tale character. Exaggerate the forms; make them larger than life. Give important parts emphasis by boldly delineating them, omitting unimportant details, or using contrasting techniques in other parts of the paper.

A room weaving can be created by stapling yarn in a weblike design to a bulletin board or across a corner. Starting at a central point, one child can weave additional yarn under and over while another "spins" an entertaining yarn verbally. The completed weaving (after many children have taken turns in both roles) can be finished into a circular rug to serve as a base for still more storytelling.

Catalogs of Animal Behavior   Read Rosalie Moore's "Catalog" (*Golden Treasury of Poetry*, Louis Untermeyer, ed., Golden Press, 1959, p. 50). How do cats "sleep fat" and "walk thin," "jump in a streak," and "spread comfort beneath them like a good mat?" Ask the youngsters to visually document the characteristic movements of a favorite animal—and their relationship to it—by drawing or cutting out silhouettes and pasting them on contrasting colors. Create a gallery of animal behavior rivaling the poem's vivid imagery. Caption the pictures and create poems "cataloging" other animals.

9. The School Environment

How do you, a teacher, think of your classroom? "Is it a home away from home or is it a workroom? Is it an exhibit area for displaying class activities or is it a barracks, a place for storing bodies? Is it a center for pleasurable activities or is it a prison in which your job is to keep order?" These are questions worth thinking about. And after you have thought about them, they are worth discussing with your class:

DESIGN OF CLASSROOMS

Ask the children and yourself, "How many waking hours do we spend together in our classroom?" Once you have recovered from that shock of discovery, ask yourselves whether the appearance of the room can affect what goes on inside it? (Please notice, the verb is affect, not determine; nothing will take the place of good teaching.) As a traveling art teacher, trudging around with my cart of materials from room to room and school to school, I cannot help noticing the variety in the appearances of the many classrooms I visit. Of course, the buildings themselves are very different, and each room has to be arranged within the framework of the building—but aesthetic readiness was part of my training. I react positively to every bit of color and imagination I see and groan at every sterile bare room I enter. But one day it suddenly came to me that my moaning and groaning was a kind of self-indulgence. The problem of the quality of the aesthetic atmosphere in schools was mine as well as that of classroom teachers. I certainly had no right to go into other teachers' rooms and dictate how they should set up the place. I did have the responsibility to raise the aesthetic questions that needed to be raised, however—this was part of my job as the art teacher.

One day when I was in a fifth-grade classroom, we were busy making prints, using potatoes, stones, shells, and twigs. We were also discussing what we called "random design," patterns created by forms repeated at random, as differentiated from "structured design" in which the forms are repeated in a clearly organized relationship. The children had reached a good level of understanding, I thought, and it occurred to me, "Why not apply it to their room?" Their classroom teacher was sitting in the back of the room, listening and marking papers.

"If you were to spend a lot of time living with a design, would it matter to you what type it was?" I asked.

"Yeah, yeah," piped up Joe. "I like excitement. Random for me!"

"No," objected Connie, "I like to wear random, but I'd rather look at structured on the walls."

I started to laugh. "If anyone heard you 'wearing random' and 'looking at structured,' they would think you were out of your minds. Let's use the words correctly. Not just 'random,' but 'random design' and not just 'structured,' but 'structured design.' Agreed? Now—look around you. Look at the walls of the room in which you and Ms. Walker live for hours every day and think about the design quality. Ms. Walker is a very busy woman. Maybe you can help her, if she is willing. Ms. Walker, do we have your permission to consider the design of this room?"

She smiled and agreed.

As we looked around, we saw one corner of the back wall covered with stories written by the children, in another section was a large calendar, elsewhere there was a list of names, indicating room responsibilities for the week, and so on. The life of the class was apparent everywhere, but . . . "it's random design," volunteered Pete.

"Is it?" I asked, "or is it no design at all—just something here and something there without much thought as to how they are related? What does the word 'design' mean anyway?"

"To make."

"To put together."

"How can you make or put things together unless you have an . . . ?"

"An idea," someone interrupted.

"A plan," offered Marie.

"Good, now we are thinking. To 'design' is to plan, to organize, to structure. Now, who put up that last group of stories back there?"

Paul spoke up, "I did."

"What do you think, Paul? Did you design your arrangement or did you just put things in any old place? Don't get nervous," I reassured him, "just think about it."

Paul smiled. "You already know," he said, "just anyplace."

At that point several children were asked to go to the blackboard and make a rough drawing of one wall in the room. When these were completed, another group went up to do more sketches incorporating some suggestions for improvement. One of the first sketches looked like this:

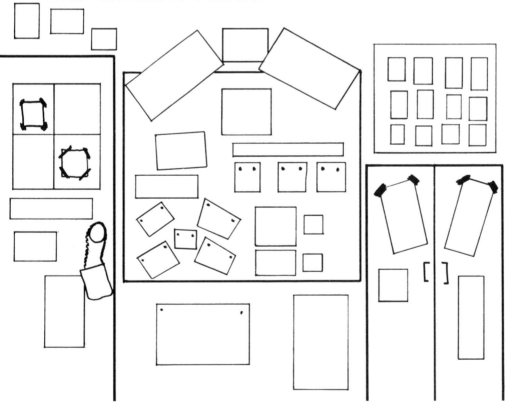

That was a busy wall the children decided. Very random. A suggestion for improvement looked like this:

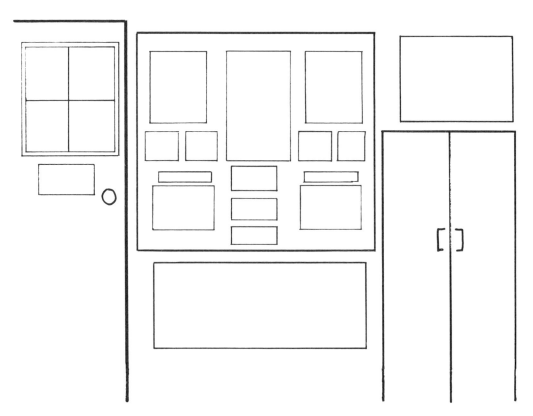

We looked and agreed that this was a more organized wall but that perhaps it was a little dull looking.

"Do you think you work better in a busy, active-looking place or in a more quiet, orderly environment?" I asked.

The answers varied. Wise children that they were, they decided that there are times for both. Sometimes people need some zip—slam—bang to pep them up (random design), while at other times a quiet order (more structured design) helps them to concentrate. Everyone agreed that an important consideration was color. "Nice bright colors make you feel good," someone said. (This has been studied experimentally, and there seems to be evidence that colors do have a physical effect and can even affect the quality of the work performed. An interesting discussion of this phenomenon may be found in James Thompson's *Beyond Words*.[1]

At this point Ms. Walker joined us. She went to her supply closet and, smiling broadly, brought out a large roll of colored papers. Magenta! Hot pink! Orange!

"Wow!"

---

[1] New York: Citation Press, 1973, pp. 58–82.

"How can we use these," she asked, "just for a splash of color—for fun? Or shall we mount our written work on them?" There was a flood of replies from the children. "Let's appoint committees who will look at the room each week to decide what needs to be done to 'pep it up' or to 'tone it down.' I'll work with the committees, but I hope that you will take charge of the design quality. What do you think?"

The children thought that this was an excellent idea. Of course, there would be disagreements and discussions about these weekly decisions. Not everyone would like every arrangement, but in the process of living with these decisions the children would not only become sensitive to their environment, they would also realize that they could change it and control it. Psychologists say that this realization is important for the development of a positive self-concept.[2] Such experiences should also assist in developing a sense of taste and of aesthetic judgment. Teachers who allow their students to participate in the design of their rooms encourage development in these areas, even though their own standards of taste may not always be met by their students' efforts.

ORGANIZING AN ART CENTER

Children who became involved in changing the design of their classroom required materials. Glue, tape, thumbtacks, staplers, scissors, marking pens, and paper were needed for mounting displays and lettering captions. The teacher found that interruptions asking for each item were a nuisance. It was far more efficient to train the children to use the various tools and supplies and then to leave them in an accessible place. Two children were asked to check the supply corner daily to make sure that everything was returned and in good order. A checklist was posted to facilitate this task.

Soon the supply corner became the art center. A wide variety of creative works, in addition to the room exhibits, were produced there. Students were able to go to the center as an independent activity. They learned to use their supplies carefully and to restore the center to its original order when they were fin-

---

2 J. Rotter et. al., "Internal vs. External Control: A Major Variable in Behavior Theory," in *Decisions, Values and Groups*, vol. 2, N. F. Washburne, ed. (London: Pergamon Press, 1962).

ished. We stressed that care and respect for materials and work space are essential skills in the field of art. Even kindergarten children can assume responsibility for maintaining an art center. As they replace scissors, sort papers, and group brushes or crayons, they are learning about their materials, improving their competence in handling them, and refining their classification skills, to say nothing about helping their teachers!

In establishing an art center the goal should be to provide a constant art "presence" where children are invited to express themselves visually. Accessible materials and uncluttered work space are the primary ingredients. It is really not necessary to list minimum and maximum amounts of supplies, except to say that the minimum is anything that permits all students opportunities for visual expression and the maximum is as much as can be kept in an organized fashion. A choice of two- and three-dimensional media is most desirable, but an overly lavish and crowded array is overwhelming and impossible to manage. (A recommended list of basic supplies is presented at the end of this chapter.) Don't wait until you have acquired everything you may want to start an art center. A quality art program can begin to grow with just paper, crayons, and scrap articles if that is all that is accessible. But keep striving for a variety of media over a period of time. Whatever is available should be neatly and attractively arranged by the children in a quick, daily routine. This practice develops good work habits while maintaining the art center as an inviting place. Disorder can be confusing and discouraging to children, especially when they have ideas they are anxious to express.

If there is space to house supplies but not enough for a work area, actual work may be done on tables placed elsewhere in the room, or children may take materials to their own desks or out to a hall or corridor.

We have found that children are very responsive to activities suggested on a bulletin board in an art center on which helpful hints on procedure are given. For example, a posted sheet suggested comparing several paintings from the history of art through a series of questions that called attention to the subject matter as well as the techniques used by the artists. After responding to these questions, children were asked to produce their own works using some of the ideas stimulated by the pictures. At one art center, paintings of the sea by Winslow Homer, John Marin, and J. M. W. Turner showed the children three different ways of painting water. They were then encouraged to

Inexpensive flat pans and recycled jars, plastic containers, and cans are ideal for holding paints, brushes, and other art materials. This photograph of an art center table shows an easy way to provide individual children with paints that they can use and clean up with a minimum of mess and disorder.

do a painting of their own, not copying but portraying the sea in their own styles. Thus art appreciation and practice are combined in a meaningful way.

Another center presented views of circus life, contrasting the gaiety of the performances with the loneliness of the traveling performers, who were always on the move. Following the questions, which emphasized the different use of color, the children produced their own views of a circus. Themes popular in other centers have included a contrast between sculpture in-the-round and relief sculpture, children's games, mobiles, animal habitats, Afro-American art, and pre-Columbian and Mexican-American art.

Suggestions are left up on the poster board at the art center until all the children interested have had a chance to complete them. In the two or three weeks that this usually requires when children work in small groups, students are not only exposed to a range of art history but they learn to make a personal response to it. Along with the children, teachers have enjoyed classroom habitats where great art from many cultural heritages and their own children's art coexist harmoniously.

A WALK THROUGH THE HALLS

My first conversation with my first principal, on my first teaching job, dealt with the appearance of the halls.

"I want these halls to sparkle!" she exclaimed. "When the children or their parents come into the building, I want them to feel a sense of excitement, of activity and involvement. Exhibits on the walls of the hall also permit one class to share its interests and activities with another. And if it isn't perfectly clear who did what, or why, there should be labels to explain it all."

I had just come from practice teaching in an old building with a sickly cream-colored ceramic tile on all the walls in the halls. The terror of the school was the elderly custodian who had been there forever and ruled the place like a tyrant. He had decided that the walls must be kept absolutely clean at all times. No one was ever permitted to put anything up for a display. If a teacher objected to his arbitrary decisions, he would quote the fire code, although his interpretation of what constituted a hazard was questionable, or else he would insist that anything put on exhibit would be stolen, so why bother.

Having worked under these conditions, I found the new instructions quite startling. But what an exciting challenge! I was given specific time, two periods a week, to do this display job. Sometimes it was necessary to stay after school, but I found it interesting. After much trial and error, I learned what was effective and what was not. I learned that it was important not to leave the same items up too long. I learned that it was impossible to do the job all by myself and so I appointed student helpers from each class. I learned that a wall stapler was absolutely indispensable. I learned that corridor exhibits were important teaching devices that helped teachers, parents, and students learn more about what was going on in the school. I learned, finally, that three-dimensional displays could be very informative and attracted great interest.

The mural about evolution was very well received. Paintings of the Greek coastline made a fine display. Each was carefully placed on a piece of construction paper of a compatible color; this was easier than cutting individual mats. A large papier-mache imaginary creature, standing about four feet high, graced the front hall to greet visitors. Soon other teachers requested help in setting up exhibits on the walls outside their rooms. I was delighted. The idea was spreading. I cajoled the maintenance department into making some high wooden boxes for display purposes. They also pulled some old beat-up tables out of the junk pile. They were long and narrow, perfect for displaying assemblages, pottery, sculpture, and group projects.

In the back of my mind I carried on a constant and indignant dialogue with the custodian from the first school. "What are schools for? For children's learnings or for your compulsive needs about cleanliness? Who makes the rules? The custodian or the educators? I know that you are just trying to do your job, and a conscientious custodian is very important to the smooth running of a school. However, a school is a place for learning. If exhibits help learning, we must have exhibits."

In my fantasy I saw his resistance breaking down. There he was, on his knees begging for forgiveness. "But," he wept, "how can you hang things on ceramic tile walls. Scotch tape won't hold and it makes an awful mess."

"The answer," I declared sternly, "is to install wooden strips along the walls, possibly at two levels, expressly for the purpose of attaching large bulletin boards, or murals, or whatever is needed."

He sat there quietly in my dream and then tried again. "But vandals!" he pleaded, "they will steal everything."

"That's a risk we must take," I replied firmly. "If we involve the children in this project right from the beginning, we are apt to have little stealing and vandalism. However, we cannot eliminate all exhibits on the chance that perhaps some things will be taken or destroyed. If that happens, we'll have to deal with it. But we must try."

He was demolished; I was triumphant. But, victorious as I was in my imagination, I never did summon up the courage to go back to confront him. Many years later I found myself supervising a practice teacher in that same school. The walls were still empty and barren looking. More confident then, with many years of teaching behind me, I asked about the custodian. "Retired," I was told, "but happily he trained a young man who is carrying on exactly as Roy did."

"That," I responded, "is perfectly clear."

THE EVER-PRESENT HOLIDAYS

I have often thought that people created holidays to give themselves a certain respite from boredom. Holidays in schools can be viewed in the same way for no one can be excited and learning *all* the time. There are bound to be ups and downs for both students and teachers. If the holidays come at an "up" time for learning, they can be a terrible nuisance, but if they come at a "down" time, they can be a useful diversion.

For some reason the coming of holidays seems to be a signal for pulling out old cliches. I have a nightmarish vision of hundreds of floating pumpkins, worn-at-the-edges Christmas wreaths, strange looking paper turkeys, and lopsided Easter bunnies and Easter baskets—all made from stencils, all meant to be the same. It must be admitted, albeit reluctantly, that these are the symbols used by our culture to represent various holidays. To help teachers get out of their tired old ruts of celebrating holidays, here are some questions they might pose to their classes.

*   *   *

Halloween is a time for mystery, for imagination. There are alternatives to pumpkins, skeletons, and witches. Children can be asked:

What is the origin of Halloween?

What is the mood?

What colors can create this mood (including orange and black, but not exclusively orange and black)?

If Halloween means mysterious eerie creatures, why not create your own? In paint? Wire? Papier-mache? Linoleum blocks? Plastics? Aluminum foil?

Would you prefer to create a design that expresses this mood?

Or a repeat pattern using a Halloween symbol, something that would make handsome wrapping paper?

Or would you like to make Halloween kites—paint them, construct them, and fly them?

Thanksgiving suggests not only a history lesson, but also an opportunity for expressions of a humanistic nature. Questions might resemble the following:

How do you think the Pilgrims felt as they crossed that enormous ocean, sailing for days, and days, and days (echoes of Columbus)?

What would they have seen first as they approached the shore?

Do you think that people in a new situation like that would feel kindly toward the Indians they saw?

How do you think the Indians felt when they saw these strangers settling on their land?

Would clay sculptures be appropriate for expressing their feelings toward one another? Or drawings? Or wax resist?

Why is there so much emphasis on food at Thanksgiving?

Would it be interesting to make models (or drawings or paintings) showing how these people obtained their food or how they managed when there was no food? And then, by contrast, how they felt when things improved, thus explaining why Thanksgiving?

Christmas has a clear and straightforward meaning in religious schools, but in public schools, where the separation of church and state is meant to be operational, the meaning becomes muddied. To avoid difficulty, many schools settle for the symbols of Christmas without becoming too involved with their traditional religious significance. There are many fine ethical concepts relating to Christmas that can be stressed besides the religious ones. One way to do this is to introduce a study of Hanukkah and compare the similarities and differences of these Christian and Jewish December holidays. Children can be asked:

What would "peace on earth and good will toward men" mean if you suddenly met a person who had different color skin and hair from yours and who spoke a strange language?

If we really had peace on earth, how do you think it might affect your family—or the street where you live?

Using any of the art materials that you like, why not try to make something you feel expresses the idea of "peace on earth and good will toward men"?

Does the brotherhood of man have anything to do with Christmas?

Suppose you lived in France, or Italy, or Mexico, or Japan, or India. Do people in those countries celebrate Christmas or Hanukkah? Do they have a comparable holiday?

Would you like to do a painting that would give a feeling of what you think the holiday spirit is like in another country?

We could make programs for the school festivities or greeting cards for our families using linoleum blocks.

Or would you like to make (as one fifth-grade class did) a huge Santa Claus with children of many countries climbing all over him? (This was done by using chicken wire and papier-mache. Some serious research was done on the clothes and appearances of the foreign children. Santa was a marvelous joyous fellow, four feet high and worth the trouble.)

Would you like to make some beautiful holiday wrapping

paper by dipping tissue paper in water and then dropping bits of paint on it at random? Or string prints? Or potato prints?

Hanukkah or the Festival of Lights commemorates the return of a group of Jews, the Maccabees, to Jerusalem after their long struggle to maintain their identity against powerful oppressors. Questions might include the following:

Do Hanukkah lights and Christmas lights have anything in common?

Would you like to make a painting or sculpture that would capture the feeling of victory of the weak over the strong?

Does this make you think of David and Goliath? If so, can you think of a comparable situation in your own life? Can you tell us about it in a painting or drawing?

What images might you see in the flickering of the candles of the menorah?

There are many other minority groups in the United States who have holidays other than those listed above. The curriculum can be enriched by encouraging children of varied backgrounds to share their holidays with the rest of the class. While enjoying the diversity of different customs, children can also realize the need that all people share—to celebrate universal themes, such as a triumph over adversity, the resistance of the weak against the strong, and a sense of responsibility for others.

Here is a lesson called the crystal apple that will relate a holiday involving gifts to an appreciation of the power of the imagination. It will help children become aware of architectural shapes and shapes created by the refraction of light through glass and its separation into colors. Have available a prism and/or chandelier crystals, watercolors, brushes, water containers, sponges, white paper, crayons, and reproductions of Marc Chagall's "I and My Village" and Lionel Feininger's "Sight of a Village" (available from Shorewood Prints, New York).

Read the story of *The Crystal Apple* (Beverly Brodsky, Viking Press, 1974) in which a girl experiences her father's advice that, "Your imagination is your most precious gift." While reading, call attention to the beautiful illustrations, emphasizing the shapes and colors created by the refraction of light and the architectural shapes, such as cupolas. Briefly discuss sibling relationships, possibly acting out situations when a child's siblings broke her or his favorite toys. Next show the prism or crystals and allow the children to observe light refraction. Briefly describe and diagram the bending of light rays and their separation into different colors.

Then show the Chagall print. When he lived in France, the artist used his imagination to recall his Russian town. Note his use of color and shapes, both faceted and architectural. Elicit from the class that imagination can create combinations that don't appear in reality. Follow up by showing the Feininger print —a different artist's imaginative recollection of a village. What are the similarities (architectural and faceted shapes)? What are the differences (color, mood)?

Ask the children to illuminate their own imaginations. "What colors and shapes do you see?" Have each child use watercolors to create an allover pattern. When dry, they may define details with crayons. They may use both sides of their papers (if the paper is of good quality).

Ask each child to present his or her favorite side and to comment on the techniques employed and their observations about the media in addition to their imaginative content. Call attention to the diverse styles in the group, just as Chagall and Feininger had different styles. Hang the "Crystal Apples" as holiday decorations or as an "Imagination Tree."

*   *   *

Certainly readers can add many ideas to the above. Children will understand and enjoy holidays much more if they are stimulated to think about the meaning of each one, and if the projects involve personal effort and thought rather than long mindless copying.

RECOMMENDED BASIC SUPPLIES FOR AN ART CENTER

Similar items can be stored in shoe boxes. Every container should be clearly labeled to help maintain order.

Assorted papers in varied sizes (newsprint, manila, colored construction paper, white painting paper, rolls of mural paper, colored tissue paper)

Crayons, oil pastels, colored chalks, felt-tip markers

Tempera—powder or gel

Brushes in varied sizes (#12 is good, as a single basic size)

Containers for water (coffee cans or plastic containers from ice cream, cottage cheese, and the like)

Sponges, paper towels

Scissors

Masking tape

Stapler—staples

White glue and paste

Wet clay in an airtight container

Squares of vinyl on which to use clay

Tongue depressors as tools for carving

Plasticene

Florist's wire and pipe cleaners

Yarns and string

Boxes of paper and fabric scraps for collages

Found objects such as cardboard rolls and small wood pieces (but avoid clutter!)

Smocks (old shirts or aprons will do)

Storage space for children's folders

Picture file of art from around the world

Interesting objects to handle including natural "finds," such as sea-shells and rocks.

10. Intelligence, Creativity, and IQ Tests— The View from the Art Room

Many of the children introduced in this book have abilities that have been inaccurately evaluated. There was Chris whose intelligence was displayed only in the art room (chapter 4). There was the first-grader, Tyrone, who had to repeat a school term although he drew pictures worthy of much older children (see p. 189). And there were children who lacked self-confidence and weren't sure about their own abilities (chapter 4). In this chapter you will meet children who, having encountered racial discrimination at an early age, were so discouraged that they really don't care about school or tests associated with school.

LABELING CHILDREN

As we worked and traveled from school to school over many years, we often found children labeled on the basis of IQ scores—"low achievers," "not up to their potential," "slow developers," "below normal IQ," and so on. The IQ test was used as an absolute measure of ability, when there was nothing absolute about it. This created difficulties for high IQ children as well as low ones.

"Marie has a high IQ," I heard a teacher say. "It's 120, but she does only average work, and she looks sullen most of the time. She is a bad girl and is not working up to her potential." Had there been no IQ score on her record, the teacher might have willingly accepted Marie as an average student and adopted a more positive attitude toward her. She might have inquired about why Marie looked so sullen, which might have been more to the point.

As in other areas, teachers and parents must be wary of using labels. I frequently hear children described as "hyperactive," "disturbed," or "uncreative" without any concern for defining these terms. Positive attributes are also used loosely. Children are described categorically as "gifted" but without describing what area they are gifted in. In the case of art, it is difficult to pronounce with certainty that a child has or lacks talent, since almost all children love to draw, paint, and sculpt. There do not seem to be art prodigies of the sort that appear in music or mathematics. Often children who appear to be "artistic" turn to other things, while Cezanne, van Gogh, Matisse and others didn't begin to be serious about art until maturity.

While avoiding premature labels, it is frequently obvious that some children are especially adept at expressing themselves visually. These children should be given increased opportunities, resources and challenges so that greater and greater discipline may be achieved. An art teacher's advice should be sought, and other teachers and administrators should be alerted to the child's skills, as described in the next chapter.

Tyrone's abilities were not recognized at his school. He was regarded as the classic "disruptive" child. He frequently raced around the room when he should have been completing assignments. "Immature, hyperactive, short attention span" was the verdict on his record card. A decision was made to retain him in the first grade.

My work with Tyrone showed very different qualities of his personality and behavior. He applied himself to art projects with purpose and concentration. His finished work contained an extraordinary amount of detail and exceptional attention to composition and proportion. The use of symbols, including numbers and words, in his pictures made me wonder why he wasn't performing at a higher level in math and reading.

Tyrone's portrait of his friend Edward is reproduced here. Anyone who knows the difficulty of drawing a front view of a seated figure will appreciate its extraordinary qualities. Most seven-year-olds draw awkward people standing rather squatly on a chair or superimposed against it. They may turn the figure to show a profile view curving delicately around the chair. I have

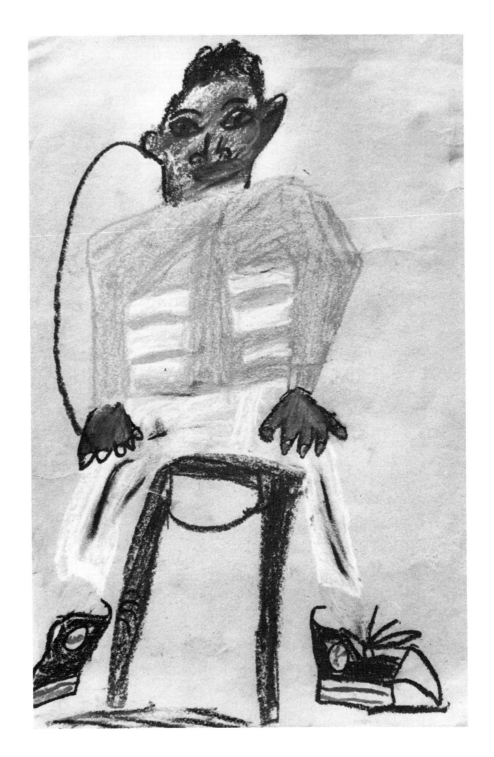

This remarkable portrait of a seated friend was drawn by a seven-year-old boy. His school had labeled him as "immature . . . and disruptive," but his artwork indicated that he was exceptionally intelligent. Few adults could draw a seated figure with such accurate foreshortening and sense of proportion. His rendition of details was also exceptional.

never encountered a solution to this problem as successful as Tyrone's.

I evaluated a number of Tyrone's drawings using standards described by Florence Goodenough and Dale B. Harris in their work, *Children's Drawings as Measures of Intellectual Maturity*.[1] I felt sure that Tyrone needed more, rather than less, stimulation since his art indicated that he was extremely bright. His interest in art could have provided an avenue for reaching him and interesting him in other subjects, but art ability was not considered important in his school, except as something to be withdrawn as a punishment. "Additional time for art might keep Tyrone out of the teacher's hair a little longer, but it won't teach him what he needs to know," the principal declared as I flinched.

It is safe to say that Tyrone had exceptional ability in art, but it must be emphasized that all the children in his class enjoyed the reflection and reconstruction of their experiences that was encouraged by their artwork.

*   *   *

The habit of labeling disserves the needs and interests of young children. It can have tragic consequences when the labels are wrong, as they often are when inadequate testing instruments are used for lack of something better. In many instances cultural differences rather than cognitive deficiencies cause children to have difficulties with standardized tests. These differences have caused many minority group children to be incorrectly labeled "retarded."

INTELLIGENCE AND IQ TESTS

When Alfred Binet devised the first examination for categorizing children in 1904, his test was not based upon any specific theory of intelligence—it was simply a tool for determining which children could or could not function successfully in French schools as they were then organized. The purpose was to eliminate children who could not function in school This approach stems from an educational philosophy very different from the American one. American schools are organized to include all children, not to eliminate some.

Lewis Terman of Stanford coined the term "intelligence

---

[1] New York: Harcourt Brace Jovanovich, 1963.

quotient" and adapted the Binet test to the American system, changing and improving upon it periodically, hence the Stanford-Binet IQ Test.

Volumes have been written about the subject of intelligence and IQ tests (see bibliography), and a complete analysis of the subject does not belong here. However, certain aspects of both the tests themselves, and the uses to which they have been put are more apparent to people working in the arts than to others. These effects need to be called to the attention of parents and the educational community at large. Since the Stanford-Binet and the Wechsler Intelligence Scale for Children (WISC) are most commonly used in schools, it should be understood that these are the tests referred to in this discussion.

Is intelligence one specific human characteristic that can be tested? Hardly. Most psychologists today agree that the word "intelligence" covers a large number of abilities, many of which IQ tests do not even pretend to measure. David Wechsler, father of the WISC, stated "Intelligence is not a unique entity, but a composite of traits and abilities recognizable by the *goals and ends* it serves [my italics] rather than the character of the elements which enter into it."[2] The phrase "the goals and ends it serves" is important. It has often been stated that artists are concerned with goals different from those of other people. Artists' goals usually involve a commitment to expressing those insights that may originate in intuition, or perception, or imagination.

DIVERGENT THINKING AND CREATIVITY

In the course of working out a formal expression of these insights, most artists (and children when they make art) explore many different possible solutions to any given problem. In the art process there is a constant weighing of and playing with different ideas, any number of which might solve the problem at hand (see chapter 2). In the choice of solution artists show their insight and artistry. This process involves what is called divergent thinking. Wilbert McKeachie and Charlotte Doyle have written:

---

[2] "Intelligence: Definition, Theory and the IQ," *Intelligence: Genetic and Environmental Influences*, Robert Cancro, ed. (New York: Grune and Stratton, 1971), p. 50.

Intelligence tests have tended to emphasize verbal contents, information and comprehension (cognition), logic (convergent thinking) and memory. One process which standard intelligence tests have not included is what Guilford called "divergent thinking," the ability to generate a variety of ideas or approaches to a problem. . . . Divergent thinking, in which the person must conceive of a variety of answers, contrasts with convergent thinking, in which the person is to discover the one correct answer.

A variety of ideas—logically or by association—is a very important part of the problem-solving process, especially in the solution of the problems posed to himself by the creative artist or scientist. By omitting divergent thinking from the domain sampled in intelligence tests, one of the crucial abilities for creative work has been overlooked.[3]

What they are saying, of course, is that intelligence tests do not test creativity. It has been noted that a fair number of creative people score high on tests both of creativity and of IQ, but the number of creative individuals who go unnoticed because of low IQ scores is impossible to estimate. Frequently the unrecognized creativity of children is squashed precisely because their styles of thinking do not conform to the standard categories prevalent in education. Perhaps this is why creative people are often attracted to art fields where standardization has no place.

E. Paul Torrance, a leading psychologist in the study of creativity, has reported on some of the personality characteristics of creative children at the elementary school level. Important characteristics related to children's drawings were originality and a large number of unique or unusual details. Mr. Torrance has written, "This finding helps to explain why some of these highly creative children do not show up better than they do on traditional intelligence tests. Their ideas simply do not conform to the standardized dimensions, the behavioral norms, on which responses are evaluated."[4]

Elsewhere he describes the abilities involved in creative thinking as, "fluency of ideas, flexibility, originality, sensitivity to problems, defects, and missing elements, and the ability to re-

---

[3] *Psychology* (Reading, Mass.: Addison-Wesley Publishing Co., 1966, 1970), p. 353.
[4] *Creativity* (Belmont, California: Feron Publishers, 1969), p. 15.

define and restructure problems, all of which exemplify divergent thinking." He went on to state, "Traditional measures of intelligence emphasize memory, recognition, and logical reasoning and call for convergent thinking or getting the one correct or best answer."[5]

This confirms what most art teachers have known to be true, namely, that any evaluation of children's abilities should include some consideration of their artwork. Youngsters who are more visually than verbally oriented may be equally intelligent but may express their insights in different ways. There is a wealth of information to be found in children's artwork that relates directly not only to their degree of intelligence and creativity but also to their developmental level.

Torrance also reported that creative children, "sometimes insist on learning in creative ways rather than by authority. . . . Highly creative children have a reputation for producing wild or silly ideas, especially the boys. . . . Their productions are characterized by humor, playfulness, and relative relaxation." Teachers will recognize that if these characteristics are put together, they can easily cause what is not-so-fondly known as a "discipline problem."

CARL, A "DISCIPLINE PROBLEM" Carl, a third-grader, was one of these problems. He fidgeted and fussed much of the time. His teacher found herself disliking him intensely since his humorous remarks, received with delight by the other children, were extremely disruptive. In the art room I noticed that he could, if he wished, dominate the entire class by his comic antics and sly remarks. The work he did was original and often amusing, but its casual quality told me that thus far his involvement was still at a somewhat superficial level.

One day he was particularly rambunctious. We were working with ceramics. Some children were making sculpture, while others chose to do pottery. Carl began to make clay spitballs, lining them up, ready to fire. The children watched with interest, a ready audience. Since I am a sculptor, I have a particular respect for clay, and to me he was really violating the material.

"Oh Carl," I protested, "what a waste! That's not just a soft mushy material. With clay you can express something that's important to you. It's a means of using your brain in a different

---

[5] *Ibid.*, p. 8.

way. Are spitballs all that you have on your mind? I hope not!"

He was startled and perhaps a little insulted. "Well," he countered, "there's not enough there to do anything with anyway. It's nothing." He pointed to the ball of clay, the size of a fist, which he had taken from the bin.

"Very well—come!" Somewhat irritated, I went to the clay bin and pulled out a large chunk of clay, about ten pounds worth. Not enough, I decided. I was on a limited budget, but something drastic had to be done with this boy. So I removed all of the rest of the clay that was there.

"Here," I said, presenting him with about twenty pounds of clay on a large board. I led him to a corner of the room so that he would be removed from his audience and left him there to work by himself.

At first he looked astonished and then (lucky for me) interested. *This* was a challenge.

Ten minutes later he was beside me, pulling at my smock. "I need a big tool," he announced excitedly. His facial expression had totally changed. Instead of his usual somewhat insolent look, he had a serious intent expression. I did not have any large tools, so I showed him how he could use a piece of two-inch board to pound the large chunk of clay into the desired shape. I explained how one could rough out the large forms first and then follow by developing details.

Much to everyone's amazement, including my own, in the course of the next month Carl made a fine clay head, far beyond the level of work one expects from a third-grader. He became so interested that many days he asked to stay after school to work on it! My "discipline problem" had become a devotee of art.

His classroom teacher and I both felt that there was much to be learned from this experience. We decided together that Carl was probably a very creative child who did not find school stimulating enough. His teacher decided to give him more leeway in terms of work and not to hold him too strictly to the class activities. Rather, she found more advanced materials for his use and encouraged him to go off in his own direction when something interested him. She wondered whether he should be advanced a grade. After some consideration it was decided that emotionally and socially Carl was a normal third-grader, but he had a creative mind, and when it was not being utilized, he became a real nuisance, a "discipline problem."

*   *   *

Of course, every child who is disruptive is not necessarily a creative one. However, when teachers frequently face chaos and begin to despair, it is time to look at themselves and their curriculum before blaming the children. "Is the work at a sufficiently interesting level for the age group? Is it introduced in a stimulating manner? Are the children really involved in determining the direction the work will take? Is it meaningful to them?" These and similar questions must be asked and answered before a child is blamed for a problem. There are countless possible explanations for difficult classroom behavior. Behaviors that are unacceptable to one teacher may seem perfectly normal to another. This in itself can be confusing for children. Certainly any consideration of this complex matter should include creativity as one possible cause of restlessness and disruptive behavior. It's too important to be passed over.

Creativity is one of the most precious qualities human beings possess, and so is intelligence. These two qualities are needed by society to help us deal with the enormously complicated problems we constantly face. Creativity and intelligence are probably equally complex since both are multifaceted. Individuals can be talented in some aspects but average or poor in others. This is why it is so essential that teachers and parents be wary about applying labels, both other people's and their own. They should look for strengths, help with weaknesses, and see both as clues for understanding the child. It is surely the responsibility of schools to seek out children who are gifted and to help them grow and develop in every way possible. But if schools are committed to using tools of measurement that identify only one type of intelligence, neglecting the types associated with creativity, clearly reevaluation is very much needed.

To suggest that the arts are the only fields that attract creative people would clearly be nonsense. However, divergent thinkers probably attract one another and the general atmosphere of the arts, plus the nature of the work itself, tend to make the art center in a school a comfortable place for creative children.

JAMES, WHO HAD A "LOW" IQ   James was about thirteen years old when he came to an after-school art class that was part of an experimental art education laboratory. He was number two in a black family with eight children. One younger brother and a younger sister came to class with James from time to time, and I noticed that they were unusually beautiful children. There was also a sweet quality to their personalities, which made me want to know them better.

James came to the class regularly, but I was not sure if it was the artwork that attracted him. I noticed that although he listened closely to what was being said, he rarely finished a piece of work, and whatever he did finish was about average in quality. But there was a special air about him that aroused my curiosity. He usually arrived somewhat early and before the class started he would wander about the room looking around and examining whatever he could find.

This laboratory class took place at an art college. The classes were taught by art education students under my supervision. The large airy room was carefully arranged, with several small exhibits we thought would interest the children. In one corner were live animals—gerbils, birds, turtles, snakes, a rabbit, and even a parrot. In another was an assortment of plants, including a small orange tree. (We watched the oranges grow and change, and when they were ripe, each child was to have one. When the great day arrived, the first ripened oranges were distributed, but, as the children eagerly popped them into their mouths, there were shrieks. They were so bitter! Like lemons! What a disappointment!) There were changing exhibits on the walls and tables, sometimes work done by the children and sometimes work done by the student teachers.

James found all of this very intriguing, but in addition to looking at all these things, I noticed that he would carefully examine such objects as a staple gun, or the lock on the door, or a pencil sharpener, or a desk chair on a swivel.

"What's so interesting?" I asked him laughingly, when I saw him screwing and unscrewing the back of an easel. He was sliding the canvas support up and down.

"I like to see how it works," he smiled shyly, his hands falling to his sides as he looked down at the floor.

"So—perhaps you'll be an inventor when you grow up," I offered.

"My father is a inventor—kind of," he responded, looking up eagerly. "He can't talk much, so he makes things for us kids all the time. Made us a play yard out back of our house. It's real good!" he declared, nodding his head.

"What do you mean—he can't talk much?" I asked.

"Well," he hesitated and then went on. "He was in the war

and got hurt in his neck. So he has a little box in his throat, and he talks funny—with a kind of machine. But *I* understand him." His expression was intense and a little defiant now. But then he sighed and said sadly, "I guess he wanted to be an inventor, but he won't be one now."

We stood silently for a minute or so, and then I said, "James, if you have some special idea about something you'd like to make, we have lots of materials here, as you know. Why not try making a small model or else just play around with the nuts and bolts and corrugated paper and paper clips and small pieces of metal—maybe you'll get an idea."

"I'd rather do that than paint," he replied.

So he tried. And that was when I learned about what happens to a bright child who has a low frustration threshold. If something didn't work after several efforts—and he did make many efforts as he tried to create a "something" involving gears—he would toss the piece down and pace around the room, furious with himself. I would plead with him to just calm down and try to think it through. But there were thirty other children in the class as well as a practice teacher who needed frequent attention, so there were interruptions and I didn't have the time necessary to really help this boy. It was very disturbing to me as a teacher. He was obviously unusually observant and curious about the structure of things, but he couldn't seem to handle his own feelings of inadequacy. If I urged him to try something more simple, he would look down scornfully and say, "Aw, that's not worth trying." He needed "know-how" but his mind went faster than his fingers, and he became impatient and frustrated.

One day I decided that perhaps art and design just weren't his thing. "What is your favorite subject in school, James?" I asked.

"Aw, school," he shook his head, "well, I guess science. My science teacher, he's real nice. And I'm his helper."

This sounded encouraging. "I know a man who is a real scientist," I told him. "He does research on viruses. Would you like to visit his laboratory?"

He was delighted with the idea, and the next week I arranged for an after-school visit. The scientist took James around and explained in simple terms what was going on. James was beside himself with excitement and delight. After the tour, the scientist said to me, "You know, he asked excellent questions. And he was so interested in the equipment. He must be a very good student in school."

In the car on the way back to his home I told James what had been reported. He immediately started to sulk. "I don't like school," he finally volunteered. "My daddy gives me a quarter for every good mark I get, but I don't get them often. Those teachers, and that big old building. . . . I just hate bein' in school." I immediately envisioned the restless boy bored to death, soon not caring what went on. It was a depressing thought.

After a few minutes of quiet, James turned to me and said, "And tests! They're always giving tests. And they're always in a hurry. Even if the test is interesting, I can't stop and think about it, have fun with it. No, I have to hurry up, hurry up, and we had one today, the dumbest thing. There were all these questions, and one didn't have anything to do with the one before. No sense at all to them. Why should I try to answer stupid things like that!"

I had been thinking about contacting his school to find out what his scholastic standing was. Maybe some sort of scholarship could be obtained for him, but after hearing this, I felt doubtful. "James," I said, deciding to make a try, "those tests may not make sense to you, but they have been carefully written by educators, and they do make sense to them. If you would only try to do better in school and on those tests, you could learn the things that would make it possible for you to be a scientist when you grow up. Just think, going to college and then working at things that interest you all the time. Wouldn't that be worth the effort now?"

The thirteen-year-old boy turned and looked at me pityingly. "My big brother wants to be a architect. But we don't have money for his school. Now he carries blueprints around in those rolls, you know? Just no use . . ." and he shook his head like an old man.

"James, you can't give up before you have even tried! You have the brains. With some hard work you could get your grades up and maybe your school could help you to find a scholarship so that you could go on to college."

"Yeah, they wanted to give my brother a scholarship, but he'd have to play football. No architecture scholarship. He hates football. Gets his head broken every time."

It was the end of the school year. I phoned his science teacher to ask whether anything could be done to shake James from his cynicism. "No," the science teacher replied, "I haven't had any luck, although I've tried. I think he's a really superior type of person. But his IQ scores are low, his teachers find him uncooperative, and he seems to save his curiosity for those things that have nothing to do with school. So the school has labeled him as a poor student, and I have not been able to change that picture of him. He just rejects formal schooling, although his parents plead with him to try. They are loving, gentle people who have not had much education but who would love to see their children get some. Occasionally James will make an effort in order to please them, but he finds his classes boring. He was discouraged by his brother's experience, and now he has just given up."

Torrance suggests that a careful observer can often spot a creative child and he offers a list of behaviors that might give teachers or parents a clue.[6] I think that some of those listed describe James very well:

- Intense absorption in listening, observing, or doing
- Intense animation and physical involvement
- Tendency to challenge ideas of authorities
- Taking a close look at things
- Showing relationships among apparently unrelated ideas
- Various manifestations of curiosity, of wanting to know, digging deeper
- Excitement in voice about discoveries
- Penetrating observations and questions
- Self-initiated learning

*   *   *

This incident happened many years ago, but I have never forgotten James, whose talents were lost, not only to himself, but to all of us as well. Many factors were probably responsible for his IQ scores. His cognitive style made it difficult for him to check off right and wrong answers that represented fragments of information. He was concerned with relationships, how things work, and with the organization of information. He was not success-oriented. He didn't respect his school, and so he didn't care whether or not he did well on tests given there. This attitude, combined with a lack of knowledge about the skills needed for test-taking, such as timing one's responses, produced a creative but frustrated child with a low IQ score. James was probably

---

[6] *Ibid.*, p. 36.

attracted to the art class, not because he had any special aesthetic insight, but because the style of thinking in it was close to his own and so he felt comfortable there.

WHAT DO IQ TESTS TEST?

We have discussed what abilities IQ tests do *not* test, and the next question must be, "What is it they *do* test?" What is being tested is the ability to function successfully in today's schools, according to the standards of the white middle-class community. Until 1974 all children tested were measured against a norm which, in the case of the Stanford-Binet, was based on a standard population of 3,184 white, native-born people. Obviously this sample was not genuinely representative of the whole population. What meaning did these tests have when given to Puerto Ricans, blacks, Chicanos, or Orientals? To evaluate all children more accurately, a "culture-fair" test based upon a more representative norm was needed. In the absence of such tests, many large cities with minority populations stopped using IQ tests at all (New York, Philadelphia, Los Angeles, for instance).

It has been said that at times IQ tests reveal surprisingly high scores for children who have, until tested, been considered of low or average ability. There was, therefore, a loud outcry by some against the elimination of the IQ tests. It would seem that some harm could be done in following either course; the different degrees of harm would have to be weighed. Apparently the cities mentioned decided that IQ tests harm more than they help.

What is meant by the term "culture-fair?" Here is a very simple example. In one of these tests there might be a picture of what some call a "fire-hydrant." In some cities or in some neighborhoods, it is called a "fireplug," in others a "pump," while in some farm communities, it may not exist at all. An individual's designation of such an object depends upon where one grew up, not upon understanding what the object is or what its function is. Yet a word such as "hydrant" can be used in an intelligence test perhaps to test children's understanding of relationships or their understanding of synonyms. A child who grew up saying "pump" may receive a lower score than the one who grew up saying "hydrant," although both are equally acceptable designations.

The people who write these tests incorporate their own cultural experiences into what is meant to be an objective test. This happens, not because they are being devious, but because they tend to generalize from their own limited experience.

Art teachers are especially aware of the inadequacy of IQ tests—or they should be if they are not. Predictably, when working in poverty areas where culturally different children are apt to be found, teachers may notice extremely able young artists who do poorly in academic work and who have been already tagged as "low IQ." We have seen children who for years have made their way through dangerous neighborhoods, have been surrogate parents, have taken care of disabled grandparents, and whose experiences make their way into their paintings and other artwork. Such children know the meaning of the word "survival." Sometimes they don't like to think about this, and then their paintings are full of fantasies that help them forget what is unpleasant. These children's knowledge about real conditions of existence is beyond the level of experience of many adults, and many are exceedingly clever in these harsh conditions. If then, a school official tells us that they have low IQs and are therefore unintelligent, we can only conclude, as we look over their drawings, constructions, and sculptures, that there is something wrong with the tests.

THE WISC-R

To counter all these criticisms David Wechsler published the Wechsler Intelligence Scale for Children—Revised (WISC-R) in 1974. The purpose of this test, as stated in the instruction handbook for administering it, is "for assessing the individual's potential for purposive and useful behavior." In this test an individual who is culturally different has a little more chance. Wechsler used a stratified sampling plan based upon reports of the 1970 U.S. Census. His variables included age, sex, race, geographic region, occupation of the head of the household, and urban or rural residence. The sample includes designations such as "white" or "nonwhite." Nonwhite includes most blacks, American Indians, and Orientals. Puerto Ricans and Chicanos are designated as white or nonwhite depending upon their physical characteristics. This presents problems, of course, for the light-skinned black and anyone else who does not fit into a tidy category. However, it does represent an improvement over the samples previously used.

Although the WISC-R made some changes in the performance section of the test, it still largely favors children who are high in verbal ability. Interestingly enough, Wechsler's handbook also points out what he calls the "nonintellective factors of intelligence." Some of these were discussed in relation to James' inability to score high on IQ tests. Wechsler states that they are not so much skills and know-how but such characteristics as drives, attitudes, sensitivity to social, moral or aesthetic values, persistence, zest, impulse control, and goal awareness. These "nonintellective factors" are close indeed to Torrance's list of characteristics suggesting creativity.

Wechsler says that these "factors of intelligence are not substitutes for other basic abilities," which he defines as "facility with abstract reasoning, memory, and verbal fluency." There is no doubt that these are important skills, but, by assuming that words are the only medium for expressing understanding (or intelligence), he leaves little room for children who are different and who may be musically oriented, or visually oriented, or movement oriented.

There are other questions regarding the items in the section of the WISC-R concerned with comprehension. The answers to some of these involve value judgments of an ethical nature. Consider, for example, these questions: "What are you supposed to do if you find someone's wallet or pocketbook in a store?" "What are some reasons why we need policemen?" "What is the thing to do if a boy (girl) much smaller than yourself starts to fight with you?"

Children living in a poverty area could understand these questions perfectly well, but their answers may differ from those of middle-class children. They may not think that the policeman on the beat is their best friend; if they are very poor, they may think it a real piece of luck to find a wallet. If they struggle for survival in a tough neighborhood, they may think it reasonable to knock a small child down. For one thing, the aggressor might be small but very strong, and for another, he or she had better learn not to start trouble with kids bigger than him or herself.

Lastly, the symbols or drawings used in most IQ tests have been drawn by adults. Numerous art teachers have asked why children's drawings aren't used instead. Of course, the drawings would have to vary as the age levels advance, but an acceptance of one another's drawings has been observed among many youngsters, indicating that perhaps they understand one another's symbols better than adults do. The question can logically be asked, "Would the use of symbols drawn by their contemporaries affect test scores with regard to comprehension? with regard to a feeling of relaxed familiarity with the material? or with regard to making the tests more interesting to children?

Our main points concerning divergent thinking, creativity, and art-minded youngsters are rarely discussed in relation to IQ tests. We would be the first to agree that, "Love is not enough," for if we are to seriously assist children who are "different" or "unusual," it is not helpful to disparage all attempts at testing and leave it at that. Testing represents an effort to learn more about children, and the more knowledge teachers have about children, the more they can do to encourage their development. But as long as tests produce half-truths about children, which are then treated as if they were definitive evaluations, these criticisms must be made loud and clear. J. McVicker Hunt, who has headed up evaluating teams for the Head Start program, points to the inadequacy of what he calls our "psychological technology,"[7] meaning our testing devices.

---

[7] *Reflections on a Decade of Early Education*, commissioned paper by Clearinghouse in Early Childhood Education of the Educational Resources Information Center, ERIC, 1975.

11. Some School Problems and Prospects

With inflation rampant, school boards and state departments of education have watched their expenditures increase at an alarming rate, even as enrollments go down. They have noted that there are still high school students who read at a fourth-grade level—and some of these students have not learned how to do simple arithmetic. Where, officials ask, are the returns for all the money they are spending? At the same time that they must deal with these worries, school boards are pressured by disturbed parents who see their children adopting very different living and learning patterns from their own. Uneasy community leaders have turned to their schools and said, "Account for yourselves. Why should we give you all this money unless we know that you are spending it effectively?"

ACCOUNTABILITY

The degree of effectiveness can only be determined by careful evaluation procedures. At first glance, the demand for these appears to be simple and reasonable. Why, then, has accountability become a touchy problem? If it means that teachers should be able to explain to themselves and to others what their educational objectives are, surely there should be no objections to this. If accountability means that teachers should be able to demonstrate how they work to achieve their objectives and how they evaluate their own results, that too seems perfectly reasonable. Surely as teachers we should know what we are doing. We are accountable to ourselves as professionals, to our school boards who are responsible to the community, to our fellow educators, and, most important, to the children.

The point at which the accountability process ceases to be simple and straightforward is when an attempt is made to treat all types of education in exactly the same way. In a period of growing technology, people tend to develop a kind of faith in, and dependence on, the tools of technology. This has been as true in education as it has been in industry, government, medicine, and other fields. There is a general belief that everything can be put into a computer; everything can be measured in mathematical terms; everything about human beings can be explained. It is assumed that a tool used satisfactorily for evaluation in one field should be applicable to all other fields as well.

Unfortunately this is a simplistic view. It leaves no room for differences in objectives. Perhaps in a very general sense educational objectives are similar, but when one gets down to particulars, there can be large areas of difference. Objectives in art education have been discussed throughout this book. Stated simply, its concerns deal with the development of perceptual awareness, sensitivities, skills, and humanistic attitudes. These very real phenomena are not mere words. But although a trained observer can clearly see when they are operating, it is very difficult to pinpoint the depth or extent to which they have been learned.

How is learning in art measured? Do teachers look at children or at their products? Or both? Does it make sense to count the number of paintings or sculptures they make without regard for quality? Or should teachers count the number of times a child stops to look and think about a work of art. If French teachers wish to evaluate their teaching, their students can be asked to speak, to listen and respond, to read, or to write in French. Each of these is a process, and each produces an easily identifiable product. Students may excel in one or another process, but it is perfectly clear if they have learned French or not. Their learning can be tested. In art classes, however, evaluation is not so simple, as the following actual situation demonstrates.

* * *

As I approached Terry, a boy of seven, I saw that he was deeply involved in making a mosaiclike picture, using little bits of colored tissue paper. He looked up and then waved me away impatiently. He was busy. Good. About fifteen minutes later I looked to see what he had done and saw that the bits of paper had been glued to the background sheet, covering it with a mass of variegated forms. The colors were carefully arranged to focus one's attention on a central point, which was itself an assortment of different kinds of yellow.

"Nice picture, Terry," I commented. "Want to tell me about it?"

He looked down at the floor a bit shyly and then, looking at me tentatively, he replied, "It's heaven."

*   *   *

How does a teacher evaluate a piece of work like that? Does the picture show evidence of some technical facility? It shows some but nothing very special. Does Terry's concept show sensitivity, which was one of the initial objectives in art education? Yes, it clearly does, but how much? Do teachers know how to measure sensitivity? Not really. If an observer stopped to look at Terry's picture and its title but did not know his age or the intensity with which he worked, would the picture alone be a basis for measuring Terry's sensitivity? Should teachers care only about the quality of the picture (the product) or should they be equally concerned about what went on in a child's mind as she or he made the picture (the process)? Clearly, both the product and the process give useful information. Even if teachers are interested in evaluating all aspects of children's learning in art, there is still another factor to be considered. How does a particular picture differ from those made when the child first entered the art class at the beginning of the year? And how does his or her attitude toward art differ? Has his or her attitude toward him or herself shown any change?

If teachers are to be held responsible for the learning in their classes, the first thing that is needed is an evaluation of the work of their students. By taking a close look at Terry and his picture as suggested above, some of the problems involved in this evaluation are identified. Obviously the quality of a work cannot be measured by means of standardized tests or norms—they simply do not exist. Viktor Lowenfeld's art norms for different age groups may cast some light on the developmental levels of certain groups of children (see chapter 3), but that is not the primary concern here. For purposes of evaluation the only meaningful measurement of growth will be that which measures children against themselves.

EVALUATION QUESTIONS IN ART

To do this, it is necessary for all students to keep a representative cumulative portfolio of their work from the beginning of a year until the end. As teachers and evaluators examine the work, they must ask:

> Does children's work show any conceptual growth? If they started the year doing pictures of Superman, are they still doing the same thing by the end of the year? If there are changes, are they just growing up or has their teacher stimulated them to expand their thinking and express their ideas and feelings visually?
>
> Have they experienced work in new media? Has their range of performance expanded?
>
> Have they developed some technical facility in any or all of these new media?
>
> Has their knowledge of art vocabulary increased? (The portfolios will not answer this; only direct contact with the children can provide the answer.)
>
> Is there any indication at all that they have learned to see more perceptively?
>
> Do they work more imaginatively than before?
>
> Is there any indication that they approach art more enthusiastically?
>
> Have they learned that evaluating their own work and that of others is part of the art process?

Of course teachers cannot ask these questions about their students without asking themselves similar questions regarding their own teaching and their art curriculum:

> Does the art curriculum provide experiences that will encourage conceptual growth or does it provide experiences that encourage sameness and copying? Is originality encouraged?

Does the art curriculum provide opportunities for work in new media, increasing the children's scope as they advance grade by grade?

Does the teacher attempt to assist children in increasing their technical facility (without touching a child's work, we hope) or does the teacher see him or herself as a distributor of materials only?

Does the curriculum provide "seeing-touching-feeling" experiences?

Does the teacher use progressively sophisticated art vocabulary while talking with the children?

Does the teacher introduce fantasy, poetry, artifacts from past and foreign cultures, or other methods of stimulating the children's imaginations, and inventiveness?

Does the teacher approach the subject enthusiastically with the awareness that art is more than just playing around with materials? Do they define this awareness for students, parents, and administrators?

Is evaluation a routine activity as work is concluded so that children can develop high standards and a sense of taste?

As readers consider these questions they must recognize that growth and learning are tricky subjects. Schools cannot be held completely responsible for everything that children learn. Biological growth, social growth, changes in the family, changes in personal friendships . . . all these outside factors affect the learning that goes on in classrooms.

Still, it is true that responsible educational groups in a community have every right to ask for some degree of accountability. However, they must understand that there are no simple answers when it comes to evaluating human beings; measurement in this area is extremely difficult.

PROMISING RESEARCH FINDINGS

There is a growing body of information with highly significant results attesting to the relationship between participation in art activities and learning in many areas. Among the most important contributors to this field have been three consecutive programs in "Learning to Read Through the Arts."[1, 2, 3] These programs involved children who were initially at least two years below their expected reading levels. After participating in an intensive arts project where reading was taught in the context of art activities, the children were found to make significant gains in their reading scores as well as exhibiting increased enthusiasm for and application to academic learning in general. The Howard Conant evaluation of the first of these programs states categorically:

> *It is possible to effectively teach reading in a program of instruction primarily focused upon the arts.*

> *The California Achievement Test [Reading] was administered to all children on a pre/post basis, and an exceptionally significant reading score gain of 8.4 months over a four-month chronological period was determined. [The program was designed for children who were performing two years below grade level in reading and/or math.]*

> *Attitudes toward academic curriculum subjects in general can be enhanced through an arts and reading enrichment program.*

> *The hundred or so children in this program not only grew remarkably in reading ability, they also learned to express themselves creatively and significantly in at least two of the arts as well.*[4]

Interesting positive results were also reported in the area of self-concept.

Another study was called Arts IMPACT (Interdisciplinary

[1] Howard Conant, Evaluation Director, *An Evaluation of the 1972–1973 Guggenheim Museum Children's Program "Learning to Read Through the Arts,"* ESEA Title I Program, Function No. 09–31699, Center for Educational Research and Field Services, School of Education, New York University, July 1973.
[2] Sheldon Marcus, *Title I Guggenheim Museum Children's Program, Learning to Read Through the Arts, 1973–1974,* Evaluation Report, Function No. B/E #09–41699, Board of Education of the City of New York, Office of Educational Evaluation, 110 Livingston Street, Brooklyn, N.Y. 11201.
[3] Bernadette C. O'Brien, Project Director, *The Title I Guggenheim Museum Children's Program, Learning to Read Through the Arts, 1974–1975;* Report available from the Solomon R. Guggenheim Museum, 1071 Fifth Avenue, New York, N.Y. 10028.
[4] Conant, op. cit.

Model Program in the Arts for Children and Teachers).[5] Initiated at Pennsylvania State University, work was done at five sites in Ohio, Oregon, California, Pennsylvania, and Alabama. The general conclusion, developed in detail in the project reports, is that education is made more effective for both teacher and learner when the arts are utilized.

Still another report by Stanley S. Madeja, called *All the Arts for Every Child*, is part of the Arts in General Education Project.[6]

The study of the relationship of the arts to the learning process is still unfinished business in today's world. Therefore, there must be enough flexibility to permit each discipline to set up its own standards for evaluation, standards that have meaning in terms of basic objectives. Evaluation involves not only the skill of the teachers but also the substance of the curriculum, the philosophy of the school, and the quality of the students. Accountability thus becomes a more complicated matter than apparent at first, but the climate created by the studies cited here, as well as by additional Elementary and Secondary Education Act, Title III projects currently underway, makes the prospects for constructive use of the arts in elementary schools most encouraging.

---

[5] *Arts Impact: Curriculum for Change—A Summary Report*, Robert L. Lathrop, Director of Evaluation Team, The Arts Impact Evaluation Team, Pennsylvania State University, University Park, Pa. 16802. Final three hundred page report available from ERIC Document Reproduction Service.

[6] *All the Arts for Every Child: Final Report on the Arts in General Education Project in the School District of University City, Mo., 1973.* Report available from J.D.R. 3rd Fund, Inc., 50 Rockefeller Plaza, New York, N.Y. 10020.

12. A Word to Parents

Dear Parent:

Your reaction now—as your child brings home his or her "precious" paintings may well affect the whole attitude toward art training in the next few years. Therefore, may I urge you to proceed with caution!

Remember that things must appear very different to a little person only three feet high. Life does not appear the same from down there as it does to adults. The decision as to what is important is also different. So please—don't ask, "What is it?" as you look at the painting. Try "Tell me about your painting" instead. Frequently the importance to the child lies not in WHAT it is, but rather HOW ·it was done, or what colors were used. A blob of blue paint may be just a blob to you. But the other day a child said to me," "What a beautiful ball of blue color!" It was the pleasure in the use of the color that was important, not that it was a ball.

So please be sympathetic and admiring even if you don't understand it all. If you laugh or joke about the work, you may destroy that joy in the color which is such an important experience for your youngster.

Remember—"Tell me about it." And thank you for your help.

Your Child's Art Teacher

This letter, addressed to the parents of first-grade children, has been attached to the first batch of artwork sent home each year. It has been used year after year and has provoked an enthusiastic response from parents, which surprised me very much. Apparently it met a need.

"I never knew what to say when my little one showed me something that she had done," one mother remarked. "Now when I ask, 'Will you tell me about it?' her responses are really surprising. What I thought was a badly drawn triangle turned out to be a tepee with smoke coming from the top. The strange shape above it on the top of the same picture was 'a bird flying.' I never realized that she thought about so much."

Another parent showed me a drawing of a face. "When I asked her to tell me about it, my child pointed to the eyes and told me that they showed what the person was seeing. What an astonishing idea!" This four-year-old had also indicated the teeth in a most detailed and unusual fashion.

Being a good responsive parent is sometimes difficult. The stresses involved in making a living and meeting everyday demands leave many parents drained. They sincerely wish to do the best for their children but often lack not only the energy, but also the knowledge needed to meet their children's needs. Loving parents often face the eager eyes of their youngsters as they proudly display pictures or objects that are completely incomprehensible to the adult. "Look what I made!" the children exclaim happily.

This book contains many ideas that will help parents deal with such situations in ways that will maintain children's pride and enthusiasm and will enable parents to share them. Although the content material is primarily addressed to school people, the authors have included parents in their thinking as well.

Perhaps as a parent you have been thinking that all those scribbles of your four-year-old mean that your child cannot draw. You can obtain some sense of what may be expected at different age levels by reading chapter 3 where art is discussed as a record of developmental levels. These levels should be loosely interpreted since, for example, no child demonstrates three-year-old behavior on the very day when he or she turns three. The categories are broad and roughly drawn. After reading this section, you will probably discover that the work your child is doing is fairly characteristic of her or his age group. If not, a visit with your child's art teacher may be helpful.

Until her little daughter explained this picture, her mother thought it was a large person with un-related shapes in the background. It turned out that the girl had very deliberately drawn a hill in the upper left corner on which sat a teepee with smoke billowing out the top and a bird flying overhead.

If your child tends to disparage his or her artwork, or if you do, chapter 4 should be of interest. The information about art and self-concept presented here should be useful to both of you. The suggested related activities at the end of the chapter can all be done at home as well as in school.

If you have wondered how you can help your child to draw or paint, read chapter 6 entitled "Learning to See." You will find, among other things, that after an initial period of scribbling, children draw and paint what they know, not what they see. You will also learn how different people mentally process what they see in different ways. Therefore, until age seven or eight, children are best left alone with regard to the actual forms they draw. At that point they can be helped by activities that aim at expanding their perceptual experiences but that still leave them free to interpret what they see in their own personal idioms. You will find in this chapter many such activities that have been successful with children as young as first-graders. These too can be tried at home if the children seem to respond to what is suggested. However, if there are signs that the children are resisting your efforts, it is better to stop. Every activity is not necessarily appropriate for every child. You may, once you acquire the feel for the type of activity that works, devise other ways of introducing color, form, and texture that may be more appealing to your children.

Obviously one cannot draw or create other art objects without thinking. Chapter 5 discusses why it is important to provide art materials for children's use so that art processes can assist them in learning to think.

But please, when you provide materials, never give your children a coloring book. These books do not help children to develop their own ideas; rather they say, "This is the way (for example) to draw a cow." Instead of providing a drawing of a cow, it would be preferable to present a photo (if a real cow is not available) and ask children to make their own pictures of a cow. Perhaps children will observe characteristics of the animal that an adult might not even notice. It is in the act of observing and selecting what a child considers to be important that significant learning takes place. Just filling in colors not only prevents learning but also instills wrong ideas. "Filling in" tells children that what is important in drawing is keeping within the lines in a neat and tidy way. This actually has nothing to do with the essential part of drawing, which is the act of putting down one's own ideas in line.

Art is described by the authors as being a language, a means of communication. Parents need to know what their children are thinking and feeling, and chapter 7, "Learning about Feelings," will be most informative in this regard. Since young children often don't have the verbal facility to express their feelings fully, their art should be examined carefully for the messages that are being sent. However, this too must be handled with care. Praising everything indiscriminately will lead children to distrust what you say.

For example, I am reminded of Arthur, who, as he rolled up his paintings to take them home, said, "Now I'll show my mother all of these rabbits."

"But Arthur," I protested, "those are not pictures of rabbits."

"Well," he explained sadly, "my mother always thinks that I do beautiful rabbits. Everything looks like rabbits to her. So, now when I bring home some paintings, I say, 'Look at the rabbits I have done,' and then she is happy."

But, important as the learnings may be, the rich source of pleasure in colors, forms, and textures that art provides is what art education is all about. Sharing these experiences with your children can create a lasting bond, important for all of you. Such experiences are discussed with respect to teachers in chapter 2. Many adults share some of the inhibitions that many classroom teachers feel about art, and if you do too, you will respond to many of the points raised in this chapter.

Finally, the whole book emphasizes and documents the need for art teachers and for art in the general curriculum. It is hoped that a thoughtful reading of this book will prompt you to bring the problems of providing top quality art education to the attention of your PTA or other parent organizations. Parent pressure is essential to assure action in this important area.

13. Some Human Concerns

Many thorny questions are facing educators today, and teachers must ask themselves:

> How can we help children to deal effectively with their world in ways that are satisfying both to themselves and to their communities?

> How can we help children to be self-motivated and to want to learn?

> How can we help them to enjoy reading?

> How can we help them to learn necessary mathematical skills?

> How can we deal with, and even eliminate, the serious discipline problems that plague our schools?

> How can we help children to feel more confident about their own abilities?

This book has suggested specific ways in which art can help teachers to deal with these questions because art, when well taught, involves the enthusiastic participation of children. We have discussed art as it relates to learning problems, learning styles, self-concept, self-motivation, and personal feelings. These problems are not the special concerns of any one group of children—they are human problems. We have not focused on the cultural backgrounds of the children described because we have preferred to discuss them within the context of all children. Art is important for everyone.

ART AND MINORITY CHILDREN

Where poverty and prejudice exist in severe forms, school problems are exacerbated; they become more painful, more bitter, and more difficult to handle. Sensitive teachers in these situations want to help their students deal with and overcome their difficulties. As has been shown, art is particularly adaptable for meeting these needs, especially those of minority children who need new ways of learning about themselves and each other. Through art they can begin to experience some sense of mastery over their environment, an important experience for anyone. Art certainly will not solve all educational problems, but it can make a substantial contribution.

Not all minority children are poor just as not all poor children belong to minority groups. The special needs of each must be considered. There are numerous middle-class children from minority families who, although free of the economic pressures of the poor, face troubled situations simply because of the color of their skins. These children require special help if they are not to be victimized because of their ethnic or racial backgrounds.

Many of the problems that loom so large for poor minority children stem, not from the children themselves, but from the social and educational framework in which they find themselves. Persuaded by the neon light, plastic culture glowingly presented by the mass media, many minority children have moved toward conformity, separating themselves from their origins, frequently in a self-deprecatory manner. This kind of integration is unhealthy and very different from integration built upon an acceptance and respect for differences. People need to know who they are and how to appreciate their diversity. The cultural backgrounds and physical differences that set people apart from each other should be highly valued sources of pride. It is the tremendous variety and interaction of different kinds of people that make for the vigorous entity that is the United States. It is the richness of diversity that has helped this country grow. How can teachers convince young people of the validity of this point of

Art experiences won't eliminate all the problems minority children face in most schools, but they definitely can help these youngsters learn about themselves and others in positive ways.

view? The best way is to try to develop these attitudes among the very young, before they become enveloped in hard, cynical, protective coverings. And teachers can begin with art where human creativity is immediately obvious.

I once worked as an art specialist in a Title I school whose students were about 60 percent Chicano, 30 percent black and 10 percent white, or Anglo as they were called. It was agreed with the Follow-Through supervisor, that we would spend one week on pre-Columbian art, combined with a clay experience, and another week on African art, combined with the mask experience described in chapter 4. This was hardly enough exposure to ensure a lasting effect, but it was assumed that the classroom teachers would build on the experiences after I left. Children in grades one, two, and three were to be included.

In a class of third-graders we sat on the floor in a circle and passed around reproductions of pre-Columbian ceramic objects, which had been borrowed from the local art resource department expressly for this purpose. Beside me I had books of photographs of the real things, so the children would learn the difference between an original and a copy.

The children admired the ways the artists had made objects such as pitchers and bowls using human and animal forms. They loved the small clay figures, which were small enough to sit in the palm of one's hand. They enjoyed the Mayan masks and the Aztec snakes, and, most of all, a small round clay rattle that must have had beans inside.

"What material do you think was used to make these things?" I asked.

"Cement."

"Stone."

"Clay"—Finally one child produced the right answer.

The children decided that these people had been pretty "smart" to have found clay in the ground and to have figured out how to bake it to make it hard.

"Yes, they were smart," I agreed. "But do you know what happened to them?" I asked in a dramatic tone.

"What—what?"

"Well, let's give these ceramics to Maria to put away, and I'll show you some slides that will help to tell the story." Slides of the dramatic murals made by Orozco at Dartmouth College, which tell the history of Mexico, were flashed on the screen.

As we looked, the children listened to the story of Cortez who came to Mexico "a long, long time ago," looking for gold and for power. I used as my source of information the fascinating book, *The Discovery and Conquest of Mexico* by Bernal Diaz.[1] Diaz was actually there, on the spot with Cortez. From the murals we learned how Cortez and his men crossed the ocean from Spain, how he tricked and robbed the Indian tribes that he met, and how he used Donna Marina, a native Indian woman, as interpreter.

Suddenly a small voice interrupted. "She was a traitor to our people!"

Pedro, who had spoken up without realizing it, covered his face with his hands in embarrassment.

I was a bit startled, having never heard this point of view before. "That's really interesting, Pedro," I said. "Can you explain to us why?"

"No, no," he murmured and would not say another word. I coaxed a little, but no, he was overcome with shyness. So I went back to the story.

These were third-graders, such little children, but they looked very serious as they listened to the rest of the story. Pedro's comment, obviously something that he had heard at home, gave this tale a new significance. It was not just a story now—it related to them, to their lives. When the story was finished, they sat quietly, thinking for a moment. Then I asked, "Would you like to make some things in clay too, like the pre-Columbians?" (I had explained that they were called pre-Columbians because they represented the dominant culture in that area of the world before Columbus came.)

"Yes! Yes!"

The classroom teacher helped, and soon each child had a square of plastic material on which to work, a chunk of clay (about one pound) and a tongue depressor for cutting and shaping.

"Let's try not to copy what those Indian artists did," I suggested. "Rather, let's make our own clay designs so that we'll find out how they felt when they were working."

Some children made small pieces of pottery; some made animals; some made people. They learned how to water and score the clay in order to connect two pieces so that they would not

---

[1] Bernal Diaz del Castillo, *The Discovery and Conquest of Mexico* (New York: Grove Press, 1956).

fall apart. They enjoyed the feel of the material as well as the freedom to make whatever they chose.

Later, one child called out, "This is fun, but it ain't so easy. Those people sure knew how to do it." He shook his head in appreciation and went to take another look at the reproductions in the box.

The next day I asked, "Would you like to take a trip to Mexico today?" and showed them where it was on a map. I had brought some slides of Mexico and of Mexican art as well. Most of the class watched the slides with interest. The paintings of Diego Rivera were meaningful now that they knew some history. But a few children were fidgeting. I could see that I had to get them involved.

"Do you know anyone who comes from Mexico?" I turned off the projector for a moment and addressed the most restless child, a boy named Bernard. He was a black child, taller than the others and clearly very alert.

"Sure," he laughed. "Pedro!" pointing to the small boy near him. The others turned to look.

Pedro was startled. Then he threw back his little shoulders and said, "Not me. But my father—he comes from Mexico." And, gaining courage, he pointed to the screen. "See—see— what a pretty place that is? My father he told me that, but I did not ever see it before." He cast a brief glance in my direction and then looked away shyly.

"You are right, Pedro," I nodded, "Mexico *is* a beautiful country. Those mountains outside of Mexico City are a little bit like our mountains here in Colorado, aren't they?"

He relaxed, pleased with the support for his idea.

Bernard listened closely. "But Pedro's father is Mexican. He isn't Indian. You said yesterday that it was Indians who had a fight with that Spanish guy," he protested. "Jim, here, he's Indian," pointing to another boy in the class.

Jim, a North American Indian boy, lifted his chin and listened cautiously.

Again a deep breath from Pedro, who then said, "No, not Jim's kind of Indian. But my grandfather's grandfather's grandfather's kind of Indian." The class laughed.

"Some of those Indians married Spanish people and got to be Mexicans," he explained urgently. "My father came from Mexico, but he is American now," he added.

I returned to the map and pointed out the different parts of

America—South, Central, and North. "The United States where we live is part of North America. Different kinds of Indian people lived throughout all of the Americas over a long period of time, and they mixed with other peoples who came to this part of the world," I concluded.

"Oh!" Bernard was satisfied and then volunteered, "My momma came from Texas."

"That's very interesting," I replied. "My mother was born in Chicago, but her parents came to the United States from Europe. I guess that most North Americans are people whose families came from someplace else . . . except North American Indians, of course." Jim's eyes accepted that, but he didn't say a word.

By now Pedro was shaking his head in approval, Bernard was slapping him on the back, and the room was full of chatter as most of the children busily told their neighbors where their families had come from. They were very excited. It was good and very acceptable to have a family who had come from someplace else, even though you were part of the United States now. When their pleasure began to border on bedlam, I decided we had had enough. I flashed the lights for quiet, and we returned to the rest of the slides.

As I was about to leave that day, a small boy came over and pulled at my smock. "That's a pretty dashiki," he smiled. "That comes from Africa, doesn't it?"

"It doesn't, but it's very much like the ones that do," I replied. "I'm glad that you like it. Would you like to see some things that really came from Africa?"

"Yeah!" he was enthusiastic.

"Well, maybe we can take a trip to Africa next week."

"Wow! Hey, guys, we gonna see Africa next week."

Some nodded their heads, pleased. But others looked non-committal—still a little distrustful, still waiting to be shown.

*   *   *

The next week I followed a similar procedure, introduced African artifacts, showed slides, and then made masks. The slides showed Abidjan, the capital of the Ivory Coast, which I had visited. The children were astonished to see a beautiful modern city with paved streets and high buildings. They admired the women wearing gaily printed fabrics and noticed that many were carrying their babies on their backs.

"That's not Africa," protested one little girl. "Where are the animals?" I explained that there are animals in some parts of Africa but not everywhere. Although there are parts of Africa that are jungle and parts that are desert, there are many large modern cities that look much like the cities in our country. I used a map to give them some idea of the various regions.

The children found the wood carving slides very exciting. They saw pictures of a tool used to pound grain, which was in the form of a woman. It stood about two feet high and looked like a long pole. The bottom of the wood was rounded so that the pounding could be done in a bowl. They saw masks used for ceremonial purposes and a stool made especially for the chief of the tribe. All these pieces, and others, showed a marvelous sense of design. They were highly decorated, and the decorations always followed the basic form of the piece. There was nothing accidental in the way these sculptures were done. Everything seemed to be carefully planned and showed fine workmanship.

When I projected a particularly colorful picture of a market place outside Abidjan in a town called Buake, one child murmured, "Look, so many black people!" I took that as a cue and asked whether they knew how black people from Africa came to the United States. We discussed the story of the slave trade and its ramifications at length.

"The way they treated those people, that wasn't very nice," a little girl with a red ribbon remarked, shaking her head in disapproval.

"No, it wasn't," I agreed. "Do you know that it's said that they even brought some tribal princes over on those slave ships?"

The irrepressible Bernard jumped up at that and started to dance around, shouting, "My granddaddy wuz a prince." He pounded his chest proudly, and everyone started to laugh. His clowning relaxed the atmosphere in the class. Our observations of artifacts and discussions of tribal life had touched on the role of masks. Now it was time to make some, and we all became very busy (see chapter 4 for details on mask making).

* * *

The art of a people can introduce the sense of pride in one's own heritage that is so badly needed by many minority children. It can also introduce respect for others' achievements, which is equally needed by all children. It is important to note that the backgrounds of many Americans do not necessarily fall into obvious or clear-cut categories. We can ask children what their family origins are and build lessons around their responses. Perhaps their families can contribute skills and ethnic items for observation and discussion. Teachers can also bring in varied materials showing the creativity of many different groups, even those not represented in the class population. Forming a healthy self-concept and becoming appreciative of people different from one's self can occur hand in hand, especially when art activities are the vehicle of understanding.

The first requirement is to involve the children, using whatever experiences they can bring to the subject. The second, equally important, is the interest and respect shown by the teacher. A teacher's attitude can indicate that it is desirable to learn about Orozco's murals because some of the class are Mexican-Americans and proud of their history; also the murals are so interesting and beautiful that they can enrich the lives of everyone. And the children may go on to express something about themselves in murals of their own. What will people who see our murals learn about us?

ART AND POOR CHILDREN

While poor children may lack many of the advantages others enjoy, they frequently develop resources that compensate for material possessions. Self-reliance is one such resource found in large measure among poor children. In situations where more protected children might be helpless or terrorized, children of the poor may take charge with strength, humor, and responsibility. It is therefore ironic to see young children shopping for food, tallying prices, and counting change accurately, when only minutes earlier they failed a simple arithmetic test at school. The same children may seem totally at a loss verbally when asked to respond to simple questions at school, but when confronted by derelicts on the way home, they have no difficulty letting loose a verbal barrage with impressive color and vehemence.

Obviously such children regard street and school settings as totally separate and unrelated; one stimulates their intelligence and creativity and the other leaves them hopeless. Teachers who wish to relate education to the lives of their students can rely on art to help bridge the gap. Art activities such as murals, puppets, portraits, films and photographs of interiors and street scenes, sensory collages, and sculptures of found objects can encourage children to express their own experiences.

When children are given opportunities to imaginatively reconstruct experiences, they will discover new resources for dealing with problems and new reasons for developing interest in the skills school can provide. To foster these changes in attitude, teachers must be willing to receive as well as to impart information. They must be sincerely interested in the realities of their students' lives and not merely in teaching a prescribed curriculum. When students become aware that their words, actions, and achievements are important to school authorities, they will be more interested in making them known. Herbert Kohl made this point in *Teaching the Unteachable*:

> *A student will only be concerned with his own use of language, will only care about its effectiveness . . . when he is talking to an audience, not just one that allows him to say what he wants as he wants, but one that takes him and his ideas seriously.*[2]

Teachers can persuade students of their serious interest in what they have to say by responding with respect to their art ideas as well as to their verbal ideas. In many instances, visual ideas may emerge more easily and may provide a basis for increased verbal communication.

ART AND BILINGUAL CHILDREN

Bilingual children who speak a language other than English at home often find it very difficult to keep up with their work when they are in English-speaking schools. School programs that incorporate both the home language and English are beng tried in many parts of the country. In the Southwest especially there is growing recognition of the need for bilingual, bicultural schools.

How does art fit into this picture? Children who are confused about language in school are likely to talk much less than others. This makes it harder for teachers to learn about their abilities and interests. However, the natural urge to draw, which *all* children have, can be helpful here. It is up to teachers to encourage this form of communication to facilitate becoming acquainted with the children and establishing the friendly kind of relationship that will help learning to take place. A sensitive

[2] *Teaching the Unteachable, The Story of an Experiment in Children's Writing* (New York: New York Review, 1967), p. 8.

consideration of children's drawings can give teachers insight into children's developmental levels (see chapter 3), family relationships (see chapter 7), and interests.

Psychologist Wayne Dennis[3] reports studies suggesting that the group values taught at home are expressed in children's drawings. By examining the drawings of children from various socioeconomic groups in thirteen different countries, Dennis discovered how the drawings reflect the kinds of people the societies admire, the attitudes toward masculinity, the attitudes toward work, religious attitudes, and other social values. If psychologists can use children's drawings to learn more about them, teachers should learn to do the same.

Chapter 4 discussed in detail the ways in which success in art can affect a child's self-concept. This is especially important for the children of migrant workers, many of whom not only speak two languages, but often speak both of them incorrectly. Moving frequently from place to place, there is little time to build up relationships with friends and teachers or even with adult family members who must work long hours. In each new place the inadequacy of their language ability presents new hurdles. The frustration level among these children is especially high. Any tool that will help them to express their own personalities should be used to its utmost by teachers. Once again it must be stressed that art media can provide exactly those tools, if used in the open-ended, flexible way advocated in the preceding pages.

Verbal communication based on children's artwork will be much clearer, easier, and more interesting to students and teachers than discussions of remote abstract subjects because the art is concrete and personal. There are now many fine picture books with short texts in several languages.[4] These, combined with children's responses in art media, can provide a much stronger language program for bilingual children than strict adherence to basal readers designed for speakers of English alone. As in most other areas of the world, bilingual skills should

---

[3] *Group Values Through Children's Drawings* (New York: John Wiley, 1966).

[4] Cat Stevens, *Teaser and the Firecat* (New York: Four Winds Press, 1972) and Gabriella Mistral, *Crickets and Frogs*, translated and adapted by Doris Dana, illustrated by Antonio Frasconi (New York: A Margaret K. McElderry Book, Atheneum, 1972) are two examples.

be recognized as strengths to be maintained and encouraged rather than as hindrances to be overlooked or demeaned.

Many educated adults in the United States regret a lack of fluency in other languages. Children who speak other languages can actually help their teachers attain this fluency. Children's art and the art of cultures that differ from our dominant Western European one can provide a powerful educational base for mutual benefit in these situations.

ART AND NONVERBAL CHILDREN

Although the term nonverbal is used widely, its definition is vague. Are nonverbal children those who can't speak, don't speak, won't speak, those who speak differently from the majority, or those who don't respond to others' speech?

Frequently children who are labeled nonverbal in one setting are voluble in other settings. Their language in voluble situations may be very different from the standard English expected in school, however. To us, Hal was a nonverbal child. He was quite able to speak, but words were definitely not his preferred mode of communication.

When there are thirty active children in a room, teachers tend not to notice the quiet ones as much as the others. On occasion I observed that when eleven-year-old Hal arrived in the room, he would look around to see what was going on and then quickly find some supplies and go to work. If it took ten minutes before the teacher was ready and the class settled, Hal usually spent this time drawing. Other children would sit and talk to their friends or they would wander around the room, but not Hal. It was not that he was unfriendly, simply that he was busy. His drawings were full of very carefully drawn details. I knew that he was in the room, but he was so undemanding that somehow I didn't talk to him very much. My student teachers, however, noticed the detailed quality and sensitivity of his work and reported that he was a talented child.

One young teacher became especially interested in Hal. "He doesn't want to talk," he reported. Could it be that Hal was just shy? Was he distrustful of the authority figures around him? Did he feel uneasy in this somewhat strange atmosphere, so different from home or school? Or was he too busy looking and thinking? We just didn't know.

Each student teacher was responsible for one session with the children. There was also an assistant teacher who was available to help out in emergencies. Most sessions were active ones, so that Hal was constantly involved in working with his hands. One day we brought in found objects, and the children made assemblages. Hal's work was so imaginative and humorous that it caught everyone's attention. He clearly enjoyed the recognition. And why not?

Then came the day that Margaret, a student teacher, decided that the children needed some exposure to the history of art. Instead of a work session, she prepared a slide presentation. I warned her that a whole hour of slides and talk might be too much for young children who ranged in age from eight to twelve and suggested that perhaps she should combine slides with some other activity in the session. But no, Margaret was adamant. The class of student teachers discussed the problem and felt that Margaret should have the chance to try the slide presentation. Besides, they all wanted to see how the children would react. So I agreed, on the condition that her assistant be prepared with an alternate activity in case Margaret should need some help.

When Hal arrived that day he looked around for the supplies, but they were closed up in the cabinets. "Something special today!" Margaret told him happily. "Find a chair and we'll get started soon." He sat down with a sullen expression on his face, not saying a word. He waited restlessly for the class to begin. Finally, after giving a vigorous introduction, Margaret turned off the lights and began to show the slides. For the first few minutes all was well but unfortunately she was overeager. She wanted to tell the children absolutely everything she knew about each slide. The time between slides became longer and longer.

Hal's special friend suddenly nudged me. "Look at Hal," he whispered excitedly. Through the darkened room I located Hal. He was sitting behind a little boy, pulling at the collar of the boy's jacket. The boy was wiggling around, trying to get free. As I watched, he turned around and gave Hal's arm a wallop. Hal raised his hand to hit him back when one of the student teachers leaned over and stopped him. We were surprised but did nothing further. It was the first time that Hal had ever gotten into a fight here. Maybe it was just a quirk.

Five minutes later Margaret stopped her talk, complaining, "Someone is tapping on the table. Will you please stop? It is very disturbing." Looking around, we saw that Hal was smiling sheepishly. The tapping stopped. Soon after that we were startled to hear a chair fall over. It was the empty chair just behind Hal's. He had been kicking at it and knocked it down. At this point Margaret became excited. "If you can't behave yourself," she stormed, "you can leave the room."

"I'm sorry," he muttered, embarrassed to find everyone looking at him. Actually the other children seemed to be grateful for the diversion. They were getting a little bored themselves. Some were wiggling, while others sat vacant-eyed, almost asleep. The slides were good, but there was too much talk that went on and on.

From the back of the room Margaret's assistant signaled to her, pointing at her watch. Responding to the hint, Margaret stopped the slide projector and turned to the children. "Would you like to see more pictures?" she asked, "or should we stop now and do something else." Immediately they were wide awake. "Something else," they replied eagerly.

Wire and styrofoam were quickly distributed. The children were reminded of the slides of sculptures they had just seen and then they got busy. The session was saved from disaster.

I tried to comfort Margaret, who was obviously disappointed with the children's response. "They did listen for almost a half hour and you were flexible enough to change direction in midstream, which many teachers wouldn't be willing to do," I added.

"What about that Hal?" she asked. "He certainly was a nuisance."

"Yes, what about Hal? Let's go and talk to him."

We found him hard at work, busy, involved, a very different boy from the Hal who had kicked over the chair.

"Didn't you enjoy seeing those beautiful pictures?" I asked him curiously.

"Uh-huh," he looked guiltily at Margaret.

"Then what was wrong?" she asked.

"Don't know," he turned back to his work, obviously finished with this conversation.

The student teachers stayed after the children left so that we could evaluate the session as we did every week. They agreed that although slides could be very informative for young children, they had to be combined with questions and discussion as well as with some related activity to maintain interest.

However, it seemed that Hal had a different kind of problem.

We had learned enough about him from his artwork to know that he was not only interested in the subject but intelligent and creative as well. We knew that he must be very observant or he could not make such detailed drawings as he consistently did. Obviously, he was visually alert. We could only conclude that it was the talk that provoked his poor behavior. Since he loved to work with his hands, it seemed that art was his best means of communication; he seemed to be more visual than verbal.

Our observations of Hal in the art room were helpful to his teachers in other subject areas. Instead of regarding him as a disruptive child who was perpetually distracted, they became aware of methods to involve him purposefully in the work at hand (literally). Hal is no longer required to "just sit still and listen!" His lessons are related to projects that involve his art interests and abilities. Of course, he must be willing to receive verbal information, but he no longer regards listening as an uncomfortable and interminable activity. He is interested in information that will help his projects. His visual transcriptions of some lessons have been a great help to other children with similar learning styles (see chapter 6). Hal himself has been most interested in the verbal descriptions of some of his completed art projects. Providing for Hal's preferences for the visual and the manipulative has enabled his teachers to communicate with him successfully.

ART AND AFFLUENT CHILDREN

"Wendy has *nine* television sets in her house," several fourth-graders reported to me excitedly.

I looked at Wendy, whose wary brown eyes were appraising my reaction. Her expression reminded me of Maurice Sendak's dog Jenny who said, "I am discontented. I want something I do not have. There *must* be more to life than having everything."[5]

This wistful, somewhat fretful child lived in a luxurious home where the emphasis was always on material things: what they were, how they were obtained, and the prestige attached to owning them. Wendy's parents cared a great deal about what she wore, that she looked pretty and ladylike, that she was

---

[5] *Higglety, Pigglety Pop: Or, There Must Be More to Life* (New York: Harper & Row, 1967).

attending a fashionable school, and whether she came home with As on her report card. The same intelligence and intensity that had helped her father to produce this wealth was present in Wendy, except that she didn't know what to do with it. The truth was that the girl's intellectual development was being stifled. She had no one to talk with about the serious questions that bothered her. She was eager to communicate with her parents, but her perceptive mind was stimulated only in school and even there she exhibited her confusion about her own identity. Only in her paintings and her literary efforts did her strong, vigorous personality became apparent. Here she felt free to use bright, vibrant colors, expressing feelings that were not particularly "ladylike" and "sweet." In her art she became an independent thinking person.

"Do you watch those TV sets all at once or one at a time, Wendy?" I asked jokingly.

She smiled and replied, "Mostly when my parents go out—which is a lot!"

"Why not do some drawings instead sometimes? That might be fun."

"Oh no," she cried in horror, "not at home."

For Wendy, home and school were two separate departments. If she showed her school personality at home, she knew it would not be treated with favor. She was safer sitting passively and watching TV like so many other children she knew.

Wendy's case is, of course, somewhat more extreme than most, but there are other affluent children who have similar problems. Some middle-class families also have aspirations akin to those of Wendy's parents. As a result, there is a tendency toward the same impersonal "interior decorator" look in their homes, many of which are overstuffed and ornate, and the desire to have conforming children. Aesthetic considerations do not figure actively in the lives of these people probably because their usefulness was never demonstrated during their education.

Other well-meaning parents who sense that "there must be more to life than this" drag protesting children to museums to expose them to "culture." This impulse is a healthy one, but anyone who knows the discomfort of tired feet after more than one hour at a museum can appreciate the resistance of the children. Short fun visits, perhaps a half-hour long, to see two or three special paintings or sculptures can be far more rewarding then several hours of tired looking. A welcome trend in current museum development is the creation of special rooms for children's visits that involve direct participation.

For many parents the art of their young children is hardly considered important, and, at an early age, the children get the message. It is easier to succumb to the fascination of TV rather than struggle to assert their creativity and individuality. This is not meant as a blanket condemnation of all television; potentially it is a rich visual medium, both for entertainment and education. However, since it does not involve active viewer participation, long periods of watching are hardly conducive to children's growth. Growth requires the chance for thoughtful questioning and responding and the opportunity to experiment with ideas of all sorts, visual as well as others. Some television programs do expand the children's horizons and are useful in this sense, but too many hours of watching can be deadening and even frightening, particularly when children see things that they do not understand.

Passivity, an absence of defined goals, identity crises, and communication failures are all problems that can trouble any socioeconomic group. Affluence is no protection against them. Quality art activities are one means of tackling these problems. They probably will not solve them—they are too complex for that—but art can help develop healthy means of self-expression.

ART AND THE "GIFTED"

Enduring music was composed by Mozart and Beethoven when they were very young children. In contrast, there are no known child prodigies in the visual arts. Many highly revered painters and sculptors manifested no special talent until they were mature. Nonetheless, alert art teachers know that certain children are unusually capable draftsmen, sensitive colorists, or bold designers. Other children pursue art projects with extraordinary intensity and perseverance, translating their perceptions into forms having unique styles.

Frequently these characteristics are overlooked. Neat copying, precise control of media, or adult habits of representation are often rewarded as artistic talent. These criteria tend to identify children who are doing well in other academic subjects as "gifted." But in art educators need to look separately at each child's use of line, color, form, space, texture, and composition, paying attention to unusual rather than standard combinations and observations. Children who produce these are truly creative. They may come from the dreamers, or fiery activists, or shyly reticent, or seemingly strange or contrary youngsters in a group, as well as from those already commanding attention for excellence in other subjects.

When artistic interests and abilities have been identified, children possessing them should receive special attention and recognition. They should be directed to look seriously at nature and at art. They should be questioned intently about their observations. They should meet artists and be permitted to question them. They should be given added time for reflection and production of their own art. They should be guided and challenged to expand their techniques and helped to evaluate their progress rigorously. They should learn responsible work habits that will sustain interest, overcome frustration, and maintain high standards. They should learn to communicate with one another about their efforts and be made aware of the contributions their art makes to others. In all these efforts, the skills of an art teacher are especially needed. The story of Chris in chapter 4 describes the guidance of a talented child.

The special services recommended for talented children must not be syphoned off from the curriculum at the expense of other children. A high quality art program must be provided for everyone. It should be remembered that the tastes and preferences that determine evaluations in art are highly subjective. Those identified as talented (or untalented) by one judge may be evaluated quite differently by a different judge. It is also sad but true that fads and fashions have been very influential in the art world. Children should not be denied experience in art because of these characteristics of adult society. Yes, talented children exist and merit special attention; concentrated art programs can have highly beneficial and far-reaching effects on their development.

But educators must be open to reappraisals of their judgments. Those designated as talented may lose interest and others in the general population may possess latent talents that appear as they mature. This occurs frequently in art. All children should be assured opportunities to reveal artistic talent, and at the same time, the needs of those obviously gifted should be met. This can best be accomplished when the entire curriculum is not changed to meet the needs of a special group. Rather, additional avenues for enriching the curriculum through after-school clubs, special projects, and integration of the arts as described here should be provided. These activities should be open to all according to their interests, and gifted students can be steered to them.

ART AND THE HANDICAPPED CHILD

Because of her sensitivity and expertise, Ms. Wallace was asked to include children with special problems in her kindergarten class. The group was smaller than most because so many of its members had physical handicaps, learning disabilities, and emotional disturbances. Ms. Wallace was determined to provide all the children with a rich program, one that would encourage individual strengths. She introduced me to the children first through their drawings.

"We have two very repressed children," she said. "I'm sure you can pick them out in these self-portraits." I immediately noticed that two of the students had used fewer lines, smaller forms, and very limited portions of their papers.

"Yes," Ms. Wallace commented as I pulled out the two drawings. "This is Joan and this is Tom. We rarely get them to talk or participate. We really don't know the extent of their problems."

Five-year-old Joan would never have any teeth of her own, and she was too young to be fitted with false teeth. This was probably one of the reasons why she rarely spoke or smiled. She had other severe physical birth defects that affected her appearance and behavior, but whether or not she was mentally retarded had not yet been determined. As we examined her self-portrait, we observed that although it seemed constricted, she had included many details and located them all precisely. This was not true for many of the more expansive representations of her classmates. Ms. Wallace commented that Joan had been engrossed in completing her picture, a contrast to her usual preference for sitting out activities on the sidelines.

Tom appeared robust and handsome physically—but he usually disappeared. That is, he chose hiding places in remote corners of the room and only occasionally peered out from these vantage points. His speech and coordination seemed significantly behind normal expectations for his age. "Frankly," Ms. Wallace recalled, "I was surprised to see him approach the drawing table at all, and I was overjoyed to see him beam broadly when I hung his picture on the bulletin board with the others. He does enjoy looking at pictures, even when he is sitting alone. Perhaps we can encourage him to do more."

As the art program progressed, both Joan and Tom made more and more art objects, and showed more and more enthusiasm as they did so. Joan worked at collages with serious intensity, making studied arrangements notable for their balance and symmetry. She painted with verve and a happy smile, and she began to talk aloud while drawing and painting. The children who stood near her at the art table came to understand her speech easily, and she smiled proudly when they explained phrases to me or when they registered excitement about a beautiful painting she had made. "She has made friends as well as pictures at this table," Ms. Wallace declared.

Tom's work developed strength and vigor. He wasn't always willing to work alongside his classmates. He sometimes took his supplies to a separate area. Nor would he always hold up his work at the close of each session, but he would allow me to hold it up while he stood at the periphery of the group. He was delighted to have classmates add to my comments about his use of color, space, line, or texture. He even began to add to the discussion when he felt we had overlooked something significant.

Tom and Joan are exceptional children. They are fortunate to have an exceptional teacher who emphasizes their abilities and encourages their growth in many areas. Rather than focusing on their limitations and providing a limited program for them, Ms. Wallace recognizes that her students have many dimensions apart from their disabilities. For this reason she requested the arts program in which I participated. She frequently points out to her students that everyone delights in using colors, lines, shapes, and all the elements of art. "However," she always adds, "each of us is special and can do special and different things with our materials." In this environment, Ms. Wallace's students experience art at the many levels described in this book, developing perceptual, manipulative, cognitive, and affective skills.

Children like Joan and Tom are examples of many. They appeared severely repressed and problem-ridden at the beginning of their school experience, but art activities enabled them to make contacts with others and with their environment. Through their art experiences, they gained knowledge and pleasure and contributed to that of others. They were recognized beyond the categories of their disabilities. Everyone has limitations, but even handicapped children need not be permanently bound by them or defined solely in terms of them. In the act of compensating for handicaps, other sensitivities may become more fully developed and find expression in art.

Teachers are seldom aware at first glance of the numbers of handicapped children in elementary schools. Almost every teacher has a current story about a child with a degree of deafness, or blindness, a crippling deformity, a condition requiring unusual attention such as a colostomy, a serious disease such as diabetes or cancer, or a troubling problem at home. These children are frequently distressed and distracted. They may be absent for long periods, causing gaps in their schooling that compound their difficulties. Teachers commonly note how helpful art is in working successfully with such children.

14. Contributions of Art to Education

Art is usually taught in this country as something rather precious and esoteric, separate from education and from life. Rather than being separate, we contend that art is an integral part of life and can act as a cement, enriching and binding together many aspects of human experience. Aesthetic awareness, when built into every day lives, can provide infinite pleasure and deepen understanding of ourselves and our world.

If teachers and parents feel remote and intimidated by art, they will pass this feeling on to their children. This book has attempted to break down some of this remoteness by suggesting ways in which persons who lack formal art training may approach the subject side by side with children and begin to derive some of its benefits. Some understanding of the many simultaneous learnings that take place when children make art is necessary to this approach. A brief recapitulation of these areas of learning is presented in the following visual section.

Art experiences can do the following:

COMMUNICATE IDEAS

This charming drawing of a bear done by a child in kindergarten became even more interesting when the teacher discovered that the child's mother was pregnant. Very often children tell us what is on their minds through their drawings and paintings. In the chapter on "Learning About Feelings" we describe the troubled child whose parents were in the process of divorce. This child had not discussed her dismay with anyone, but it became quite apparent when she did a painting about her home. We made no effort to intrude on the child's privacy, but when her call for help was so apparent, we tried to be responsive.

Then there was the little girl who thought of her father as the top of a head shown over the page of a newspaper. That particular bit of communication was a bit of a shock to the father, but helped to make for change in that household.

Another title for this book may well have been "Art: Another Language for Communicating."

By looking around us we become aware of the design elements that are everywhere. This painting, done by a child living in Jerusalem, shows that an awareness of architectural design can provide a rich source of pleasure at the visual level. Although the colors are not available to us in this reproduction, they did indeed show a marvelous mosaic that could shine even on a cloudy day.

Drawing is a marvelous tool in the service of careful observation. Children learn to think about proportion, quality of line, textural differences, and relative importance of the various parts of whatever the subject is at hand.

They often derive great pleasure from seeing how differently some people see what appears to be the same subject. Is the beaver running from the fox? Or do they just happen to be there at the same time? Is there a difference in the texture of their coats? And the colors of the fur? And the expression in their eyes? So many questions can be raised and answered in the course of drawing. Note the intent concentration of these students.

We have discussed the communication aspect of expressing human feelings, but what about physical aspects of feelings? What of lightness, or buoyancy? or heaviness, or roundness? Or imagining creatures from outer space, or another planet? What about closeness? or tightness? or feelings of being isolated—far away from others? So many insights can be expressed in visual terms, eliminating the need for words which sometimes represent pitfalls for small children.

Eileen was a first grader who was not very sure of herself. After working with the art teacher for several months things began to look up for Eileen, who did the self portrait above. Note the firmness of the outline drawing; see the pleasant contented look on the face with the mouth turned upward and the rosy cheeks.

This child has filled her whole page in contrast to the timid child who will place herself off in a corner of the page, or swimming around at the very top of the sheet. Eileen has said, "Here I am," firmly and confidently. How refreshing!

The building of this papier-mâché sculpture involves many skills. To build an armature one must know about flexible materials: one must be able to consider questions of balance, support and structure. The cognitive skills involving the organization of ideas, orientation in time and space, quantification, etc. are all involved in the building of a sculpture. This child is working in a determined, purposeful way.

History is not just the study of dates and places. History is about people, and where there are people there are always feelings and emotions. When this sixth grader studied events in ancient Greece and Rome, he felt the urgency and involvement of charioteers. Using linoleum block printing techniques, he imagined the intensity of these men as they forced their horses forward. What excellent imagery! Of course, the facts of chariots and dress of the period were also called upon for depiction of this subject.

These children are engaged in lively interaction about a shared pursuit. They are helping each other towards a goal. As they do so, they discover that many ideas are needed, more than those that occurred to each of them along the way. In this case, the children combined their efforts to create a beautiful wall-hanging for the school. The final product was composed of many contributions, each different yet related through color and texture. The unified whole was a source of great gratification to the contributors and pleasure to the community.

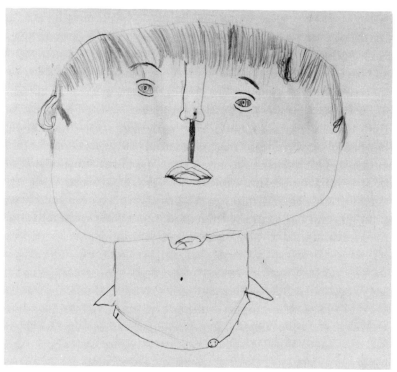

PROVIDE A RECORD OF GROWTH

The two drawings on the left were done by the same boy, but approximately five years apart. What a marvelous record of his development! The drawings tell much more about him than the marks of his report card. His definition of fingers, so carefully moving from four to five as the drawing progressed, identifies his thought process. The details of the carefully drawn face are so much more refined and show his powers of observation as he grew older. This set of drawings, combined with others, can provide a valuable sense of continuity and maturation. They indicate learning and offer insights potentially useful for future evaluation of abilities and sensibilities.

DEEPEN CONCENTRATION

At a time when difficulties in concentration are so widely noted, perhaps the most striking aspect of children's art is the total absorption that goes into its production. Children making art are completely engrossed in their own creative activity. When children state that they "love art," as they repeatedly do, they are usually referring to this experience.

The artwork itself is an expression of intense engagement with ideas and emotions. It must be respected as an extension of the individual. Adult praise should be respectful of the investment of self that is made by each child but this praise shouldn't be automatic. Those who insist that the young artist is Rembrandt incarnate are immediately distrusted. "Isn't that weird?" say the exchanged glances of youngsters following such praise. Instead, a thoughtful response is needed, one that indicates some effort to understand what is really being attempted. At the close of each art session in the school setting a teacher might comment that "We used the same materials and had the same instructions, time frame and even subject matter, yet each of us produced something entirely different. Let's think about why that happened and what it would be like if it didn't." In this way students learn to take themselves and their efforts seriously. They become confident about pursuing their own ideas.

Through art education we try to reach the minds and emotions of young children in such a way that an awareness and love of color, form, and line can be built into their everyday lives, helping them to grow up to be individuals with discriminating taste. We hope that they will be unafraid of their own responses, not only to the physical world but also to the world of feelings. We hope that they will develop a sense of wonder at the extraordinary diversity of people's minds as exhibited in the art objects that have been produced over the centuries. We hope that as they begin to understand that art is essentially a quest for order, they might consider more thoughtfully the possibilities of ordering their own selves and even, perhaps, their environment.

Selective Bibliographies

PHILOSOPHY AND METHODS

Arnheim, Rudolf. 1969. *Art and Visual Perception.* Berkeley: University of California Press.

———. 1971. *Visual Thinking.* Berkeley: University of California Press.

Bank, Mirra. 1979. *Anonymous Was a Woman.* New York: St. Martin's Press.

Barclay, Doris L., ed. n.d. *Art Education for the Disadvantaged Child.* Washington, D.C.: National Art Education Association.

Barkan, Manuel. 1955. *Through Art to Creativity.* Boston: Allyn and Bacon.

Blandy, Doug, and Kristin Congdon. 1990. *Culture and Democracy.* New York: Teachers College Press.

Bloom, Benjamin S. 1984. *Taxonomy of Educational Objectives: The Classification of Educational Goals.* New York: Longman.

Broudy, Harry S. 1972. *Enlightened Cherishing: An Essay on Aesthetic Education.* Urbana: University of Illinois Press.

Burkhart, Robert. 1966. "The Relationship of Creativity to Intelligence." In *Readings in Art Education*, edited by Elliot Eisner and David Echer. Waltham, MA: Blaisdell.

Chapman, Laura H. 1982. *Instant Art, Instant Culture: The Unspoken Policy for American Schools.* New York: Teachers College Press.

Churchill, Angiola. 1970. *Art for Preadolescents.* New York: McGraw-Hill.

Clark, Gill, and Enid Zimmerman. 1987. *Educating Artistically Talented Students.* Syracuse, NY: Syracuse University Press.

Clements, Claire, and Robert Clements. 1984. *Art and Mainstreaming: Art Instruction for Exceptional Children in Regular School Classes.* Springfield, IL: Charles C. Thomas.

Davis, Don Jack. 1990. *Behavioral Emphasis in Art Education.* Reston, VA: NAEA.

Dewey, John. 1958. *Art as Experience.* New York: Capricorn.

Dimondstein, G. 1974. *Exploring the Arts of Children.* New York: Macmillan.

Efland, Arthur. 1990. *A History of Art Education: Intellectual and Social Currents in Teaching the Visual Arts.* New York: Teachers College Press.

Eisner, Elliot. 1972. *Educating Artistic Vision.* New York: Macmillan.

———. 1979. *The Educational Imagination: On the Design and Evaluation of School Programs.* New York: Macmillan.

———. 1987. *The Role of Discipline Based Education in America's Schools.* Los Angeles: The Getty Center for Education in the Arts.

Ernst, Karen. 1993. *Picturing Learning: Artists and Writers in the Classroom.* Portsmouth, NH: Heinemann.

Faulkner, Ray, and Edwin Ziegfeld. 1969. *Art Today.* New York: Holt, Reinhart and Winston.

Fein, Sylvia. 1993a. *First Drawings: Genesis of Visual Thinking.* Portsmouth, NH: Heinemann.

———. 1993b. *Heidi's Horse.* Portsmouth, NH: Heinemann.

Feldman, Edmund Burke. 1970. *Becoming Human Through Art.* Englewood Cliffs, NJ: Prentice-Hall.

———. 1985. *Varieties of Visual Experience.* New York: Prentice Hall.

Freeman, Nancy. 1980. *Strategies of Children's Drawings*. New York: Academic.

Freeman, Nancy, and M. V. Cox, eds. 1985. *Visual Order*. Cambridge, England: Cambridge University Press.

Gaitskell, Charles D., Al Hurwitz, and Michael Day. 1991. *Children and Their Art: Methods for the Elementary School*. 5th Ed. New York: Harcourt Brace Jovanovich.

Gagne, Robert. 1975. *Essentials of Learning*. New York: Dryden.

Gardner, Howard. 1973. *The Arts and Human Development*. New York: Wiley.

———. 1980. *Artful Scribbles: The Significance of Children's Drawings*. New York: Basic Books.

———. 1982. *Art, Mind, and Brain: A Cognitive Approach to Creating*. New York: Basic Books.

———. 1983. *Frames of Mind*. New York: Basic Books.

Getty Center for Education in the Arts. 1986. *Beyond Creating: The Place for Art in America's Schools*. Los Angeles.

Getxels, Jacob, and Mihalyi Csikszentmihalyi. 1976. *The Creative Vision: A Longitudinal Study of Problem Finding in Art*. New York: Wiley.

Goldstein, Ernest, Theodore Ketz, Jo D. Kowalchuk, and Robert Saunders. 1986. *Understanding and Creating Art*. Dallas: Garrard.

Goodlad, John. 1984. *A Place Called School: Promise for the Future*. New York: McGraw-Hill.

Goodman, Nelson. 1979. *Languages of Art: An Approach to a Theory of Symbols*. Indianapolis: Hackett.

Goodnow, J. 1977. *Children Drawing*. Cambridge, MA: Harvard University Press.

Greenberg, Pearl. 1966. *Children's Experiences in Art*. New York: Van Nostrand Reinhold.

———. 1970. *Art and Ideas for Young People*. New York: Van Nostrand Reinhold.

———, ed. 1972. *Art in the Elementary Schools*. Washington, D.C.: National Art Education Association.

Hart, Kate. 1988. *I Can Draw! Ideas for Teachers*. Portsmouth, NH: Heinemann.

Heberholz, Barbara. 1974. *Early Childhood Art.* Dubuque, IA: William C. Brown.

Heberholz, Donald, and Barbara Heberholtz. 1967. *A Child's Pursuit of Art.* Dubuque, IA: William C. Brown.

————. 1990. *Developing Artistic and Perceptual Awareness.* Dubuque, IA: William C. Brown.

Horn, George G., and Grace Sands Smith. 1971. *Experiencing Art in the Elementary School.* Worcester, MA: Davis Publications.

Hubbard, Ruth. 1989. *Authors of Pictures, Draughtsmen of Words.* Portsmouth, NH: Heinemann.

Hurwitz, Al. 1983. *The Gifted and Talented in Art: A Guide to Program Planning.* Worcester, MA: Davis Publications.

Jackson, Margaret. 1994. *Creative Display and Environment.* Portsmouth, NH: Heinemann.

Jameson, Kenneth. 1968. *Art and the Young Child.* New York: Viking.

————. 1971. *Primary School Art.* New York: Van Nostrand Reinhold.

Johnson, Paul. 1992. *A Book of One's Own: Developing Literacy Through Making Books.* Portsmouth, NH: Heinemann.

————. 1993. *Literacy Through the Book Arts.* Portsmouth, NH: Heinemann.

Kramer, Edith. 1972. *Art as Therapy with Children.* New York: Schocken Books.

Krantz, Stewart, and Joseph Deley. 1970. *The Fourth "R."* New York: Van Nostrand Reinhold.

Lark-Horowitz, Betty, Hilda Lewis, and Mark Luca. 1973. *Understanding Children's Art for Better Teaching.* Columbus, OH: Merrill.

Lewis, Richard. 1992. *When Thought Is Young: Reflections on Teaching and the Poetry of the Child.* Minneapolis, MN: New Rivers Press.

Lewis, H. P., ed. 1973. *Child Art—the Beginnings of Self-affirmation.* Berkeley, CA: Diablo Press.

Linderman, Earl W., and Donald W. Heberholtz. 1969. *Developing Artistic and Perceptual Awareness.* Dubuque, IA: William C. Brown.

Linderman, Marlene. 1990. *Art in the Elementary School: Drawing, Painting, and Creativity for the Classroom.* Dubuque, IA: William C. Brown.

Lindstrom, Miriam. 1962. *Children's Art.* Berkeley: University of California Press.

London, Peter. 1994. *Step Outside: Community-based Art Education.* Portsmouth, NH: Heinemann.

London, Peter, Judith Burton, and Arlene Linderman, eds. 1990. *Beyond DBAE: The Case for Multiple Visions of Art Education.* North Dartmouth, MA: Southeastern Massachusetts University.

Lowenfeld, Victor, and Lambert W. Brittain. 1964. *Creative and Mental Growth.* 4th Ed. New York: Macmillian.

Marshall, Sybil. 1963. *An Experiment in Education.* New York: Cambridge University Press.

Mattil Edward L. 1965. *Meaning in Crafts.* 2nd Ed. Englewood Cliffs, NJ: Prentice-Hall.

Mattil, Edward L., and Betty Marzan. 1981. *Meaning in Children's Art: Projects for Teachers.* New York: Prentice-Hall.

McCann, Michael. 1985. *Health Hazards Manual for Artists.* New York: Nick Lyons Books.

McFee, June K. 1970. *Preparation for Art.* 2nd Ed. Belmont, CA: Wadsworth Publishing.

Mendelowitz, Daniel. 1963. *Children Are Artists.* Rev. Ed. Stanford, CA: Stanford University Press.

Merritt, Helen. 1964. *Guiding Free Expression in Children's Art.* New York: Holt, Rinehart and Winston.

Montgomery, Chandler. 1968. *Art for Teachers of Children.* Columbus, OH: Charles E. Merrill.

Nicolaides, Kimon. 1941. *The Natural Way to Draw.* Boston: Houghton Mifflin.

O'Brien, Bernadette C. 1978. *Tapestry: Interrelationship of the Arts in Reading and Language Development.* New York: New York City Board of Education.

Olson, Janet L. 1992. *Envisioning Writing: Toward an Integration of Drawing and Writing.* Portsmouth, NH: Heinemann.

Pickering, John M. 1971. *Visual Education in the Primary School.* New York: Watson-Guptil.

Pile, Naomi. 1973. *Art Experiences for Young Children: Threshold Early Learning Library.* Vol. 5. New York: Macmillan.

Read, Herbert. 1958. *Education Through Art.* Rev. Ed. New York: Pantheon Books.

Richardson, Elwyn. 1964. *In the Early World: Discovering Art Through Crafts.* New York: Pantheon.

Rowe Gaelene. 1989. *Guiding Young Artists: Curriculum Ideas for Teachers.* Portsmouth, NH: Heinemann.

Roy, Susan, and Jeremy Steele. 1989. *Young Imagination: Writing and Artwork by Children of New South Wales.* Portsmouth, NH: Heinemann.

Schaefer-Simmern, H. 1961. *The Unfolding of Artistic Activity.* Berkeley: University of California Press.

Schirrmacher, Robert. 1988. *Art and Creative Development for Young Children.* Albany, NY: Delmar.

Schools Council. 1974. *Children's Growth Through Creative Experience.* New York: Van Nostrand Reinhold.

Schwartx, Fred R. 1970. *Structure and Potential in Art Education.* Waltham, MA: Gin-Blaisdell.

Silberstein-Storfer, M., and M. Jones. 1982. *Doing Art Together.* New York: Simon and Schuster.

Smith, Nancy R. 1982. *Experience and Art: Teaching Children to Paint.* New York: Teachers College Press.

Szekely, George. 1988. *Encouraging Creativity in Art Lessons.* New York: Teachers College Press.

——. 1991. *From Play to Art.* Portsmouth, NH: Heinemann.

Taylor, Harold. 1960. *Art and the Intellect.* New York: Museum of Modern Art.

Thistlewood, David, ed. 1991. *Critical Studies in Art and Design Education.* Portsmouth, NH: Heinemann.

Uhlin, Donald M. 1979. *Art for Exceptional Children.* Dubuque, IA: William C. Brown.

Wachowiak, Frank, and Robert D. Clements. 1993. 5th Ed. *Emphasis: Art.* New York: HarperCollins.

Weismann, Donald L. 1970. *The Visual Arts as Human Experience.* Englewood Cliffs, NJ: Prentice-Hall.

Wilson, Brent, Al Hurwitz, and Marjorie Wilson. 1987. *Teaching Drawing from Art.* Worcester, MA: Davis Publications.

Wilson, Brent, and Marjorie Wilson. 1982. *Teaching Children to Draw.* Englewood Cliffs, NJ: Prentice-Hall.

Winner, Ellen. 1982. *Invented Worlds: The Psychology of the Arts.* Cambridge, MA: Harvard University Press.

MATERIALS AND THEIR USES

Anderson, Yvonne. 1970. *Make Your Own Animated Movies* and *Teaching Film Animation.* New York: Van Nostrand Reinhold.

Ballinger, Louise Bowen, and Thomas F. Vroman. 1965. *Design Sources and Resources.* New York: Van Nostrand Reinhold.

Bedor, John. 1968a. *Creating and Presenting Hand Puppets.* New York: Van Nostrand Reinhold.

———. 1968b. *Rubbings and Textures: A Graphic Medium.* New York: Van Nostrand Reinhold.

Borgeson, B. 1983. *The Colored Pencil: Key Concepts for Handling the Medium.* New York: Watson-Guptill.

Brockie, K. 1984. *One Man's Island, a Naturalist's Year.* New York: Harper & Row.

Brommer, Gerald F. 1968. *Wire Sculpture.* Worcester, MA: Davis Publications.

Brown, L. 1960. *Map-making, the Art That Became a Science.* Boston: Little, Brown.

D'Amico, Victor, and Arlette Buchman. 1972. *Assemblage.* New York: Museum of Modern Art.

Dendel, Esther Warner. 1974. *African Fabric Crafts.* New York: Taplinger Publishing.

Dunn, Susan, and Rob Larson. 1989. *Design Technology: Children's Engineering.* Bristol, PA: Falmer Press.

Erikson, Janet, and Adelaide Sproul. 1966. *Printmaking Without a Press.* New York: Van Nostrand Reinhold.

Grummer, A. E. 1980. *Paper by Kids.* Minneapolis, MN: Dillon Press.

Guyler, Vivian. 1970. *Design in Nature.* Worcester, MA: Davis Publications.

Hofsinde, Robert. 1971. *Indian Arts.* New York: William Morrow.

Ikegami, K. 1986. *Japanese Bookbinding.* Adapted by B. Stephan. New York: Weatherhill.

Jackson, Paul. 1993. *The Pop-up Book.* New York: Henry Holt.

Johnson, Paul. 1992. *Pop-up Paper Engineering.* Bristol, PA: Falmer Press.

Johnson, Pauline. 1977. *Creative Bookbinding.* Seattle: University of Washington Press.

Kaupelis, Robert. 1966. *Learning to Draw.* New York: Watson-Guptill.

Keightley, M. 1976. *Investigating Art.* London: Elek.

Klager, Max. 1975. *Letters, Type and Pictures: Teaching Alphabets Through Art.* New York: Van Nostrand Reinhold.

Krevitsky, Nik. 1965. *Stitchery: Art & Craft.* New York: Van Nostrand Reinhold.

Laliberte, Norman, and Shirley McIlhany. 1966. *Banners and Hangings: Design and Construction.* New York: Van Nostrand Reinhold.

Laliberte, Norman, and Alex Mogelon. 1966. *Masks, Face Coverings, and Headgear.* New York: Van Nostrand Reinhold.

———. 1967. *Painting with Crayons: History and Modern Techniques.* New York: Van Nostrand Reinhold.

Lane, S. M., and M. Kemp. 1973. *An Approach to Topic Work in the Primary School.* London: Blackie and Son.

Lesch, Alma. 1971. *Vegetable Dying: 151 Recipes for Dyeing Yarns and Fabrics with Natural Materials.* New York: Watson-Guptill.

Levitan, E. 1962. *Animation Techniques.* New York: Van Nostrand Reinhold.

Leyh, Elizabeth. 1975. *Children Make Sculpture.* New York: Van Nostrand Reinhold.

Lidstone, John. 1965. *Building with Balsa Wood.* New York: Van Nostrand Reinhold.

———. 1968. *Building with Cardboard.* New York: Van Nostrand Reinhold.

Marcousé, R. 1974. *Using Objects: Visual Awareness and Visual Learning in the Museum and Classroom.* New York: Van Nostrand Reinhold.

Morman, Jean. 1989. *One- Two- Three Murals: Simple Murals to Make Using Children's Open Ended Art*. Everett, WA: Warren.

Neuman, Lee S., and Jay H. 1974. *Kite Craft*. New York: Crown.

Perrins, L. 1985. *How Paper Is Made*. New York: Facts on File.

Rainey, S. 1966. *Weaving Without a Loom*. Worcester, MA: Davis Publications.

————. 1971. *Wall Hangings: Designing with Fabric and Thread*. Worcester, MA: Davis Publications.

Rottger, Ernst. 1961. *Surfaces in Creative Design*. London: Batsford.

————. 1963. *Creative Clay Design*. New York: Van Nostrand Reinhold.

————. 1969. *Creative Wood Design*. New York: Van Nostrand Reinhold.

————. 1970. *Creative Paper Design*. New York: Van Nostrand Reinhold.

Schwartz, Alice M. 1972. *Images and Things*. Bloomington, IN: National Instructional Television Center.

Seidelman, James E., and G. Mintouye. 1967. *Creating with Clay*. New York: Macmillan.

Shahn, Ben. 1963. *Love and Joy about Letters*. New York: Grossman Publishers.

Shannon, F. 1987. *Paper Pleasures*. New York: Weidenfeld & Nicolson.

Shuman, J. M. 1981. *Art from Many Hands*. Englewood Cliffs, NJ: Prentice-Hall.

Southworth, M., and S. Southworth. 1982. *Maps: A Visual Survey and Design Guide*. Boston: Little, Brown.

Sproul, Adelaide. 1968. *With a Free Hand*. New York: Van Nostrand Reinhold.

Stacy, Donald L. 1975. *Experiments in Art*. New York: Four Winds Press.

Topal, C. W. 1983. *Children, Clay and Sculpture*. Worcester, MA: Davis Publications.

Trogler, George E. 1972. *Beginning Experiences in Architecture: A Guide for the Elementary School Teacher*. New York: Van Nostrand Reinhold.

Wasserman, R. 1979. *The Mathematics of Islamic Art: A Packet for Teachers of Mathematics, Social Studies and Art.* New York: The Metropolitan Museum of Art.

Wilson, Forest. 1988. *What it Feels like to Be a Building.* Washington, D.C.: Preservation Press.

Wood, P. 1982. *Scientific Illustration.* New York: Van Nostrand Reinhold.

PSYCHOLOGY AND EDUCATION

Biber, Barbara, E. Shapiro, and D. Wickens. 1971. *Promoting Cognitive Growth.* New York: Bank Street College of Education.

Bruner, J. S. 1960. *The Process of Education.* New York: Random House.

Coles, Robert. 1967. *Children of Crisis.* Boston: Little, Brown.

———. 1970. *Teachers and the Children of Poverty.* Washington, D.C.: The Potomac Institute.

Dennis, Wayne. 1966. *Group Values Through Children's Drawings.* New York: John Wiley.

Di Leo, Joseph H. 1970. *Young Children and Their Drawings.* New York: Brunner-Mazel Publishers.

Featherstone, Joseph. 1971. *Schools Where Children Learn.* New York: Liveright.

Ginsburg, Herbert, and Sylvia Opper, eds. 1969. *Piaget's Theory of Intellectual Development.* Englewood Cliffs, NJ: Prentice-Hall.

Golomb, Claire. 1974. *Young Children's Sculpture and Drawing: A Study in Representational Development.* Cambridge, MA: Harvard University Press.

Guilford, Joy P. 1968. *Intelligence, Creativity and Their Educational Implications.* San Diego, CA: Robert R. Knapp.

Harris, Dale B. 1963. *Children's Drawings as Measures of Intellectual Maturity.* New York: Harcourt Brace & World.

Jones, Richard M. 1970. *Fantasy and Feeling in Education.* New York: Harper & Row.

Kellogg, Rhoda. 1969. *Analyzing Children's Art.* Palo Alto, CA: National Press Books.

Kohl, Herbert. 1994. *"I Won't Learn from You" and Other Thought on Creative Maladjustment.* New York: The New Press.

Mooney, R. L., and S. Smilansky. 1973. *An Experiment in the Use of Drawing to Promote Cognitive Development in Disadvantaged Preschool Children in Israel and the U.S.*, Project No. 2-0137. Washington, D.C.: Office of Education, U.S. Health Department of Health Education and Welfare.

Murphy, J., and R. Gross. 1967. *The Arts and the Poor.* Washington, D.C.: Government Printing Office.

Piaget, Jean. 1963. *The Origins of Intelligence in Children.* New York: W. W. Norton.

Piaget, Jean, and B. Inhelder. 1969. *The Psychology of the Child.* New York: Basic Books.

―――. 1971. *Mental Imagery in the Child.* New York: Basic Books.

Platt, Penny. 1971. *Platt Early Reading Program.* Menlo Park, CA: Addison-Wesley.

Postman, Neil. 1985. *Amusing Ourselves to Death.* New York: Penguin.

―――. 1994. *The Disappearance of Childhood.* New York: Penguin.

Schewbel, Milton, and Jane Ralph. 1973. *Piaget in the Classroom.* New York: Basic Books.

Sharp, Evelyn. 1972. *The IQ Cult.* New York: Coward, McCann and Geoghegan.

Silberman, Charles E., ed. 1973. *The Open Classroom Reader.* New York: Vintage Books.

Witken, H. et al. 1962. *Psychological Differentiation: Studies of Development.* New York: John Wiley.

Young, John Z. 1971. *An Introduction to the Study of Man.* New York: Oxford University Press.

BOOKS FOR CHILDREN

Anno, M. 1978. *Anno's Journey.* New York: Philomel.

Balet, J. 1969. *The Fence.* New York: Delacorte.

Bang, B., and M. Bang. 1978. *The Old Woman and the Rice Thief.* New York: Greenwillow.

Baskin, L. 1984. *Imps, Demons, Hobgoblins, Witches, Fairies and Elves.* New York: Pantheon.

Batterberry, A. R., and M. Batterberry. 1976. *The Story of American Art.* New York: Pantheon.

Baylor, Byrd. 1972. *When Clay Sings.* New York: Scribner's.

———. 1974. *They Put on Masks.* New York: Scribner's.

Behrends, Rainer, and Karl Max Kober. 1975. *The Artist and His Studio.* New York: St. Martin's Press.

Belvés, Pierre, and Fancois Mathey. 1966. *Enjoying the World of Art.* New York: Lion Press.

Bryan, A. 1977. *The Dancing Granny.* New York: Atheneum.

———. 1992. *Sing to the Sun.* New York: HarperCollins.

Carle, E. 1991. *Dragons, Dragons.* Compiled by Laura Whipple. New York: Philomel.

———. 1993. *Today Is Monday.* New York: Philomel.

Cohen, C., and S. Begay. 1988. *The Mud Pony.* New York: Scholastic.

Cohen, M. 1980. *No Good in Art.* New York: Greenwillow.

Craft, R. 1975. *Pieter Brueghel's "The Fair."* Philadelphia, PA: Lippincott.

Delaunay, S. 1972. *Alphabet.* New York: Crowell.

Demi. 1993. *Demi's Secret Garden.* New York: Henry Holt.

Douglas, E. 1987. *The Magic Carpet and Other Tales.* Illustrated by Walter Anderson. Jackson: University Press of Mississippi.

Ehlert, L. 1990. *Fish Eyes.* New York: Harcourt Brace Jovanovich

Fern, E. 1991. *Pepito's Story.* New York: Yarrow.

Frasconi, A. 1974. *The Elephant and His Secret.* New York: Atheneum.

Gerstein, M. 1986. *Tales of Pan.* New York: Harper & Row.

———. 1987. *The Mountains of Tibet.* New York: Harper & Row.

Glubok, Shirley. 1965. *The Art of Africa.* New York: Harper & Row. (One of a fine series on the art of diverse cultures.)

Holme, B. 1979. *Enchanted World.* New York: Oxford University Press.

Hogrogian, N. 1976. *The Contest.* New York: Greenwillow.

Isadora, R. 1979. *Ben's Trumpet.* New York: Greenwillow.

Janosch. 1968. *Joshua and the Magic Fiddle.* Cleveland: World.

Keats, E. J. 1965. *John Henry*. New York: Pantheon.

Kesselman, W. 1980. *Emma*. New York: Doubleday.

Lasker, J. 1976. *Merry Ever After*. New York: Viking.

Lawrence, J. 1968. *Harriet and the Promised Land*. New York: Simon & Schuster.

———. 1993. *The Great Migration*. New York: HarperCollins.

Lionni, L. 1966. *Frederick*. New York: Pantheon.

Longfellow, H. W. 1983. *Hiawatha*. Pictures by Susan Jeffers. New York: Dutton.

Macagy, Douglas. 1959. *Going for a Walk with a Line*. Garden City, NY: Doubleday.

Manniche, L. 1981. *The Prince Who Knew His Fate*. New York: The Metropolitan Museum of Art.

McDermott, Beverly Brodsky. 1974. *The Crystal Apple*. New York: Viking Press.

McDermott, G. 1993. *Raven*. New York: Harcourt Brace Javonovich.

Moore, Janet G. 1968. *The Many Ways of Seeing: An Introduction to the Pleasures of Art*. Cleveland: World Publishing.

Melville, H. 1991. *Catskill Eagle*. Paintings by Thomas Locker. New York: Philomel.

Niland, K. 1980. *Feathers, Fur and Frills*. Sidney: Hodder and Stoughton.

Nomura, T. 1991. *Grandpa's Town*. Brooklyn, NY: Kane/Miller.

Otsuka, Y. 1981. *Suho and the White Horse*. New York: Viking.

Paine, R. M. 1968. *Looking at Sculpture*. New York: Lothrop, Lee & Shepard.

Paul, A. W. 1991. *Eight Hands Round*. New York: HarperCollins.

Piatti, C. 1964. *The Happy Owls*. New York: Atheneum.

Pinkwater, D. 1977. *The Big Orange Splot*. New York: Hastings House.

Price, Christine. 1975. *Dancing Masks of Africa*. New York: Scribner's.

Raboff, Ernst. 1968. *Marc Chagall*. New York: Doubleday. (One of an excellent series of profiles on artists.)

Ringgold, F. 1991. *Tar Beach*. New York: Crown.

————. 1992. *Aunt Harriet's Underground Railroad in the Sky*. New York: Crown.

Roth, S. 1988. *Fire Came to the Earth People*. New York: St. Martin's Press.

Ruskin, Ariane. 1964. *The Pantheon Story of Art for Young People*. New York: Pantheon.

Sandburg, Carl. 1993. *Arithmetic*. Illustrations by Ted Rand. New York: Harcourt Brace Jovanovich.

Schick, E. 1977. *One Summer Night*. New York: Greenwillow.

Seeger, E., and M. Hays. 1986. *Abiyoyo*. New York: Macmillian.

Sendak, M. 1963. *Where the Wild Things Are*. New York: Harper & Row.

Sis, P. 1991. *Follow the Dream*. New York: Knopf.

Spencer, C. 1963. *How Art and Music Speak to Us*. New York: John Day.

Stern, Philip Van Doren. 1973. *The Beginnings of Art*. New York: Four Winds Press.

Tison, Annette, and Talus Taylor. 1971. *The Adventures of the Three Colors*. New York: World Publishing.

————. 1972. *Inside and Outside*. New York: World Publishing.

Tanobe, M. 1976. *Quebec, Je T'aime, I Love You*. Plattsburgh, NY: Tundra.

Testa, F., and A. Burgess. 1979. *The Land Where the Ice Cream Grows*. New York: Doubleday.

Ungerer, T. 1991. *Moonman*. New York: Delacorte.

Velthuijs, M. 1975. *The Painter and the Bird*. Reading, MA: Addison-Wesley.

————. 1987. *The Little Boy and the Big Fish*. Faellanden, Switzerland: North-South Books.

Wildsmith, B. 1985. *Fishes*. New York: Oxford University Press.

Williams, K. L., and C. Stock. 1990. *Galimoto*. New York: William Morrow.

Williams, Vera. 1986. *Cherries and Cherry Pits*. New York: Greenwillow.

Winter, J., and J. Winter. 1991. *Diego*. New York: Knopf.

Yani, W. 1987. *Yani's Monkeys*. Beijing: Foreign Languages Press.

Yashima, T. 1967. *Crow Boy*. New York: Viking.

Yolen, J. 1972. *The Girl Who Loved the Wind*. New York: Thomas Y. Crowell.

Young, Ed. 1992. *Seven Blind Mice*. New York: Philomel.

Index

crayons, 77, 120
experimenting with, 21
markers, 141
paint/chalk on wet paper,
121
papier-mâché, 140, 158
photography, 53–54
sandpaper, 117
scissors, 51
stencils, xiv, 181
tissue paper, 74, 140
wood, 223
Arts in General Education Project,
210
Arts IMPACT, 209–10
art teachers. *See* teachers
assimilation, 68

Bailey, Charity, 16, 17
Beitlel, Kenneth R., 58
Binet, Alfred, 190
black children, *See also* minority
children
African art activities, 50–52,
222–23
racism and, 138
self-concept of, 50–53, 58
Bowra, C. M., 155
Braque, Georges, 168
Briggs, Edith, 165
Brittain, Lamber W., 93
Brodsky, Beverly, 184
Brookover, Wilbur B., 57
Brown, B. R., 52
Bruner, Jerome, 65

Calder, Alexander, 91
California Achievement Tests,
209
cameras, being and using, 53–56
cave paintings, 159
celluloid, colored, 121
Cézanne, Paul, 72, 133, 188
Chagall, Marc, 184, 185
chalk, 89, 121, 140
Chardin, Jean Baptiste, 133
Chicano children, pre-Columbian
art activities, 217–22
children, *See also* black children;
Hispanic children;
minority children
affluent, 230–32

bilingual, 225–27
condition of, 2
disruptive, 187–90, 193–95,
227–30
gifted, 232–33
handicapped, 5–6, 234–36
labeling, 187–90
of migrant workers, 226
minority, 5–6, 217–24
nonverbal, xv–xvi, 127–28,
227–30
poor, 217, 224–25
with special needs, 6–7
troubled, 4, 124–29, 238
children's art, *See also* art
child's self-evaluation of, 24
as expressionist art, 39
vs. fine art, 21–22
nature of, 26–43
parents and, xiii–xiv, 48, 57,
211–15
point of view in, 100–101
significance of, 1–7
Christmas, xiv, 55, 56, 183–84
Clark, K. B., 52
Clark, M., 52
class albums, 61
classification collages, 91
classroom design, 172–85
clay, 77, 114, 121, 140, 154,
193–94, 219
cognitive skills, *See also* learning
abstract thinking, 70–71
art and, 64–92, 243
figurative aspects of, 69
generalizing, 161
learning, 64
linguistic skills, 65
logical thinking, 89
mental imagery, 31
operative aspects of, 69, 81
Piaget's stages of development, 20–21, 32
reading, 64, 65
symbolization, 64, 65, 67–68,
81
Coleman, James S., 57
Coles, Robert, 39
collage, 74–76, 91, 115, 122, 140
color, *See also* art activities;
painting
expression through, 39

individual choice of, 45, 60,
106, 120, 204, 211
mixing, xvi, xviii, 24, 60, 68,
109–10, 120, 121, 126,
148, 149, 152, 154
perception of, 106–11
physical effects of, 175
primary, xv–xvi, 109–10
colored celluloid, 121
coloring books, xiv, 214–15
communication, 23, *See also* language; poetry; reading;
writing
art as, xv–xvi, xviii–xix, 2,
36–37, 39–42, 69,
125–29, 215, 224–25, 238
by bilingual children, 225–27
learning and, 26
with self, 69
texture and, 115
comparisons, art project, 92
computers, 3
Conant, Howard, 209
concentration, 247–48
conformity, in minority children,
217–19
construction, 101
construction paper, 74, 84,
165–66
Courbet, Gustav, 55
crayons, 77, 120
creativity, 19, 28
divergent thinking and, 192
encouraging, 233–34
intelligence and, 187–203
recognizing, 199, 232–33
television and, 3, 232
Crite, 133
crystal apple, art project, 184
culture
art as, 10, 18, 36
of children, 18
intelligence and, 190
intelligence tests and,
200–201
perception and, 105
pride in, 223–24
self-concept and, 57–58
valuing diversity in, 217–18
curriculum, *See also* art education; education
evaluation of, 207–8

feelings and, 132–35
history, 152–56
integrating art into, 4–5,
145–71
language arts, 160–64
mathematics, 164–68
science, 156–60
social studies, 149–56

dance, 135
Davis, Stuart, 89
daydreaming, channeling in positive direction, 135–36
Dennis, Wayne, 226
design
art activities, 165–68, 170,
173–76, 239
random vs. structured, 173–76
school environment, 172–76
development, *See also* art development
aesthetic experience and,
28–29
art, 30–33, 65, 67, 100,
207–8, 247
cognitive, 30–33
image, 69, 104
imagination, 81
new situations and, 68
stages of, 13, 28–33
symbols, 64, 65, 67–68
Dewey, John, 35, 90, 106
Diaz del Castillo, Bernal, 220
Dickinson, Emily, 84
discipline, in art, xviii
discovery, 28
disruptive children, *See also* children; troubled children
intelligence and, 187–90,
193–95
nonverbal, 227–30
divergent thinking, creativity and,
191–200
diversity, *See also* individual
variation
appreciation of, 217–18, 245,
248
cultural, 217–18
Doyle, Charlotte, 191
dramatic play, dressing up for, 62
drawing, 94–100, *See also* art
activities

individual variation, *See also*
    diversity
    in aesthetic experience, 60
    in art activities, 33–36, 60
    cultural diversity, 217–18
    intelligence and, 196
    learning and, 49, 51–52
    in observation, 95–108
    in perception, 33, 57, 58, 63,
      77, 95–108
    in response to poetry, 81
    self-concept and, 50–52
    in talent, 100–101
intelligence, 13
    art development and, 45–49
    creativity and, 187–203
    culture and, 190
    individual variation and, 196
    intelligence tests and, 190–91
    underestimated, 195–99
intelligence tests, 13, 45
    creativity and, 192
    culture-fairness of, 200–201
    drawing and, 202–3
    qualities measured by,
      190–91, 200–201
interdisciplinary education, 4–5,
    145–71, *See also* curricu-
    lum

Jacobson, Lenore, 49
Jones, Richard M., 49, 100, 130

kindergarten, 63, 78, 118, 177
Kohl, Herbert, 225
Kollwitz, Kathe, 55

Langer, Susanne, 67
language, *See also* communica-
    tion; poetry; reading;
    writing
    alphabet, 36, 160–61
    as art, 136
    art as, xviii–xix
    linguistic skills, 65
    understanding through art,
      160–64
Lawrence, Sir Thomas, 133
Lawson, Robert, 149
learning, *See also* art education;
    cognitive skills; educa-
    tion

    aesthetic experience and,
      28–29
    art and, 208–10, 237–48
    individual variation and, 49,
      51–52
    as organization, 69
    repetition and, 69–73, 76
    styles, of nonverbal children,
      230
    through play, 90
Liverant, S., 58
loneliness, 138
Lowell, Amy, 81, 132
Lowenfeld, Viktor, 30–31, 32, 36,
    69, 70–71, 93, 100, 106,
    206

Machover, Karen, 104
McKeachie, Wilbert, 191
Madeja, Stanley S., 210
Malinowski, Bronislaw, 105
map making, 86–89
Marin, John, 177
markers, 141
masks, 117, 120
    African, 50–52
mathematics
    dimensions, 112–15
    studying through art, 164–68
Matisse, Henri, 55, 72, 188
"Me" games, art activity, 60–61
migrant workers, children of, 226
minority children, 17–24, *See*
    also children
    pride in heritage, 219–22,
      223–24
    racism and, 138
    self-concept of, 50–53, 58,
      219–22, 223–24
    value of art to, 5–6
mobiles, 91
models, drawing from, 76–78
Mondrian, Piet, 89, 168
Montessori, Maria, 32, 35, 65, 69,
    90
motion, expressing, 78
motion pictures, art activity, 92
motivation, 73, 164
murals, 74–76
museums, visiting, 231–32

natural dyes, 159

Taylor, Harold, 130
teachers
    art and classroom teacher
        roles, 148–49
    art workshops for, 15–16
    encouragement by, 25, 51, 60
    evaluation by, 24, 25
    expectations of students by,
        57
    feelings of, 139
    as models, 15–17
    passion and, 130–31
    resistance to art by, xiv,
        14–17, 237
    roles of, xvi, 148–49
technology, art education and,
    2–4
television, 3, 232
Terman, Lewis, 190–91
tests. *See* intelligence tests
texture
    communication and, 115
    drawing, 120
    perception of, 115–20
Thanksgiving, 182
Thompson, James, 175

tissue paper, 74, 140
Torrance, E. Paul, 192–93, 199
troubled children, *See also* chil-
        dren; disruptive children
    communicating with, 4,
        124–29, 238
trust, 137–39
Turner, J. M. W., 133, 177

values, group art and, 226
van Gogh, Vincent, 55, 72, 188

Wechsler Intelligence Scale for
        Children (WISC), 191
Wechsler Intelligence Scale for
        Children—Revised
        (WISC-R), 201–3
Wilson, A. B., 49
wood, texture, 116–18
writing, *See also* communication;
        language; poetry
    about feelings, 136, 158–59
    as art form, 136
    drawing and, 161–62
    readiness, 161–64

DATE DUE

DEC 1 3 1995			
1 4 1998			
DEC 0 9 1999			
FEB 0 6 2001			
MAR 2 0 2004			
APR 2 2 2004			
OCT 1 4 2004			
GAYLORD			PRINTED IN U.S.A.